The Virgin of Guadalupe

Celebrating Faith
Explorations in Latino Spirituality and Theology
Series Editor: Virgil P. Elizondo

This series will present seminal, insightful, and inspirational works drawing on the experiences of Christians in the Latino traditions. Books in this series will explore topics such as the roots of a Mexican American understanding of God's presence in the life of the people, the perduring influence of the Guadalupe event, the spirituality of immigrants, and the role of popular religion in teaching and living the faith.

The Virgin of Guadalupe

Theological Reflections of an Anglo-Lutheran Liturgist

MAXWELL E. JOHNSON

ROWMAN & LITTLEFIELD PUBLISHERS, INC.
Lanham • Boulder • New York • Oxford

ROWMAN & LITTLEFIELD PUBLISHERS, INC.

Published in the United States of America
by Rowman & Littlefield Publishers, Inc.
A Member of the Rowman & Littlefield Publishing Group
4720 Boston Way, Lanham, Maryland 20706
www.rowmanlittlefield.com

PO Box 317
Oxford
OX2 9RU, UK

British Library Cataloguing in Publication Information Available

Library of Congress Cataloging-in-Publication Data

Johnson, Maxwell E., 1952–
　　The Virgin of Guadalupe : theological reflections of an Anglo-Lutheran
liturgist / Maxwell E. Johnson
　　　　p.　cm.—(Celebrating faith)
Includes bibliographical references and index.
　　ISBN 0-7425-2284-9 (alk. paper)
1. Guadalupe, Our Lady of.　I. Title　II. Series.
　　BT660.G8 J57　2002
　　232.91'7'097253—dc21

　　　　　　　　　　　　　　　　　　2002006954

Printed in the United States of America

⊖ ™
　　The paper used in this publication meets the minimum requirements of American
National Standard for Information Sciences—Permanence of Paper for Printed Library
Materials, ANSI/NISO Z39.48–1992.

Contents

Foreword

It is a great honor and pleasure to introduce the fabulous and ground-breaking work of my good friend and colleague Dr. Maxwell E. Johnson. Max and I are very different in many ways, yet we have one thing in common: our transforming experience through contact with Our Lady of Guadalupe and our desire to make her better known and appreciated.

I was very hesitant to accept his invitation to write this foreword because so much of the book is based on my own writings; on the other hand, it has been a great joy for me to do so. For even though much of this book is based on my own efforts to gain a better and deeper understanding of this religious tradition that has illuminated the lives of millions since the beginning of America, reading through Max's manuscript has given me many new, profound, and exciting insights. He has opened the doors to many more aspects of the Guadalupe tradition than I had ever imagined.

Out of his own expertise as a Lutheran, liturgical historian, and theologian, Max Johnson has done a marvelous job in creating a beautiful and powerful mosaic of the multifaceted theological meaning of the image, narrative, and devotion of Guadalupe. By carefully interweaving history, devotion, tradition, theology, and liturgy, he allows the reader to appreciate Guadalupe as a dynamic parable of justification and a beautiful New World parable of the reign of God. He refers to Guadalupe as "a vehicle for the doctrine of justification through grace." It is the grace of God proclaimed in and by the Guadalupan event that justifies Juan Diego, Juan Bernardino, and even Bishop Juan de Zumárraga.

Guadalupe is not just a feel-good, touchy devotion. It can be truly appreciated only in the context of the terrific crucifixion that the entire Mexican people were living at that moment, only ten years after the final defeat of the Indian nations. We are told by historians that these were the worst years of cruelty and horror. It was so bad that the people as a whole had a collective death wish: "If you love us, let us die! You have killed our warriors, destroyed our cities, raped our women, and now you tell us our gods are not true. If this be so, why live? Let us die." This was truly a collective crucifixion. Guadalupe, like the cross and resurrection of Jesus, thus becomes the great reversal. It becomes nothing less than a *theologia crucis.*

It is the experience of this unconditional and unmerited grace of God that not only rehabilitates but even re-creates all people so as to bring them into a new common household, into the new family bonds beyond all the blood bonds of this world. This is the temple of living stones requested by La Morenita. Through her, one experiences a new space of love in which everyone is welcomed, everyone is respected, everyone is valued, and everyone is listened to. But even more, one experiences in one's heart a new freedom and joy of living, a new serenity and peace, a new reason for living that heals and liberates from the sufferings of this world. What has been divided and segregated by society finds equality and unity in the mother's household. Her very image is like a mirror reflection of the bodily features of the various peoples of the hemisphere. As such, Max writes that "the image itself is revelatory of the multiracial, multiethnic, multicultural, mestizo 'church' " and that, as Martin Luther viewed Mary theologically, she thus functions as a *typus ecclesiae,* a type or image of the church itself.

Although Max clearly works out of a Lutheran theological framework in this study, the title of the book could easily have been "The Virgin of Guadalupe for All Christians." But even more than being a book about Guadalupe, this book, through the medium of Guadalupe, challenges the reader to a new and greater understanding of several key themes of the Christian tradition, and thus it makes a great contribution to the ongoing growth in the understanding of the faith and the worship aspect of faith. The Virgin of Guadalupe is a divine intrusion into the humanly created liturgical cycles of the church, a divine gift that enriches and expands our cycles of worship.

For too long, Guadalupe has been seen as a major source of division between Catholic and Protestant Christians. Many have felt that until we Mexicans give up Guadalupe, no true ecumenism will be possible. Max clearly demonstrates that the very opposite is true. She will be the medium of the deepest and tenderest ecumenism. Our Lady of Guadalupe is not a dry and complex dogmatic truth of the church but the beautiful and melodious truth of the tenderness of God's love. She is especially precious precisely because she is not necessary for salvation, for ever more precious than that which is necessary is that which is a gift of pure love! In one of the greatest moments of need and divine healing, this great gift came from the infinite graciousness of God's love.

Our best Christian doctrines of redemption, salvation, and justification can be found poetically expressed in the Guadalupe tradition and even more lived out by devotees throughout the world. This poetic expression of saving truth stimulates the mind, heart, senses, and entire person to want to enter into the realities expressed.

Guadalupe, properly understood, can become the deepest source of unity not only of Christians but also of people of all religions. She is, in her own words, "the mother of *all* the inhabitants of this land." She made no qualifications, no distinctions, no conditions. She is the loving mother of all the inhabitants, no matter how different they may be; whether they recognize her or not, she continues to be present, offering her loving love and compassion. She was able to reconcile and bring together what appeared to be two very different and contradictory religions. By so doing she enriched them both, purifying their destructive elements and bringing out the best of each. She offered a win-win situation for everyone. This in itself was a far greater miracle than anyone could imagine, and one that is very much needed today. She can continue to show us how various religions can help each other become better rather than seek to destroy each other.

She did not complete the task of unifying all the inhabitants of this land into a household of love and justice any more than Jesus completed the task of bringing about the reign of God, but she initiated the process, as Jesus did. In visiting her home at Tepeyac or taking part in Guadalupe celebrations anywhere in the world, one gets a foretaste of what has indeed begun but is not yet complete. In her presence, everyone experiences the profound joy of being together without any distinctions; we are all together as a loving family in our mama's home. In this millennium, hungry for affection, unity, and harmony, there will no more powerful source of bringing us together as one family of men and women than a loving, inviting, and compassionate mother.

In *The Virgin of Guadalupe: Theological Reflections of an Anglo-Lutheran Liturgist,* Max Johnson has rendered a great service to the entire Christian world by demonstrating that even though Guadalupe started in Mexico, as Jesus started in Palestine, she, like Jesus, is for all Christians. The more we probe the mystery of her tradition, the more we appreciate the way she gave American flesh to Christianity. Her presence and her message become all the more relevant and urgent in our world today. What had been seen as a major barrier to ecumenical unity will in effect become the tenderest and most beautiful source of unity.

Thanks, Max, for being a Juan Diego for us today, for as Mary appeared on the Tilma of Juan Diego for all to see and appreciate, so a new and dynamic image of her presence is masterfully painted through the pages of your book.

VIRGIL ELIZONDO
University of Notre Dame

Acknowledgments

The English translation of the *Nican Mopohua* and notes by Virgil Elizondo in chapter 1, pages 20–29, from *Guadalupe: Mother of the New Creation,* by Virgil Elizondo (Maryknoll, N.Y.: Orbis Books, 1997), and other quotations from Orbis Books, appear with permission of Orbis Books.

The lengthy quotation from Rubén Martinez, "The Undocumented Virgin," in chapter 4, pages 117–19, from *Goddess of the Americas, La Diosa de las Americas,* ed. Ana Castillo (New York: Riverhead Books, 1996), appears with permission of Riverhead Books.

The photograph of the icon Roses in December, by Brother Claude Lane, OSB, Mount Angel Abbey, St. Benedict, Oregon, in chapter 5, page 163, appears courtesy of Brother Claude in the photographic format graciously provided by Gerald Nelson, director of information technology, Conception Abbey, Conception, Mo.

The photograph of the icon Nuestra Señora del Programa Misionero from Coachella, California, in chapter 5, page 164, appears courtesy of the Reverend Daniel Groody, C.S.C., Department of Theology, University of Notre Dame, Notre Dame, Ind.

Introduction: An Apologia

From December 12, 1531, the date of her alleged appearances to the recently converted Aztec native, Juan Diego, on the hill of Tepeyac, north of Mexico City, until the present, the image and cult of Our Lady of Guadalupe have been defining religious and cultural expressions of especially Mexican and Mexican American identity and spirituality. Juan Diego himself was beatified, that is, declared "blessed," by Pope John Paul II in 1990, the next-to-the-last step in his canonization as a saint of the Roman Catholic Church, an event that is currently scheduled to take place in Mexico City in July 2002. And, as recently as 1999, the celebration of Our Lady of Guadalupe on December 12—already, of course, a *solemnity* in Mexico—was raised in status by Pope John Paul II from a *memorial* on the liturgical calendars of many dioceses and a *feast* on the liturgical calendars of some, to the rank of feast for *all* Roman Catholic dioceses of North, Central, and South America. Indeed, Hispanic-Latino Catholicism, especially in its Mexican and Mexican American expressions, is, in no uncertain terms, Guadalupan in its form, character, and identity.

Since this is the case, there are, undoubtedly, several reasons why a Protestant liturgist, specifically a Lutheran liturgist, and an *Anglo male* Lutheran liturgist at that, should probably not even venture to write a book on the Virgin of Guadalupe, a phenomenon so readily identifiable as simultaneously Roman Catholic, Hispanic-Latino (especially Mexican or Mexican American), apparitionist, and, depending on one's perspective, either feminist or misogynist in orientation. At least four reasons spring to mind from the outset.

First, the connection between Protestantism and Mariology has longed seemed to many to be such an obvious contradiction in terms that anything resembling an attempt at a "Protestant" or "ecumenical" Mariology might be readily dismissed by some beforehand as an oxymoron. That is, in spite of the potentially and ecumenically significant theological treatment of the

1

Virgin Mary in the writings of the sixteenth-century Protestant Reformers themselves, Mariology has not been a traditional characteristic of
Protestant theological thought in general. Rather, at least in the not-too-
distant past, the presence of Marian theology or traces of continued Marian devotion in the writings of some of the Reformers were often dismissed, somewhat condescendingly, as but vestiges of the late medieval
Marian devotionalism in which they were raised or from which they were
unable to escape or divorce themselves completely in their subsequent
thought. Until only recently, if modern Protestant theologians treated the
question of Mary at all, Mariological issues were often dealt with in a relatively negative or dismissive manner.[1] The influential Lutheran theologian
Paul Tillich, for example, critiqued even the "virgin birth" of Christ as
something that "by excluding the participation of a human father in [his]
procreation . . . deprive[d] him of full participation in the human predica-
ment."[2] And, in spite of his strong differences with Tillich in theological
method, the great Reformed theologian Karl Barth was also very critical in
his approach and once categorized and castigated Roman Catholic Mariology in an oft-quoted statement as "an excrescence, i.e., a diseased construct of theological thought . . . [which] must be excised."[3]

Second, the narratives of the Virgin of Guadalupe as they appear in the
earliest extant written accounts in 1648[4] and 1649, the second of which
was composed in the ancient Aztec language Nahuatl and called from the
first two words of the account *Nican Mopohua* ("it is narrated"),[5] are, of
course, the narratives of a series of alleged apparitions or visions of Mary
experienced by Juan Diego, his uncle Juan Bernardino, and the local bishop of what is today Mexico City, Juan Zumárraga, in December of 1531.
And, in spite of several theophanies in the Hebrew Bible, the New Testament post-Resurrection appearances of Christ to the apostles and others
on Easter night (see Luke 24 and John 20), the vision of St. Paul on the
road to Damascus (Acts 9), or even Paul's own description of the risen Lord
appearing to him after having appeared to five hundred others (1 Cor. 15:
3–11), Protestantism has had little room or time for apparitions in general,
especially Marian ones, and has been able to dismiss them readily from theological consideration. It may have been Martin Luther himself who set the
theological precedent for this kind of Protestant approach to apparitions in
his *Lectures on Genesis* (sometime during the 1530s), saying that:

> The monks extol the legends of their fathers Benedict and Bernard, but
> surely God generally speaks at far greater length and associates far more in-
> timately with any Christian whatever than they boast about their fathers.
> Indeed, if I had the matter under my control, I would not want God to

speak to me from heaven or to appear to me; but this I would want—and my daily prayers are directed to this end—that I might have the proper respect and true appreciation for the gift of Baptism, that I have been baptized, and that I see and hear brothers who have the grace and gift of the Holy Spirit and are able to comfort and encourage with the Word, to admonish, warn, and teach. For what better and more profitable appearance of God do you want?[6]

Third, there is no question but that there has been what might be called an anti-Protestant Reformation, or Counter-Reformation, bias associated with the interpretation of the Guadalupan event within the history of Roman Catholicism. In his compelling 1994 doctoral dissertation on several published Guadalupan sermons preached in Mexico during the seventeenth to nineteenth centuries, Francisco Schulte, OSB, notes a connection made between the spread of Protestantism throughout sixteenth-century Europe and the missionary planting of Roman Catholicism in the New World. In one eighteenth-century sermon studied by Schulte this connection appears clearly:

To repair the ruins [i.e., the Protestant Reformation] of holy religion by planting it anew in America by means of the apparition of Mary of Guadalupe was the beloved design of God in this work; a work by no means less of the love and the wisdom of God than of the power of God: the most admirable work that the ages have seen; and, finally, a work which shows us that Mary in the image of Guadalupe was the voice of God directed to repair the ruins that religion suffered in the old world, establishing it in the new: ego vox clamantis in deserto ["I am the voice crying in the wilderness"].[7]

Fourth, on the basis, undoubtedly, of the recent and highly critical historical study of the Guadalupe narrative and events by Stafford Poole (although she does not refer to this study directly),[8] Lutheran author Gail Ramshaw draws the following negative conclusions about the narrative, image, and implications of the Guadalupan phenomenon:

Women's studies books trace a lineage that sounds highly likely, from the Aztec goddess Cihuacoatl, Mother Serpent, to the sixteenth-century image of Mary. However, the latest meticulously footnoted historical study indicates that, sad to say, Mary was not in fact seen by a goddess-worshipping Indian peasant in 1531. Rather, she was concocted in 1648 by Mexico's Spanish clergy and back-dated to the conquest. You see, the clergy had a pressing need to prove that the Mexican-born Spanish community enjoyed as high a social and religious status as that of the more recent Spanish immigrants. How better to achieve this upgrade, than for Mary to appear in Guadalupe, Mexico, just as she had done before in Guadalupe, Spain? Thus, once again, the male hierarchy found veneration of a goddess handy for their own self-aggrandizement, and the oppressed peoples of the land, all the Juan Diegos, were manipulated to support the desires of the upper class. Now when I see contemporary women appealing to Mary, I wonder if they know to what degree she has been invented by misogynist males. To sum this all up: the apparition of our Lady of Guadalupe was neither Mary nor a transmogrified Aztec goddess, since she never appeared at all. . . . My mind knows this disturbing history, this pathway laid down with centuries of human hearts. Yet my eyes watch Indian families "creeping to Guadalupe," inching on their knees at least the last mile of their pilgrimage to give homage to Our Lady. Many carry bouquets of flowers to lay before the image, which they believe either Mary herself or God painted. I think of Dostoyevski's Grand Inquisitor commenting on our desire for miracles. The historical study of Guadalupe documents that in the sixteenth century a painting of Mary was acclaimed for being able to produce miracles. A century later, the people claimed that the painting itself had been miraculously produced.[9]

Hence, the fourth reason for my not writing this book would seem to be, on the basis of implications from the conclusions of *some* contemporary historical studies, that the entire Guadalupan narrative, image, and "history" are but a sham in the first place, a cleverly crafted story and "painting" with a deliberate intent to keep the oppressed indigenous poor locked in their oppression and poverty and women kept in patriarchal servitude in imitation of a most passive Mary, whose very passivity is used to justify an ultimately unjust social and ecclesiastical order.

In light of the above reasons, therefore, it would seem that the deck is stacked from the start clearly and decidedly against anyone who seeks to write a Protestant, ecumenically sensitive, or specifically Lutheran interpretation of the Virgin of Guadalupe. Mariology itself has not been a traditional forte in Protestant thought. Apparitions, *especially* those of Mary, have not been a significant part of Protestant theological worldviews or the Protestant religious imagination. The narrative and image of the Virgin of Guadalupe have been invoked at times in support of Roman Catholicism as the one "true" religion against the very existence of Protestantism itself. And serious doubt has been cast by recent historians and others not only on the reliability and authenticity of the standard account of the Guadalupan events but also on the actual historical existence of Juan Diego himself, and suspicion has been raised about an antipoor and antiwoman bias reflected in its development. These reasons, coupled with the clear Hispanic-Latino and Roman Catholic context and orientation of the Virgin of Guadalupe, which I, as an Anglo Lutheran, cannot possibly know from the inside, would seem to make this venture little more than an exercise in futility. So, with all of this apparently against me already, why am I bothering to attempt writing this book in the first place? Perhaps the following may help to serve as clarification and provide some kind of apologia for this attempt.

First, a Protestant Mariology is no longer the obvious oxymoron that it once may have been. Recent books, such as Anglican theologian John Macquarrie's *Mary for all Christians* and (former) Lutheran Jaroslav Pelikan's *Mary through the Centuries,* provide ecumenically sensitive Protestant assessments of Marian doctrine and devotion.[10] Since 1967 there has been in existence the international Ecumenical Society of the Blessed Virgin Mary, organized to promote both devotion and study.[11] And Evangelical Lutheran Church in America (ELCA) Lutherans and Roman Catholics in the United States produced in 1992 a joint statement, *The One Mediator, the Saints, and Mary,* in which was achieved, if not full doctrinal consensus, at least enough theological convergence and clarity to state that this issue need no longer be viewed as "church dividing" in the continued quest toward full and visible communion. With specific regard to the question of the invocation of Mary and the saints in the church, the following statement from this document is quite telling ecumenically: "Saints on earth ask one another to pray to God for each other through Christ. They are neither commanded *nor forbidden* to ask departed saints to pray for them."[12] At the same time, the highly significant 1999 officially accepted Lutheran–Roman Catholic *Joint Declaration on the Doctrine of Justification* raises to a new level the ecumenical conversation on this and other topics. As the *Joint Declaration* asserts: "By grace alone, in faith in Christ's saving work and not because of any merit on our part, we are accepted by God and receive the Holy Spirit, who renews our hearts while equipping and calling us to good works. . . . Through [Christ] alone are we justified, when we receive this salvation in faith."[13]

And further: "Justification is more than just one part of Christian doctrine. It is to serve as a criterion which constantly orients all the teaching and practice of our churches to Christ, whom alone we ultimately trust as the one Mediator (1 Tim 2:5–6) through whom God in the Holy Spirit gives himself and pours out his saving gifts."[14]

Consequently, at least ELCA Lutherans and Roman Catholics are now enabled to approach issues like Marian doctrine and devotion from a common and agreed-upon starting point. That is, if justification by grace alone through faith is a criterion for orienting all the teaching and practice of the church to Christ alone, then Marian doctrine and devotion also need to be tested and oriented by this criterion. With specific regard to the Virgin of Guadalupe, this criterion would seem to function in such a way as to ask whether or not the narrative, cult, and image are compatible with justification by grace alone through faith and whether they actually support and underscore this doctrine. In other words, might the Virgin of Guadalupe be somehow interpreted as a concrete or incarnated expression of justification by grace alone through faith, or does she actually contradict this doctrine outright? If, in light of the *Joint Declaration,* Roman Catholics now must also increasingly employ this criterion theologically in their own soteriological, Christological, and ecclesiological evaluation of Marian doctrine and devotion in general, any kind of Protestant assessment or reassessment of the Virgin of Guadalupe will need to employ this doctrinal criterion as the primary litmus test. Virgil Elizondo draws indirect attention to this criterion when he writes: "Protestants tell me: 'But Christ alone is necessary for salvation.' And I say to them: 'You are absolutely right. That is precisely what makes Guadalupe so precious. Precisely because she is not necessary, she is so special! She is a gift of God's love.'"[15] If, indeed, it is the case that the Virgin of Guadalupe is a "gift," a gift of God and a gift of Mexican and Mexican American Catholicism to the wider Catholic Church, is she a gift also to be received by Protestants and/or by the wider ecumenical Church? If not, why not? If so, then how?

Second, in spite of the antiapparitionist bias in much of Protestantism noted above, even within the Roman Catholic Church apparitions are not accorded the kind of official acceptance or authorization that is often assumed, even if, as in the case of Pope John Paul II in recent years, personal papal piety tends to display public support and preference for the various devotional expressions associated with the major Marian shrines. Out of the sheer thousands of alleged Marian (and other) apparitions throughout history,[16] the officially approved ones are very few indeed (Lourdes, Fatima, and, of course, Guadalupe are the best known and most popular), and approval by the Roman Catholic Church never implies official acceptance, authorization, or any kind of authentication or verification of the event, its message, or its contents. Because such events belong to the category of what is called "private revelation," in distinction to "public" or "official" revelation, approval never means that the apparition or its contents can be used for doctrinal or dogmatic conclusions or promulgations. It only means that a Roman Catholic, if so disposed, *may* engage in the devotion or cult associated with the apparition with the assent of "human" but not "divine" faith without contradicting the official faith and doctrinal positions of the church. But nothing about the apparition or its message is, or even can be, binding on the faith of individual Catholics. That is, it is quite possible and permissible for an individual Roman Catholic to assert in good conscience—and still remain a faithful Catholic—that Mary herself *never* appeared at Lourdes, Fatima, or Guadalupe or that she has never appeared anywhere at any time or place.[17]

The Virgin of Guadalupe, however, is not merely an apparition of the Virgin Mary that supposedly took place in December of 1531 and that, in spite of official recognition, an individual Catholic may choose either to accept or to reject. Rather, and more important, the Virgin of Guadalupe continues to "appear," not in the sense of other similar apparitions to individuals (although that too is sometimes claimed), but in the sense of an abiding or accompanying "presence" in the lives of many. In other words, historical questions about her appearance to Juan Diego, albeit important in historical-critical scholarship, are one thing. But whatever conclusions one reaches in that context, the theological questions about her presence and role in the lives of people are another thing altogether and are not necessarily solved at the same time or by the same historical-critical methods. That is, despite what historians may or may not conclude about the origins of the Guadalupan events and image, theological interpretation and liturgical celebration must take into account not so much the historicity of the events as the continued presence and role that the Virgin of Guadalupe plays. In his recent book, *Guadalupe: Mother of the New Creation,* Elizondo expresses it this way:

> Even if the story of Our Lady of Guadalupe were not historical (according to modern Western historiography), it is still definitely constitutive of the saving truth of the *sensus fidelium*—of the faith-memory of the people. The story, like the image, is so packed with the word of life expressed in human terms, is so beautiful and harmonious, is so critical and melodious, is so theological and poetic, is so simple and profound, and is so affirming and challenging that it can only be a very special gift of the creating and redeeming God.[18]

Third, the anti–Protestant Reformation bias associated in the past with interpretations of the Virgin of Guadalupe is not necessarily an argument that holds up as a deterrent against a Protestant reassessment today. History, together with ecumenical dialogue and convergence, has a way of leveling things out even on ecclesial planes. For example, the Solemnity of Christ the King on the last Sunday of the liturgical year (the Sunday before the season of Advent begins) in the Roman Catholic liturgy was originally celebrated on the last Sunday in October. Established by Pope Pius IX in 1926, it was placed originally on that Sunday in part, at least, to provide a Roman Catholic counterpart to the Protestant celebration of "Reformation Sunday" usually observed on the same day in commemoration of Martin Luther's nailing of the Ninety-five Theses to the castle church door in Wittenburg, Germany, on October 31, 1517.[19] But today, after the liturgical reforms of Vatican II and similar contemporary reforms in other churches, it is interesting to note how this feast of Christ the King, a feast that in its origins may easily be interpreted as one of Catholic triumphalism in juxtaposition to one of Protestant triumphalism, now appears as the last Sunday of the liturgical year in the calendars of several Protestant traditions together with the identical lectionary readings provided for liturgical proclamation. The same might be said for other feasts and occasions originally deleted but recently restored to the liturgical calendars of several Protestant churches (e.g., Holy Cross on September 14, Mary on August 15, and the Week of Prayer for Christian Unity, January 18–25, a period of time originally set apart for Roman Catholics to pray for the return "home" of Protestants to the Catholic Church). The ecumenical nature of contemporary Protestant liturgical calendars provides additional examples. The calendar of Lesser Festivals and Commemorations in the *Lutheran Book of Worship* even includes *popes* like John XXIII (June 3) and Gregory the Great (March 12), as well as Counter-Reformation figures like Jesuit missionary Francis Xavier (December 3). The recent Hispanic Lutheran resource *Libro de Liturgia y Cántico* has added Salvadoran Roman Catholic archbishop and martyr Oscar Romero (March 24), Mexican Jesuit martyr Miguel Pro (November 23), and Dominican founder Dominic Guzman (August 8) to its calendar; and *This Far by Faith,* an African American Lutheran liturgical resource, includes Jesuit Peter Claver (September 9) and Dominican brother Martín de Porres (November 3). Similarly, various devotional and liturgical practices long associated with Roman Catholic identity and self-expression in particular, such as *Las Posadas,* beginning on December 16,[20] the stations of the cross,[21] the imposition of ashes on Ash Wednesday, the distribution, blessing, and procession with palms on Palm (Passion) Sunday, the rite of footwashing on Holy Thursday, and the veneration of the Cross on Good Friday, have made their reappearance in several contemporary Protestant worship books.[22] The origins and traditional interpretations of particular feasts and practices, therefore, even of those with a decidedly anti-Protestant bias such as Christ the King, have not been strong enough deterrents in this ecumenical age to forbid their inclusion in contemporary Protestant liturgical celebration. Might the same be said, then, for the Virgin of Guadalupe, in spite of similar traditional associations and interpretations?

Fourth and finally, more so than any other religious image except perhaps the crucifix, the image of the Virgin of Guadalupe permeates Hispanic-Latino culture in the Americas. From tattoos, jewelry, fine art, folk art, home altars, yard shrines, rugs, ornaments and decorations for cars, baseball caps, T-shirts, *paños* (pieces of cloth or handkerchiefs painted by prison inmates), computer mouse pads, murals on the side of buildings and homes, all the way to banners under which her devotees process and even protest, the image of the Virgin of Guadalupe is encountered everywhere in those cultural contexts.[23] Even for those who may reject her Christian and/or ecclesial associations as Mary, the Mother of God, her image is frequently maintained and reinterpreted as "Mother," sometimes even in protest against Christianity itself.[24] Further, today Guadalupe increasingly appears outside the cultural confines of Mexican and Mexican American Catholicism with shrines or altars to her noted in Italy (inside of St. Peter's Basilica), Spain, Poland, Japan, France, Ethiopia, Sweden, Korea, Kenya, and Canada, related in some cases, undoubtedly, to growing trends in Mexican emigration and immigration around the world.[25]

Similarly, the influx of immigrants into the United States in the past decades from Mexico and Central and South America, as well as the increased tendency of former migrants toward permanent residency in several parts of the United States today, has led many to suggest that by 2010 the Roman Catholic Church in the United States will be over 50 percent Latino-Hispanic. If the projected figures, not surprisingly, are lower for other Christian denominations in the United States, the mere fact that both the Episcopal Church in the USA (ECUSA) and the ELCA, for example, have recently produced official liturgical books in Spanish (*Libro de oración común* and the above-noted *Libro de Liturgia y Cántico*, respectively) to assist in ministering to these new immigrants or permanent residents demonstrates that all churches are striving to pay attention to this changing social and cultural environment. The forming of a true multicultural, ethnically and racially diverse, and inclusive Christianity in the United States in which the gifts of the "other" are affirmed and valued is (and, of course, must be) on the agenda of most churches today. Hence, in light of such a changing social and cultural context, *not* to pay wider and close theological attention to the image, narrative, and cult of the Virgin of Guadalupe would be a serious error, especially for those seeking to address or minister to a people whose very cultural and religious identity has been shaped to some extent by this phenomenon.

Reactions to the cult and image of the Virgin of Guadalupe, of course, vary considerably outside of Roman Catholicism, although even within Roman Catholicism there is no one normative, accepted position held in common by all.[26] While some evangelical or Protestant fundamentalist Christians and others would and do reject outright anything and everything having to do with Guadalupe as a vestige of unenlightened paganism or expression of Catholic "superstition" and "Mariolatry,"[27] others have been accused of employing the image and name of the Virgin of Guadalupe

in their churches as an evangelistic ploy to attract Roman Catholic Hispanic-Latinos to conversion in their communities. The challenge of Protestant fundamentalism or evangelicalism to the Roman Catholic Church
throughout Mexico and Central and South America, as well as here within the United States, is strong indeed. But even for those churches that
share a more common sacramental and liturgical tradition with Roman
Catholicism, such as Episcopalians and Lutherans, who are similarly challenged today by various forms of fundamentalism, commemorations of
Juan Diego on December 9 or of the Virgin of Guadalupe herself on December 12 will vary. Neither, for example, has been incorporated into the
liturgical calendars of the recent liturgical books noted above. Nevertheless,
even if not "officially" included on liturgical calendars, Guadalupe's image
is encountered in some Protestant churches, and her feast day on December 12 *is* celebrated in some primarily Hispanic-Latino Protestant communities in the United States. And this is so, not because these communities
seek to do evangelistic "sheep stealing" from the Roman Catholic Church,
but because they recognize that not to somehow incorporate both this
image and some form of that Marian piety that permeates Hispanic-Latino cultures, would be tantamount to rejecting one of the powerful, identifying, and defining characteristics of such cultures. In other words, the need
for theological attention to the Virgin of Guadalupe is no longer simply a
Roman Catholic need or question but must somehow be confronted and
addressed *respectfully* by theologians from other Christian churches among
which the Hispanic-Latino presence is growing.

This book is nothing other than an attempt to do just that, and it proceeds as follows. The first chapter provides a translation of the most widely accepted Guadalupan narrative (the *Nican Mopohua*) and some discussion
of how the narrative and image of the Virgin of Guadalupe have been interpreted. The second chapter offers an investigation of the story of the
Guadalupan apparition, image, and cult in historical context and development. Here, especially, the recent work of Stafford Poole, which issues several critical challenges to the authenticity of the Guadalupan event and
image, will be surveyed critically.

The third chapter considers how some contemporary Roman Catholic
theologians treat the permeating presence of Guadalupe in what has been
called, sometimes pejoratively, "popular religiosity" among Hispanic-Latinos
in an attempt to understand her role and symbol within that cultural-religious context.[28] It also considers the possibilities of how or whether the
Virgin of Guadalupe functions theologically as a mediating symbol of the
"maternity" of God. Here, of course, as we shall see, the literature tends to
be divided, with some advocating this kind of approach directly, while oth-

ers call instead for a new way to reimage God with feminine and/or Guadalupan attributes apart from Mary herself.

Because the Virgin of Guadalupe is a liturgical feast, as well as an image and a popular devotion, the fourth chapter provides a brief overview of the development and content of this December 12 feast. This chapter includes an examination of the prayers and lectionary readings in the eucharistic liturgy currently appointed for December 12 in the official Roman Catholic liturgical books of both Mexico and the United States.[29] Since, however, this feast occurs in the middle of Advent, attention is also given to the relationship and possible tension between the "official" season of Advent with its strong eschatological focus and the more "popular" Marian focus of the season among Hispanic-Latinos. In addition, descriptions of Guadalupan celebrations in some Protestant churches today, limited here to Lutheran and Episcopal, will also be provided as a way of setting the context for the final chapter of this study.

The fifth and final chapter investigates whether and in what ways the Guadalupan image, narrative, feast, and even some forms of "devotion" might be received or integrated within an evangelical or Protestant theological perspective today. Here, in general, the above-noted criterion of justification by grace alone through faith, together with the thoughts of various Protestant scholars, including, notably, Martin Luther's own Marian theology, will be applied to the Guadalupan phenomenon.

This book is not written with the intention of trying to convince or tell Hispanic-Latino Protestants or Anglos who minister among them what they should or should not do with regard to the Virgin of Guadalupe in their communities, although it is certainly hoped that this study will be helpful in providing some kind of theological rationale in those contexts. To be prescriptive for Hispanic-Latinos on my part would be both rash and irresponsible, and I have neither the expertise nor the authority to do that. My concern in this book, rather, is more broadly theological than limited only to one culturally conditioned faith expression. Nevertheless, if the theological interpretations of the narrative and image of the Virgin of Guadalupe as advanced in recent years by such scholars as Virgil Elizondo, Jeannette Rodriguez, Richard Nebel, and several others has any credence or applicability beyond Roman Catholicism itself, or beyond the cultural and religious borders of Hispanic-Latino Catholicism, then, perhaps, it is time for Protestant Christians in the Americas—Anglo, Hispanic-Latino, and other—to ask themselves whether there is some room for this "Mother of the Americas," as she has been called, in their churches, liturgical celebrations, and theological reflections.

Every book to some extent, to borrow from the title of John Henry

Cardinal Newman's *Apologia pro vita sua,* is, ultimately, a defense of, or invitation to share, an author's own worldview, experience, or approach to a topic. Certainly this book is no exception to that rule. If it is possible to be Anglo, male, and Lutheran and yet be simultaneously "Guadalupan," without sacrificing or compromising my own Lutheran confessional and theological commitments and identity, then I suspect that I come as close as anyone can to fitting that rather odd, by some standards, combination. Although I had been well aware of the image and narrative of the Virgin of Guadalupe and her permeating presence in especially a Mexican Catholic and cultural context for some time, my first real encounter with *Guadalupanismo,* as it is sometimes termed, came almost thirty years ago, in January 1973, when, as a college-junior religion major at a small Lutheran liberal arts college, Augustana College, in Sioux Falls, South Dakota, I had the opportunity during a January term class to live and study with several classmates for three weeks at the Benedictine Priory of Our Lady of the Angels in Ahuatepec (on the outskirts of Cuernavaca), Mexico. Here I was able to visit and experience firsthand Guadalupan devotion at the former Basilica of Our Lady of Guadalupe in Mexico City. It was an experience I repeated with other classmates the next year, returning to Mexico for an independent study at the same priory during the January term of 1974. I recall being somewhat perplexed and put off at the basilica by what might be termed a simultaneous "sacramental-liturgical smorgasbord" taking place within it (i.e., three masses being celebrated at the same time, one at the high altar and two at side altars, Holy Communion being distributed not within the masses but continuously in the Blessed Sacrament Chapel, pilgrims going to confession throughout the basilica at makeshift confessionals set up for this purpose, and other devotions at various sites in the basilica with no obvious relation to the liturgical "celebrations" taking place). Nevertheless, unlike most of my collegiate colleagues, formed, as was I, by that Lake Wobegon, Minnesota, variety of midwestern United States, almost Stoic, and rather anti-Catholic, Lutheranism, I found myself strangely attracted not only to the Guadalupan image and narrative, as well as to other religious images throughout Mexico (especially those depicting Christ in various stages of his Passion and Crucifixion) having their roots in sixteenth-century Spain, but also by the displays of devotional piety that I witnessed among the pilgrims. Unlike me, they had gone to Tepeyac not as mere tourists or students but as devotees, as practitioners of a time-honored, centuries-long devotion at this spot. And, if "creeping to Guadalupe" on their hands and knees throughout the plaza leading to the image enshrined over the high altar in the basilica was, and is, not "my" piety, I was and remain, nonetheless, profoundly moved by this expression of faith and devotion. There was something there not to be readily dismissed, I concluded.

Many years have now passed since those initial encounters with the Virgin of Guadalupe at her basilica in Mexico City, but those first experiences have stayed with me somewhere in the back of my mind. And while since then a small framed reproduction of the image on Juan Diego's *tilma,* or cloak, together with Byzantine and other Eastern Christian icons of the Virgin and Child, has been a part of the religious iconography on display in my office and home, I had not been much concerned, until recently, with either the Guadalupan narratives or with the theological interpretation of Guadalupe. I was, rather, content to leave it alone as a kind of warm and somewhat "charming" characteristic of a specifically Mexican piety, and my small image itself was but a souvenir of a memorable experience from my college years. I suspect that my relatively recent return to a consideration of the Virgin of Guadalupe is due to a variety of factors. First, as the adoptive father of two African American children, the image of *La Morena* or *La Morenita* (little dark one), as the Virgin of Guadalupe is affectionately known in one her titles, presented itself as a valuable, indigenous American, ethnically and racially mixed iconographic alternative to the blond and blue-eyed European style of religious art that my children continually encountered in largely Caucasian ecclesial environments. Today, in fact, my one framed reproduction of the image on Juan Diego's tilma, together with a related burgeoning interest in the religious folk art of the *santeros* (makers and painters of wooden saints and altar screens) in Mexico, Central and South America, and New Mexico, has expanded into an ever growing collection of Guadalupan (and other) images (santos) crafted in various media. Second, if my initial concern was artistic and familial in nature, in my own work in liturgical scholarship and teaching in primarily Roman Catholic contexts, and especially in courses dealing with the feasts and seasons of the liturgical year and in graduate seminar courses specifically on the feasts and theology of Mary and the saints, I discovered that students themselves were often attracted to Guadalupe and frequently chose her as the subject of research papers. This, together with several conversations with my dear friend and former School of Theology colleague at Saint John's University, Collegeville, Minnesota, Francisco Schulte, OSB, who not only shared my artistic interest in Guadalupe but who had also recently completed his doctoral dissertation in spirituality in Rome on the theology of Guadalupe expressed in seventeenth- through nineteenth-century Guadalupan sermons from Mexico,[30] sparked my interest theologically and led me into a then unknown world of Guadalupan studies. Such studies were quite distinct in nature from the pious, apologetic, and devotional genre of literature that tends to be associated with all Marian apparitions and shrines. But together with all of this, there is no question that the most recent and even primary catalyst for this study has been the absence of, and the apparent refusal to include, even a mere December 12 "optional commemoration" of the Virgin Mary under the title of Guadalupe on the liturgical calendar of the Lutheran *Libro de Liturgia y Cántico*.[31] Hence, in part, my own creeping to Guadalupe in this study is an effort to understand whether this absence or refusal need be the final conclusion reached from within a Lutheran or Protestant theological perspective in the context of the changing face of North American Christianity.

While I have subtitled this study "Theological Reflections of an Anglo Lutheran Liturgist," my reflections tend to be more along the lines of theological musings rather than systematic reflections. Within a Hispanic-Latino ecclesial and cultural context *musa* is what takes place as reflection or conversation after *misa* (the Mass) and *mesa* (table), that is, the fiesta, party, banquet, convivium, or feast associated with communal gatherings.[32] Thus, this study does not pretend to be a systematic theology of the Virgin of Guadalupe but consists, rather, of my "musings" on the topic, my reflections on the potential significance of Guadalupe for other than Roman Catholic Christians. And I offer these musings as an Anglo Lutheran who has the privilege of working primarily in the field of liturgical studies in an ecumenical environment. Hence, while history and theology will clearly play important roles in this work, my overall interest is geared toward liturgical (and other) celebrations in the life of the church. For, indeed, it is precisely through misa and mesa, through liturgical celebration and fiesta, that the faith of the Church is most clearly expressed and people are continually formed in this faith. It is to this, in fact, that liturgical theologians often refer with the Latin patristic principle of Prosper of Aquitaine, "ut legem credendi statuat lex supplicandi" (that the law of supplication or prayer might establish the law of believing).

Finally, a book such as this would not have been possible without the generous assistance, support, and encouragement of several others. First, I wish to express my deep gratitude to Dean Mark Roche of the College of Liberal Arts, University of Notre Dame, and to Professor John Cavadini, chair of the Department of Theology, University of Notre Dame, for granting me a sabbatical leave during the fall semester, 2000, so I could complete the research leading to this book. Second, special thanks are also due to Julia Douthwaite, Kenneth Garcia, and Beth Bland of the Institute for Scholarship in the Liberal Arts, University of Notre Dame, and to Gilberto Cardenas of the Latino Studies Program, University of Notre Dame, who, through a faculty grant and other funding provided the financial support necessary for this research leave, which I spent at the Mexican American

Cultural Center, San Antonio, Texas. Third, I am in debt to dear colleagues and friends, especially to Father Virgil Elizondo, now also teaching at Notre Dame, whose own extensive and authoritative writings on the Virgin of Guadalupe are referred to or quoted often in this work, including his translation of the *Nican Mopohua* in chapter 1 and his foreword; to Father Francisco Schulte, OSB, of Saint John's Abbey and University, Collegeville, Minnesota, with whom I have had many Guadalupan discussions; to Sister Rosa María Icaza of the Mexican American Cultural Center, who generously loaned me several books from her own library; and to Lizette Larson-Miller of the Church Divinity School of the Pacific, Berkeley, California, who served as a resource in helping me discover the increasing presence of the Virgin of Guadalupe in some Episcopal contexts, especially in California. Third, I am also indebted to those Lutheran pastors who provided for me descriptions and interpretations of Guadalupe in their parishes. Here especially I wish to acknowledge the contributions of Pastors Ivis J. LaRiviere-Mestre of San Martín de Porres Lutheran Church, Allentown, Pennsylvania, and Antonio Cabello, of La Iglesia de San Estéban, Mártir, Carpentersville, Illinois. Thanks are also due to new friends, Roberto Piña of the Mexican American Cultural Center; Ramón Vásquez y Sanchez, Native American artist and arts program director of the Centro Cultural Aztlan in San Antonio; and Laura Sánchez of Proyecto Hospitalidad, San Antonio, for their conversations with me that they permitted me to record for quotation in this study. It was Laura Sánchez who, when I expressed to her certain misgivings I had about doing this project, encouraged me, saying that there was no question but that I *had* to write it because I had heard the message and received the call to do so from La Virgen herself. Thanks are also due to my graduate assistant, Notre Dame liturgy doctoral student David Pitt, for his assistance with research, with the index, and proofreading of the entire manuscript. Pitt himself, a Canadian Roman Catholic, has recently written a short article on the adaptation of the feast of the Virgin of Guadalupe in Canada.[33] Finally, I would be remiss if I did not gratefully acknowledge the support of my family, Nancy, Brynn, and Zachary, especially during the research phase of this project in the fall semester of 2000, when I was an absentee husband and father living in San Antonio. To all of these I owe an immense debt of gratitude.

Notes

1. See Hermann Sasse, "Liturgie und Bekenntnis: Brüderliche Warnung vor 'hochkirchlichen' Gefahren," *Lutherische Blätter* 11, (1959): 62, to appear in English

translation as "Liturgy and Confession: A Brotherly Warning against the 'High Church' Danger," in *The Lonely Way: Hermann Sasse—Selected Essays and Letters,* vol. 2, ed. Matthew C. Harrison (St. Louis: Concordia, 2002).

2. Paul Tillich, *Systematic Theology,* (Chicago: University of Chicago Press, 1957), 2: 160.

3. Karl Barth, "Bible Studies in the First Chapter of St. Luke," *Foi et vie* 85 (1936): 139.

4. Miguel Sánchez, *Imagen de la Virgen Maria, Madre de Dios de Guadalupe: milagrosamente aparecida en la Ciudad de México, Celebrada en su historia, con la profecía del capítulo doze del Apocalipsis* (Imp. Vidua de Bernardo Calderón, Mexico, 1648; reprint, Cuernavaca Morelos, 1952).

5. *Huei tlamahuiçoltica omonexiti in ilhuicac tlatocacihaupilli Santa Maria totlaçonantzin Guadalupe in nican Huei altepenahuac Mexico itocayocan Tepeyacac* (By a Great Miracle the Heavenly Queen, Saint Mary, Our Precious Mother of Guadalupe, Appeared here near the Great Altepetl of Mexico, in a Place called Tepeyacac).

6. Martin Luther, *Lectures on Genesis,* in *Luther's Works* (Philadelphia: Fortress Press, 1961), 3: 165. The exact date of this particular lecture during the 1530s is disputed. My thanks to Deaconess Rhoda Schuler, a doctoral candidate at Luther Seminary, St. Paul, Minn., for pointing out this reference to me.

7. José Patricio Fernández de Uribe y Casarejo, "Sermón segundo de Nuestra Señora de Guadalupe," in *Sermones de la Virgen en sus Imágenes del Pilar de Zaragoza, y Guadalupe de México,* (Madrid, 1821), 2: 52, as quoted and translated by Francisco R. Schulte, OSB, "A Mexican Spirituality of Divine Election for a Mission: Its Sources in Published Guadalupan Sermons, 1661–1821" (Ph.D. diss., Gregorian Pontifical University, Rome, 1994), 43. I am happy to note that Schulte's study will be published by Rowman & Littlefield within the same series as my study.

8. Stafford Poole, C.M., *Our Lady of Guadalupe: The Origins and Sources of a Mexican National Symbol, 1531–1797* (Tucson: University of Arizona Press, 1995).

9. Gail Ramshaw, *Under the Tree of Life: The Religion of a Feminist Christian* (New York: Continuum, 1998), 20–21.

10. John Macquarrie, *Mary for All Christians* (Grand Rapids: Eerdmans, 1990); Jaroslav Pelikan, *Mary through the Centuries* (New Haven: Yale University Press, 1996).

11. Several publications have appeared from this society. See esp. the essays in Alberic Stacpoole, OSB, ed., *Mary and the Churches: Papers of the Chicester Congress, 1986, of the Ecumenical Society of the Blessed Virgin Mary* (Collegeville, Minn.: Liturgical Press, 1987); and Alberic Stacpoole, OSB, ed., *Mary in Doctrine and Devotion: Papers of the Liverpool Congress, 1989, of the Ecumenical Society of the Blessed Virgin Mary* (Collegeville, Minn.: Liturgical Press, 1990). The society's "Ecumenical Office of Mary the Mother of Jesus" appears in Macquarrie, *Mary for All Christians,* 139–60.

12. H. George Anderson, et al., eds., *The One Mediator, the Saints, and Mary,* Lutherans and Catholics in Dialogue 8 (Minneapolis: Augsburg, 1992), 61 [emphasis added].

13. Lutheran World Federation and Pontifical Council for the Promotion of

Christian Unity, *Joint Declaration on the Doctrine of Justification* (Geneva: Lutheran World Federation, 1999), 3.15.

14. *Joint Declaration,* 3.18.

15. Virgil Elizondo and Friends, *A Retreat with Our Lady of Guadalupe and Juan Diego: Heeding the Call* (Cincinnati: St. Anthony Messenger Press, 1998), 81–82.

16. Michael S. Durham, in *Miracles of Mary: Apparitions, Legends, and Miraculous Works of the Blessed Virgin Mary* (San Francisco: HarperCollins, 1995), 11, notes that there are recorded at least twenty thousand alleged Marian apparitions in the history of the church.

17. See Richard P. McBrien, *Catholicism,* new ed. (San Francisco: Harper-Collins, 1994), 268–69.

18. Virgil Elizondo, *Guadalupe: Mother of the New Creation* (Maryknoll, N.Y.: Orbis Books, 1997), xii.

19. See John Baldovin, "On Feasting the Saints," in *Between Memory and Hope: Readings on the Liturgical Year,* ed. Maxwell E. Johnson (Collegeville: Liturgical Press, Pueblo, 2000), 379.

20. See ELCA, *Libro de Liturgia y Cántico* (Minneapolis: Augsburg Fortress, 1999), 150.

21. ELCA, *This Far by Faith: An African American Resource for Worship* (Minneapolis: Augsburg Fortress, 1999), 96–102. Only the eight "biblical" stations are provided in this resource rather than the traditional fourteen.

22. See ELCA, *Lutheran Book of Worship: Minister's* (Minneapolis: Augsburg, 1978), 129–30, 134–43.

23. See Jacqueline Orsini Dunnington, *Viva Guadalupe! The Virgin in New Mexican Popular Art* (Santa Fe: Museum of New Mexico Press, 1997).

24. See A. Castillo, ed., *Goddess of the Americas: La Diosa de las Americas* (New York: Riverhead Books, 1996).

25. See Ignacio Corona, "Guadalupanism: Popular Religiosity and Cultural Identity," *Josephinum Journal of Theology* 4, Supplement (1997): 16.

26. See George H. Tavard, *The Thousand Faces of the Virgin Mary* (Collegeville, Minn.: Liturgical Press, 1996), 182–83. Tavard, for example, simply places the Guadalupan apparition under the subtitle of "Apparitions Dismissed as Self-Induced."

27. See chap. 5, p. 133–36.

28. See C. G. Romero, *Hispanic Devotional Piety: Tracing the Biblical Roots* (Maryknoll, N.Y.: Orbis Books, 1991); Virgil Elizondo and Timothy Matovina, *Mestizo Worship: A Pastoral Approach to Liturgical Ministry* (Collegeville, Minn.: Liturgical Press, 1998); Rosa María Icaza, "Spirituality of the Mexican American People," *Worship* 63, 3 (1989): 232–46; and Mexican American Cultural Center, *Faith Expressions of Hispanics in the Southwest,* rev. ed. (San Antonio: Mexican American Cultural Center, 1990).

29. See J. J. Salazar, "'¿No estoy yo aqui, que soy tu madre?' Investigación Teológica-Bíblica-Litúrgica acerca de La Nueva Liturgia de Nuestra Señora de Guadalupe." 3 vols. S.T.D. diss., Pontificio Istituto Liturgico, 1981. 3 vols.; and Bishops' Committee on the Liturgy, *Newsletter 9: Interim Adaptation of Particular Calendars* (Washington, D.C.: National Council of Catholic Bishops, 1969); Bishops'

Committee on the Liturgy, *Newsletter 23: Feast of Our Lady of Guadalupe* (Washington, D.C.: NCCB, 1987); and Bishops' Committee on the Liturgy, *Newsletter 25: Confirmation of Proper Texts for the Liturgy of the Hours on the Feast of Our Lady of Guadalupe* (Washington, D.C.: NCCB, 1989).

30. See Schulte, "A Mexican Spirituality."

31. On contemporary Lutheran liturgical calendars, "commemorations" are always optional festivals distinct from the category of "lesser festivals," which are usually related to biblical-apostolic figures. As such, commemorations closely correspond to what are called "optional memorials" in the Roman Catholic liturgical calendar.

32. See Kenneth G. Davis, OFM, Conv., ed., *Misa, Mesa, y Musa: Liturgy in the U.S. Hispanic Church,* 2d ed. (Schiller Park, Ill.: World Library Publications, 1997), 1–5.

33. David Pitt, "Guadalupe: Beyond Mexico," *Celebrate!* 39, 6 (2000): 22–26.

1

The Apparition Narrative and Image

The Virgin of Guadalupe is a narrative, an image, and a devotion firmly embedded in the religious and cultural consciousness of, at least, Mexican and Mexican American people and, increasingly, among other Hispanic–Latinos as well. Because the story itself as it has been received and taught for several centuries is central to understanding the significance of both the image and the ongoing cult of the Virgin of Guadalupe, it is necessary in this chapter to provide some version of this narrative before proceeding.

The earliest extant *written* accounts of the apparitions of the Virgin of Guadalupe to Juan Diego and others are the *Imagen de la Virgen María, Madre de Dios de Guadalupe,* composed in Spanish in 1648 by Miguel Sánchez, a diocesan priest from Mexico City,[1] and the *Nican Mopohua* (It is narrated), part of a much larger work written in the indigenous Aztec language Nahuatl entitled *Huei tlamahuiçoltica omonexiti in ilhuicac tlatocacihaupilli Santa María totlaçonantzin Guadalupe in nican Huei altepenahuac Mexico itocayocan Tepeyacac* ("By a great miracle the Heavenly Queen, Saint Mary, Our Precious Mother of Guadalupe, appeared here near the Great Altepetl of Mexico, in a place called Tepeyacac"), composed by Luis Lasso de la Vega, the vicar of Guadalupe, in 1649.[2] The accounts are similar, although the *Nican Mopohua* lacks many of the biblical parallels provided by the Sánchez version (especially the relationship of Guadalupe to the woman clothed with the sun in Revelation 12). Both agree that the apparitions took place between December 9 and December 12, 1531, only ten years after the Spanish conquest of Mexico under Hernando Cortés and only seven years after the arrival of the first Spanish Franciscan missionaries known as *Los Doce,* "The Twelve," sent from Spain to evangelize the New World.[3] Of these two extant literary versions it is the *Nican Mopo-*

hua which has generally become the standard and most widely accepted version today. According to Lisa Sousa, Stafford Poole, and James Lockhart, "it is to its [i.e., the *Nican Mopohua's*] literary or dramatic qualities, as well as to the growing feeling over time that the indigenous aspect was central and original, that Laso de la Vega's version owes its ascendancy."[4]

Several easily accessible versions of the *Nican Mopohua* are now widely available in both Spanish and English.[5] The following English version, together with accompanying notes, was graciously made available to me for quotation in this volume by Virgil Elizondo from his recent book, *Guadalupe: Mother of the New Creation.*[6]

Title

[1] Here we recount in an orderly way how the Ever-Virgin Holy Mary, Mother of God, our Queen, appeared recently in a marvelous way at Tepeyac, which is called Guadalupe.[7]

Summary

[2] First she allowed herself to be seen by a poor and dignified person whose name is Juan Diego; and then her precious image appeared in the presence of the new bishop D. Fray Juan de Zumárraga. The many marvels that she has brought about are also told.

The Situation of the City and Its Inhabitants

[3] Ten years after the conquest of the city of Mexico, arrows and shields were put down; everywhere the inhabitants of the lake and the mountain had surrendered.

[4] Thus faith started; it gave its first buds; and it flowered in the knowledge of the One through Whom We live, the true God, Téotl.[8]

[5] Precisely in the year 1531, a few days after the beginning of December, a poor, dignified campesino was in the surroundings [of Tepeyac]. His name was Juan Diego. It was said that his home was in Cuauhtitlán.[9]

[6] And insofar as the things of God, all that region belonged to Tlatelcoco.[10]

First Encounter with the Virgin

[7] It was Saturday, when it was still night. He was going in search of the things of God and of God's messages. [8] And when he arrived at the side of the small hill, which was named Tepeyac, it was already beginning to dawn.

[9] He heard singing on the summit of the hill: as if different precious birds were singing and their songs would alternate, as if the hill was answering them. Their song was most pleasing and very enjoyable, better than that of the coyoltotol or of the tzinizcan or of the other precious birds that sing.[11]

[10] Juan Diego stopped and said to himself: 'By chance do I deserve this?

Am I worthy of what I am hearing? Maybe I am dreaming? Maybe I only see this in my dreams? Where am I? [11] Maybe I am in the land of my ancestors, of the elders, of our grandparents? In the Land of Flower, in the Earth of our flesh? Maybe over there inside of heaven?'

[12] His gaze was fixed on the summit of the hill, toward the direction from which the sun arises: the beautiful celestial song was coming from there to here. [13] And when the song finally ceased, when everything was calm, he heard that he was being called from the summit of the hill. He heard: 'Dignified Juan, dignified Juan Diego.'

[14] Then he dared to go to where he was being called. His heart was in no way disturbed, and in no way did he experience any fear; on the contrary, he felt very good, very happy.

[15] He went to the top of the hill, and he saw a lady who was standing and who was calling him to come closer to her side. [16] When he arrived in her presence, he marveled at her perfect beauty. [17] Her clothing appeared like the sun, and it gave forth rays.

[18] And the rock and the cliffs where she was standing, upon receiving the rays like arrows of light, appeared like precious emeralds, appeared like jewels; the earth glowed with the splendors of the rainbow. The mesquites, the cacti, and the weeds that were all around appeared like feathers of the quetzal, and the stems looked like turquoise; the branches, the foliage, and even the thorns sparkled like gold.

[19] He bowed before her, heard her thought and word, which were exceedingly re-creative, very ennobling, alluring, producing love. [20] She said: 'Listen, my most abandoned son, dignified Juan: Where are you going?'

[21] And he answered: 'My Owner and my Queen: I have to go to your house of Mexico-Tlatelolco, to follow the divine things that our priests, who are the images of our Lord, give to us.' [22] Then she conversed with him and unveiled her precious will. She said: 'Know and be certain in your heart,[12] my most abandoned son, that I am the Ever-Virgin Holy Mary, Mother of the God of Great Truth, Téotl, of the One through Whom We live, the Creator of Persons, the Owner of What Is Near and Together, of the Lord of Heaven and Earth.[13]

[23] 'I very much want and ardently desire that my hermitage[14] be erected in this place. In it I will show and give to all people all my love, my compassion, my help, and my protection, [24] because I am your merciful mother and the mother of all the nations that live on this earth who would love me, who would speak with me, who would search for me, and who would place their confidence in me. [25] There I will hear their laments and remedy and cure all their miseries, misfortunes, and sorrows.

[26] 'And for this merciful wish of mine to be realized, go there to the palace of the bishop of Mexico, and you will tell him in what way I have sent you as messenger, so that you may make known to him how I very much desire that he build me a home right here, that he may erect my temple[15] on the plain. You will tell him carefully everything you have seen and admired and heard.

[27] 'Be absolutely certain that I will be grateful and will repay you; and because of this I will make you joyful; I will give you happiness; and you will earn much that will repay you for your trouble and your work in carrying out what I have entrusted to you. Look, my son the most abandoned one, you have heard my statement and my word; now do everything that relates to you.'

[28] Then he bowed before her and said to her: 'My Owner and my Queen, I am already on the way to make your statement and your word a reality. And now I depart from you, I your poor servant.' Then he went down so as to make her commission a reality; he went straight to the road that leads directly to Mexico [City].

First Interview with the Bishop

[29] Having entered the city, he went directly to the palace of the bishop, who had recently arrived as the lord of the priests; his name was Don Fray Juan de Zumárraga, a priest of Saint Francis.

[30] As soon as he [Juan Diego] arrived, he tried to see him [the bishop]. He begged his servants, his attendants, to go speak to him. After a long time, they came to call him, telling him that the lord bishop had ordered him to come in. As soon as he entered, he prostrated himself and then knelt. [31] Immediately he presented, he revealed, the thought and the word of the Lady from Heaven and her will. And he also told him everything he had admired, seen, and heard. When he [the bishop] heard all his words, his message, it was as if he didn't give it much credibility. [32] He answered him and told him: 'My son, you will have to come another time; I will calmly listen to you at another time. I still have to see, to examine carefully from the very beginning, the reason you have come, and your will and your wish.'

[33] He left very saddened because in no way whatsoever had her message been accomplished.

Second Encounter with the Virgin

[34] The same day, he returned [to Tepeyac]. He came to the summit of the hill and found the Lady from Heaven; she was waiting in the very same spot where he had seen her the first time.

[35] When he saw her, he prostrated himself before her, he fell upon the earth and said: 'My Owner, my Matron, my Lady, the most abandoned of my Daughters, my Child, I went where you sent me to deliver your thought and your word. [36] With great difficulty I entered the place of the lord of the priests; I saw him; before him I expressed your thought and word, just as you had ordered me. [37] He received me well and listened carefully. But by the way he answered me, as if his heart had not accepted it, [I know] he did not believe it. He told me: 'You will have to come another time; I will calmly listen to you at another time. I still have to see, to examine carefully from the very beginning, the reason you have come, and your will and your wish.' [38] I saw perfectly, in the way he answered me, that he thinks that possibly I am

just making it up that you want a temple to be built on this site, and possibly it is not your command.[16]

[39] 'Hence, I very much beg of you, My Owner, my Queen, my Child, that you charge one of the more valuable nobles, a well-known person, one who is respected and esteemed, to come by and take your message and your word so that he may be believed. [40] Because in reality I am one of those campesinos, a piece of rope,[17] a small ladder,[18] the excrement of people; I am a leaf;[19] they order me around, lead me by force;[20] and you, my most abandoned Daughter, my Child, my Lady, and my Queen, send me to a place where I do not belong.[21] [41] Forgive me, I will cause pain to your countenance and to your heart; I will displease you and fall under your wrath, my Lady, and My Owner.'[22]

[42] The ever-venerated Virgin answered: 'Listen, my most abandoned son, know well in your heart that there are not a few of my servants and messengers to whom I could give the mandate of taking my thought and my word so that my will may be accomplished. But it is absolutely necessary that you personally go and speak about this, and that precisely through your mediation and help, my wish and my desire be realized.[23] [43] I beg you very much, my most abandoned son, and with all my energy I command that precisely tomorrow you go again to see the bishop. [44] In my name you will make him know, make him listen well to my wish and desire, so that he may make my wish a reality and build my temple. And tell him once again that I personally, the Ever-Virgin Mary, the Mother of God Téotl, am the one who is sending you there.'

[45] Juan Diego answered her: 'My Owner, my Lady, my Child, I will not cause pain to your countenance and your heart. With a very good disposition of my heart, I will go; there I will go to tell him truthfully your thought and your word. In no way whatsoever will I fail to do it; it will not be painful for me to go. [46] I will go to do your will. But it could well be that I will not be listened to; and if I am listened to, possibly I will not be believed. [47] Tomorrow in the afternoon, when the sun sets,[24] I will return your thought and word to you, what the lord of the priests [has] answer[ed] me.

[48] 'Now I take leave of you, my most abandoned Daughter, my Child, my Matron, my Lady, now you rest a bit.' Then he went home to rest.

Second Interview with the Bishop

[49] The next day, Sunday, when it was still night, when it was still dark, he left his home and went directly to Tlatelolco to learn about the things divine, and to answer roll call so that afterward he could see the lord of the priests.

[50] Around ten in the morning, when they had gathered together and heard mass and answered roll call and the poor had been dispersed, Juan Diego went immediately to the house of the lord bishop.

[51] And when he arrived there, he made every effort to see him, and with great difficulty he succeeded in seeing him. He knelt at his feet; he

cried and became very sad as he was communicating and unveiling before him the thought and the word of the Lady from Heaven, hoping to be accepted as her messenger and believing that it was the will of the Ever Virgin to have him build a dwelling in the place where she wanted it.

[52] But the lord bishop asked him many questions; he interrogated him as to where he saw her and all about her so as to satisfy his heart. And he told the lord bishop everything.

[53] But even though he told him everything, all about her figure, all that he had seen and admired, and how she had shown herself to be the lovable Ever Virgin and admirable mother of our Lord and our Savior Jesus Christ,[25] yet, he still did not believe him.

[54] He [the bishop] told him that he could not proceed on her wishes just on the basis of his word and message. A sign from her would be necessary for the bishop to believe that he [Juan Diego] was indeed sent by the Lady from Heaven. [55] When Juan Diego heard this, he told the bishop: 'My patron and my lord, what is the sign that you want? [When I know, I can] go and ask the Lady from Heaven, she who sent me here.' The bishop was impressed that he was so firm in the truth, that he did not doubt anything or hesitate in any way. He dismissed him.

[56] And when he had left, he [the lord bishop] sent some people from his household in whom he trusted, to follow him and observe where he went, what he saw, and with whom he was speaking. And so it was done. [57] And Juan Diego went directly down the road. His followers took the same route. Close to the bridge of Tepeyac, in the hillside, they lost sight of him; the kept looking for him everywhere, but they could not find him anyplace.

[58] Thus they returned infuriated and were angered at him because he frustrated their intentions. [59] In this state of mind, they went to inform the lord bishop, creating in him a bad attitude so that he would not believe him; they told him that he was only deceiving him; that he was only imagining what he was coming to say; that he was only dreaming; or that he had invented what he was coming to tell him. They agreed among themselves that if he were to come again, they would grab him and punish him harshly, so that he would not lie again or deceive the people.

Juan Diego Takes Care of His Uncle

[60] On the next day, Monday, when Juan Diego was supposed to take something to be the sign by which he was to be believed, he did not return, because when he arrived home, one of his uncles, named Juan Bernardino, had caught the smallpox and was in his last moments.

[61] First he went to call a doctor, who helped him, but he could do no more because he [Juan Bernardino] was already gravely ill. [62] Through the night, his uncle begged him that while it was still dark, he should go to Tlatelolco to call a priest to come and hear his confession and prepare him well because he felt deeply in his heart that this was the time and place of his death, that he would not be healed.

Third Encounter with the Virgin

[63] And on Tuesday, when it was still night, Juan Diego left his home to go to Tlatelolco to call a priest.

[64] And when he arrived at the side of Mount Tepeyac at the point where the road leads out, on the side on which the sun sets, the side he was accustomed to take, he said: [65] 'If I take this road, it is quite possible that the Lady will come to see me as before and will hold me back so that I may take the sign to the lord of the priests as she had instructed me. [66] But first I must attend to our affliction and quickly call the priest. My uncle is agonizing and is waiting for him.'

[67] He then went around the hill; he climbed through the middle; and he went to the other side, to avoid the side of the sunrise, so as to arrive quickly into Mexico, and to avoid the Lady from Heaven delaying him. [68] He thought that having taken this other route, he would not be seen by the one who cares for everyone.

[69] He saw her coming down from the top of the hill; and from there, where he had seen her before, she had been watching him. She came to him at the side of the hill, blocked his passage, and, standing in front of him, said: 'My most abandoned son, where are you going? In what direction are you going?'

[70] Did he become embarrassed a bit? Was he ashamed? Did he feel like running away? Was he fearful? He bowed before her, greeted her, and said: 'My Child, my most abandoned Daughter, my Lady, I hope you are happy. How did the dawn come upon you? Does your body feel all right, my Owner and my Child? [71] I am going to give great pain to your countenance and heart. You must know, my Child, that my uncle, a poor servant of yours, is in his final agony; a great illness has fallen upon him, and because of it he will die.

[72] I am in a hurry to get to your house in Mexico; I am going to call one of the beloved of our Lord, one of our priests, so that he may go and hear his confession and prepare him. [73] Because for this have we been born, to await the moment of our death. [74] But if right now I am going to do this, I will quickly return here; I will come back to take your thought and your word. My matron, and my Child, forgive me, have a little patience with me; I do not want to deceive you, my most abandoned Daughter, my Child. Tomorrow I will come quickly.'

[75] After hearing Juan Diego's discourse, the most pious Virgin answered: 'Listen and hear well in your heart, my most abandoned son: that which scares you and troubles you is nothing; do not let your countenance and heart be troubled; do not fear that sickness or any other sickness or anxiety. [76] Am I not here, your mother? Are you not under my shadow and my protection? Am I not your source of life? Are you not in the hollow of my mantle where I cross my arms? Who else do you need?'[26] [77] Let nothing trouble you or cause you sorrow. Do not worry because of your uncle's sickness. He will not die of his present sickness. Be assured in your heart that he

is already healed.' (And as he learned later on, at that precise moment, his uncle was healed.)

[78] When Juan Diego heard the thought and word of the Lady from Heaven, he was very much consoled; his heart became peaceful. He begged her to send him immediately to see the lord of the priests to take him his sign, the thing that would bring about the fulfillment of her desire, so that he would be believed.

[79] Then the Lady from Heaven sent him to climb to the top of the hill where he had seen her before. [80] She said to him: 'Go up, my most abandoned son, to the top of the hill, and there, where you saw me and I gave you my instructions, there will you see many diverse flowers: cut them, gather them, put them together. Then come down here and bring them before me.'

[81] Juan Diego climbed the hill, and when he arrived at the top, he was deeply surprised. All over the place there were all kinds of exquisite flowers from Castile, open and flowering.[27] It was not a place for flowers, and likewise it was the time when the ice hardens upon the earth. [82] They were very fragrant, as if they were filled with fine pearls, filled with the morning dew. [83] He started to cut them; he gathered them; he placed them in the hollow of his mantle.[28] [84] And the top of the hill was certainly not a place where flowers grew; there were only rocks, thistles, thorns, cacti, mesquites; and if small herbs grew there, during the month of December, they were all eaten up and wilted by the ice.

[85] Immediately he went down; he went to take to the Queen of Heaven the various flowers that he had cut. When she saw them, she took them in her small hands; and then he placed them in the hollow of his mantle.

[86] And she told him: 'My most abandoned son, these different flowers are the proof, the sign, that you will take to the bishop. In my name tell him that he is to see in them what I want, and with this he should carry out my wish and my will.

[87] 'And you, you are my ambassador; in you I place all my trust.[29] With all my strength [*energía*] I command you that only in the presence of the bishop are you to open your mantle, and let him know and reveal to him what you are carrying. [88] You will recount everything well; you will tell him how I sent you to climb to the top of the hill to go cut the flowers, and all that you saw and admired. With this you will change the heart of the lord of the priests so that he will do his part to build and erect my temple that I have asked him for.'

[89] As soon as the Lady from Heaven had given him her command, he immediately took to the road that leads to Mexico. He was in a hurry and very happy; his heart felt very sure and secure; he was carrying with great care what he knew would [bring about] a good end. He was very careful with that which he carried in the hollow of his mantle, lest anything would fall out. He was enjoying the scent of the beautiful flowers.

Third Interview with the Bishop
and the Apparition of the Virgin

[90] Upon arriving at the palace of the bishop, he ran into the door-keepers and the other servants of the king of the priests. He begged them to go tell him [the bishop] that he wanted to see him; but none of them wanted to; they did not want to pay attention to him, both because it was still night and they knew him; he was the one who only bothered them and gave them long faces;[30] [91] and also because their fellow workers had told them how they had lost him from their sight when the had been following him. He waited for a very long time.[31]

[92] When they saw that he had been standing with his head lowered[32] (very sad) for a long time, that he was waiting in vain for them to call him, and that it seemed that he carried something in the hollow of his mantle, they approached him to see what he had and satisfy their hearts.

[93] And when Juan Diego saw that it was impossible to hide from them what he was carrying, that he would be punished for this, that they would throw him out or mistreat him, he showed them just a little of the flowers.

[94] When they saw that they were all different flowers from Castile and that is was not the season for flowers, they were very astonished, especially by the fact that they were in full bloom, so fresh, so fragrant, and very beautiful. [95] Three times they tried to grab some of them and take them from him, [96] but they could not do it because when they were about to grab them, they did not see any more real flowers, but only painted or embroidered ones, or flowers sewn in his mantle.[33]

[97] Immediately they went to tell the lord bishop what they had seen, and that the poor little Indian who had already come many times wanted to see him, and that he had been waiting for a very long time. [98] Upon hearing this, the lord bishop realized this meant the despicable man had the proof to convince him and bring about what he was coming to ask for.

[99] Immediately he ordered that he be brought in to see him. As soon as he [Juan Diego] entered, he knelt before him [the bishop] as he had done before, and once again he told him everything he had seen and admired and also her message.

[100] He said to him: 'My owner and my lord, I have accomplished what you asked for; I went to tell my Matron, my Queen, the Lady from Heaven, Holy Mary, the precious Mother of God Téotl, how you had asked me for a sign in order to believe me, so that you might build her temple where she is asking you to erect it. [101] And besides, I told her that I had given you my word that I would bring you a sign and a proof of her will that you want to receive from my hands. When she received your thought and your word, she accepted willingly what you asked for, a sign and a proof so that her desire and will may come about.

[102] 'And today when it was still night, she sent me to come and see you once again. But I asked her for the sign and the proof of her will that you

asked me for and that she had agreed to give to me. Immediately she complied.

[103] 'She sent me to the top of the hill, where I had seen her before, so that there I might cut the flowers from Castile. After I had cut them, I took them to the bottom of the hill. And she, with her precious little hands, took them; she arranged them in the hollow of my mantle, so that I might bring them to you, and deliver them to you personally. [104] Even though I knew well that the top of the hill was not a place where flowers grow, that only stones, thistles, thorns, cacti and mesquites abound there, I still was neither surprised nor doubted. [105] As I was arriving at the top of the hill, my eyes became fixed: It was the Flowering Earth![34] It was covered with all kinds of flowers from Castile, full of dew and shining brilliantly. Immediately I went to cut them. [106] And she told me why I had to deliver them to you: so that you might see the sign your requested and so that you will believe in her will; and also so that the truth of my word and my message might be manifested. Here they are. Please receive them.'

[107] He unfolded his white mantle, the mantle in whose hollow he had gathered the flowers he had cut, and at that instant the different flowers from Castile fell to the ground. In that very moment she painted herself: the precious image of the Ever-Virgin Holy Mary, Mother of the God Téotl, appeared suddenly, just as she is today and is kept in her precious home, in her hermitage of Tepeyac, which is called Guadalupe.[35]

Conversion of the Bishop

[108] When the lord bishop saw her, he and all who accompanied him fell to their knees and were greatly astonished. They stood up to see her; they became saddened; their hearts and their minds became very heavy.

[109] The lord bishop, with tears and sadness, prayed to her and begged her to forgive him for not having believed her will, her heart, and her word.

[110] When he stood up, he untied the mantle from Juan Diego's neck, the mantle in which had appeared and was painted the Lady from Heaven. Then he took her and went to place her in his oratory.

The Construction of the Hermitage

[111] Juan Diego spent one more day in the home of the bishop, who had invited him [to stay]. And on the next day he said: 'Let us go to see where it is the will of the Lady from Heaven that the hermitage be built.'

[112] Immediately people were invited to construct and build it. And when Juan Diego showed where the Lady from Heaven had indicated that the hermitage should be built, he asked permission to leave. [113] He wanted to go home to see his uncle Juan Bernardino, the one who had been in his final agony, who he had left to go to Tlatelolco to call a priest to come, hear his confession, and prepare him well, the one who, the Lady from Heaven had said, had been healed. But they did not let him go alone; they accompanied him to his home.

The Fourth Apparition and First Miracle

[114] When they arrived, they saw his uncle who was well and with no pains. [115] He [Juan Bernardino] was very much surprised that his nephew was so well accompanied and honored, and he asked him why they were honoring him so much. [116] He told him how when he had left him to go call a priest to come to hear his confession and prepare him well, the Queen of Heaven appeared to him over there, at Tepeyac, and sent him to Mexico to see the lord bishop so that he would build her a home at Tepeyac. [117] And she told him not to be troubled because his uncle was healed, and he was very consoled.

[118] And the uncle said that this was true, that it was precisely then that she had healed him, and he had seen her exactly as she had shown herself to his nephew, and that she had told him that he [Juan Bernardino] had to go to Mexico to see the bishop. [119] And (she told him) also that when he went to see the bishop, he would reveal all that he had seen and would tell him in what a marvelous way she had healed him and that he [the bishop] would call and name that precious image the Ever-Virgin Holy Mary of Guadalupe.

[120] They took Juan Bernardino to the bishop so that he might speak and witness before him. [121] And, together with his nephew Juan Diego, he was hosted by the bishop in his home for several days, until the hermitage of the Queen and Lady from Heaven was built at Tepeyac, where Juan Diego had seen her.

The Entire City before the Virgin

[122] And the lord bishop transferred to the major church the precious image of the Queen and Lady from Heaven; he took her from the oratory of his palace so that all might see and venerate her precious image.

[123] The entire city was deeply moved; they came to see and admire her precious image as something divine; they came to pray to her. [124] They admired very much how she had appeared as a divine marvel, because absolutely no one on earth had painted her precious image.

Thanks especially to the work of Clodomiro L. Siller Acuña and Virgil Elizondo,[36] contemporary interpretations of the *Nican Mopohua* and the image of the Virgin imprinted on Juan Diego's tilma frequently underscore several connections with indigenous Aztec religion as it was practiced in sixteenth-century Mexico and as it was encountered by the Spanish conquistadores and their missionaries. First, as noted above, the connection is often made between the site of the apparitions at Tepeyac and what has been claimed to be the location of an Aztec shrine already there and dedicated to the goddess Tonantzin, "Our Mother," and mother of the gods, one of four major ancient sites of religious sacrifice in Mexico. Indeed, the very name she reveals to Juan Diego, "Mother of the true God, Téotl," similarly underscores this relationship. Second, the fact that the *Nican Mopohua* begins its narrative by referring to Juan Diego hearing "the most beautiful singing of precious birds" and concludes with the story of the Castilian flowers growing on the barren hill of Tepeyac in December, which are instrumental for the imprinting of the Virgin's image on Juan's tilma, has been taken as pointing to the Aztec understanding that truth and divine self-revelation are encountered never in logical propositions or formulas but always in beauty, in *flor y canto,* flower and song. Third, that the Virgin hides the sun but does not destroy it and stands upon the black moon is interpreted as a sign of her transcendence over the two primary Aztec manifestations of the divine, the sun god Tecatlipoca and the moon god of the night.[37] In other words, although she does not destroy as categorically evil or diabolical the revelations of the divine already present in Aztec history, culture, and religion, she does transcend and reinterpret them. Fourth, her face, neither formless nor hidden behind a mask like the Aztec gods and goddesses, appears to be not that of the Old World Madonnas of Iberian European religious art but that of a New World mestiza, one who represents the blending of the Iberian European with the indigenous peoples of the Americas, resulting in a complexion that is not Caucasian but olive-skinned or brown. According to some, in her eyes, cast down and humbled, are reflected the mirror images of Juan Diego and Bishop Zumárraga and possibly even others.[38] Fifth, she wears a blue-green or turquoise mantle, the color of Aztec royalty and of the supreme indigenous deity, Ometéotl, father-mother of the gods, over a pale red dress often understood as symbolizing both the blood of indigenous human sacrifices to Ometéotl and certainly the blood of the indigenous peoples shed by the violence of the Spanish conquest. Similarly, the stars on her mantle have been seen as reflecting the fulfillment of an omen in Aztec prophecy about the end of their civilization seen in a comet ten years before the conquest. At the same time, it has been argued that the pattern of these stars reflects exactly the astronomical pattern of the heavens over Mexico between December 9 and December 12, 1531.[39] Sixth, the *cinta,* or black band, visible around her waist is interpreted as an Aztec band of maternity indicating pregnancy, and in the very center of the image, over the Virgin's navel, has been discerned an Aztec symbol of new life depicting the center of the universe. Together with the small cross appearing in the brooch worn around her neck, these symbols have, of course, been interpreted Christologically as indicating that it is the person of Christ who is at the very center of the Guadalupan image. Finally, it is often noted that the angel that bears her aloft underscores her importance, since in Aztec culture only those of great importance or royalty were carried by others; in her case, she is carried not by Spaniards or other human beings but by a heavenly creature, pointing to her own heavenly origins. Similarly, the image may also suggest the arrival of a new age of history.

The highly symbolic contents of both the *Nican Mopohua* and the image itself have attracted the attention and devotion of the faithful and the criticism of others for centuries. It is with this that the following chapter is concerned.

Notes

1. For text, see Miguel Sánchez, *Imagen de la Virgen Maria, Madre de Dios de Guadalupe: milagrosamente aparecida en la Ciudad de México, Celebrada en su historia, con la profecía del capítulo doze del Apocalipsis* (Imp. Vidua de Bernardo Calderón, Mexico, 1648; reprint, Cuernavaca: Morelos, 1952).

2. For the very first time a critical edition of the transliterated Nahuatl text with English translation, notes, and introduction has been provided recently. See Lisa Sousa, Stafford Poole, and James Lockhart, eds., *The Story of Guadalupe: Luis de la Vega's* Huei tlamahuiçoltica *of 1649,* UCLA Latin American Studies 84 (Los Angeles: Stanford University Press, 1998).

3. On these first Spanish missionaries to Mexico, see Virgil Elizondo, *La Morenita: Evangelizer of the Americas* (San Antonio: Mexican American Cultural Center, 1980), 47–64; and Stafford Poole, *Our Lady of Guadalupe: The Origins and Sources of a Mexican National Symbol, 1531–1797* (Tucson: University of Arizona Press, 1997), 15–25.

4. Sousa, Poole, and Lockhart, *Story of Guadalupe,* 3.

5. In addition to the recent critical edition noted in note 2, the most readily accessible translations of the *Nican Mopohua* appear in Spanish in Clodomiro L. Siller Acuña, *Para comprender el mensaje de María de Guadalupe* (Buenos Aires: Editorial Guadalupe, 1989); and Jose Luis G. Guerrero, *El Nican Mopohua: Un intento de exégesis,* Biblioteca Mexicana 6 and 7, 2 vols. (Cuautitlán: Universidad Pontifica de México, 1996, 1998); and in English in Virgil Elizondo, *Guadalupe: Mother of the New Creation,* (Maryknoll, N.Y.: Orbis 1997), 5–22. For edited versions in both Spanish and English translation, see also Virgil Elizondo, *La Morenita,* 75–81.

6. Virgil Elizondo, *Guadalupe,* 5–22.

7. Tepeyac was the sacred mountain site of the goddess Tonantzin, where she had been venerated from time immemorial. Gradually it came to be known as Guadalupe. Why it came to be known as Guadalupe (from Our Lady of Guadalupe in Estremadura in Spain) is not known, but it was certainly known by that name by 1575. Gradually Our Lady became known by that name. In the redaction of the *Nican Mopohua,* the origins of the designation are attributed to Juan Bernardino.

8. "Téotl" was the designation for the God of the Nahuatls while "true God" was the designation for the God of the Christian Spaniards. In using the phrase "true God, Téotl," the text is thus linking the God of the Nahuatls and the God of the Christians.

9. The use of the word "Cuauhtitlán" indicates that Juan Diego was from the

place of the eagles, which was symbolic of the sun; it indicates he was from the land of the people of the sun. By saying he was from there, the text is pointing out that he would be explaining the things of God (See Siller Acuña, *Para comprender el mensaje,* 60).

10. This was an ancient ceremonial center that had become a center of Spanish evangelization and spiritual domination (see Siller Acuña, *Para comprender el mensaje,* 60).

11. Birds in Nahuatl thought indicate mediation between heaven and earth; the coyoltotol was the symbol of great fecundity.

12. The heart is the active and dynamic center of the person; it is the symbolic place of ultimate understanding and certitude. Truth resides in the heart.

13. This litany of names is a most important revelation, for they are the same names that were mentioned by the Nahuatl theologians in their dialogues with the Spanish theologians and that were discredited by the Spanish evangelizers. They appeared in the purest preconquest theology of the Nahuatls. She reestablishes the authenticity and veracity of these holy names. The names refer to neither demons nor false idols; they are venerable names of God.

14. "Hermitage" could refer to a home for the homeless, an orphanage, a hospice—all would have a special meaning for a people who had been totally displaced and left homeless by the conquest.

15. Notice the progression from hermitage (home for the homeless), to a home (place of affectionate relationships), to a temple (the manifestation of the sacred). Thus, where everyone is welcomed *is* sacred earth.

16. In the presence of those in power, the poor understand very well that they are not credible.

17. The reference is to the rope that was tied around the Indians' necks as they were chained and pulled around for forced labor.

18. The Indians were "stepped" on in the process by which others climbed the ladder of social and economic mobility. They were often used as beasts of burden.

19. Dried leaves were used to wipe oneself after a bowel movement.

20. The worst part of domination is that the oppressed begin to believe what those in authority say: that they are subhuman, inferior, incapable of dignified tasks, and a burden to society.

21. The text literally says "a place where I do not walk or put my foot upon." This is the Nahuatl expression for a place where one does not belong, that is, a place where one is not wanted or allowed in.

22. This is a perfect example of the soul-crushing victimization of the victims of society: They are made to feel guilty for their situation of misery and deserving of disgust and punishment.

23. Consistent with the Gospels and the beginnings of the apostolic movement, it is precisely through mediation of the "nothings of this world" (1 Cor. 1:28), through the "stone rejected by the builders of this world" (Acts 4:11), that the reign of God will erupt into this world. In the *Nican Mopohua,* the home-temple that the Lady requests is equivalent to the "kingdom" in the Gospel stories. It will begin through the mediation of the poor and the lowly of this world, to whom the kingdom belongs (see *Catechism of the Catholic Church,* no. 544). It is they who will in-

vite all others into the new family home for God's children. The abandoned of this world act under the authority of God.

24. "In the afternoon, when the sun sets," is the Nahuatl expression for coming to an end of a period of life and expectation of something new that is about to begin. It is an expression of hope. Here it could easily mean, "Tomorrow, hoping that something new will take place . . ."

25. Note that it is Juan Diego who recognizes her as the mother of Jesus Christ. She never mentions this in her conversations with him. It is he who makes the connection and thus announces to his people that the mother of their Nahuatl God "Téotl" and the mother of the Spanish God "Dios" is likewise the mother of the one and only savior of all, Jesus Christ.

26. Notice the five identifying statements—each one deepening and expanding the meaning of the previous one. Before she had identified herself as the Mother of God; now she introduces herself as the mother of Juan Diego and of the poor; "shadow" is an image-word meaning authority; "hollow of her mantle" refers to tender service as the quality of true authority; the crossing of the arms indicates the cross of sticks that produces fire, out of which new divine life is born; Juan Diego is the firstborn of the new creation; nothing else is needed (see Siller Acuña, *Para comprender el mensaje,* 83–84).

27. Note the insistent reference to "the top of the hill"—a contrast to the top of the pyramid-temple where the old priests ascended to offer human sacrifices. Now Juan Diego (who represents the new priests) ascends to discover beautiful flowers in the place where he had first heard the heavenly music—a true place of divine-human encounter.

28. He brings the flowers (truth) to her; she touches them (confirms the truth) and places them under his care. Note the contrast to verse 76.

29. The Indian was considered to be unworthy of any trust, one who imagined things and easily lied and hence one who should be dominated and punished (see vv. 31, 32, 37, 38, 46, 54, 56, 57, 58, 59); the Lady from Heaven reverses this and brings out the ultimate truth about the Indians: they are the most trusted ambassadors of heaven. The Indians, who were declared unworthy of ordination by church regulations, were to be the trusted ambassadors—spokespersons—of God.

30. Note the reappearance of the clause "when it was still night," which refers to the moment at which the new creation is about to begin. However, those whose livelihood and identity depend on the structures of the old creation, that is, the structures of domination, try to prevent the new creation. The rise and liberation of the poor always shake the structures of unjust domination and oppression, and those who rely on those structures try everything within their means to keep that liberation from coming about.

31. The poor and undignified of the world are always made to wait. Everyone else comes before them. It is as if they do not count.

32. In preconquest art, prisoners appeared with their heads lowered. This was indicative of their shameful condition, the condition of one who was totally subjected to the will of others.

33. In Nahuatl, "sewn in his mantle" meant something had become part of one's innermost being.

34. "Flowering Earth" was the Nahuatl expression for the place where ultimate truth resides.

35. See note 7.

36. See note 4. The following description is based both on Siller Acuña, *Para comprender el mensaje,* and Elizondo, *La Morenita.*

37. On solar symbolism in Mexico and Latin America and its use in Christian iconography, see Jaime Lara, "The Sacramented Sun: Solar Eucharistic Worship in Colonial Latin America," in *El Cuerpo de Cristo: The Hispanic Presence in the U.S. Catholic Church,* ed. P. Casarella and R. Gómez (New York: Crossroad, 1997), 261–91.

38. See C. Salinas and M. de la Mora, *Descubrimiento de un busto humano en los ojos de la Virgen de Guadalupe* (Mexico City: Editorial Tradición, 1980).

39. See Juan Homero Hernández Illescas, Mario Rojas, and Enrique R. Salazar S., *La Virgen de Guadalupe y las Estrellas* (Mexico City, 1995); and Janet Barber, "The Guadalupan Image: An Inculturation of the Good News," *Josephinum Journal of Theology,* n.s., 4, Supplement (1997): 81–85.

2

Origins and Development
of the Guadalupan Narratives and Image

This chapter provides an investigation of some of the pertinent historical questions and challenges that have been raised regarding the authenticity of the Guadalupan events, including those issues raised by art historians with regard to her image. In a short book like this it would be
impossible to provide either a complete analysis of the traditional narrative
presented in the previous chapter or a complete treatment of all the historical questions and problems that have surfaced. Nevertheless, together
with summarizing the work of recent scholars, this chapter seeks to provide
a clear, if necessarily limited, critical picture of the state of the question
today. Only after looking at some of the historical issues can this study investigate theological and other questions related to Guadalupan interpretation and celebration.

Historical Studies of the
Guadalupan Narratives and Image

Contemporary historical scholarship on the Guadalupan events and image
has been quite critical in its approach with regard to questions of authenticity and historicity. Augustinian theologian George H. Tavard, for example, has no qualms about simply dismissing the Virgin of Guadalupe altogether as "an apparition for which there is no historical evidence
whatsoever." He writes:

> In the same order of things, the beatification of Juan Diego, the alleged seer
> of Tepeyac near Mexico City, would seem to imply approval of both the cult

at the shrine of Guadalupe and the alleged visions of the Virgin in December 1531. But beatification cannot do away with the likelihood that Juan Diego never existed. For there is no documentation about Juan Diego and the apparitions at Tepeyac before 1648, when a first version of the story was printed, one hundred and seven years after the reported event. In fact, the bishop of Mexico City, Fray de Zumárraga, has a major role in the story, but there is no trace of the apparitions in his writings. Tepeyac had been a shrine devoted to the Aztec goddess Tonantzin. A cult of the Virgin was attested at the spot in 1556 when a Franciscan accused some Christian Indians of worshiping Tonantzin under the guise of Our Lady of Guadalupe. In 1575 a letter from the viceroy of New Spain reports that the silver and gold image of Our Lady at Tepeyac looks like the Virgin of Guadalupe [i.e., a statue of the Virgin under the same name venerated at Estremadura, Spain]. Hernán Cortéz himself came from Estremadura and must have imported the devotion that had been popular in his native province since the fourteenth century. In 1582, as seen by an English visitor, the Virgin was represented at Guadalupe by a traditional statue, just as in Spain. The statue must have been replaced by an Aztec painting at some point in the seventeenth century when the cult of Guadalupe was being indigenized.[1]

Similarly, it is well known that the former abbot of the Basilica of Our Lady of Guadalupe in Mexico City, Monsignor Guillermo Schulenberg Prado, the one whose name over the last four decades has appeared ironically as the guarantor of authenticity on every image of the Virgin reproduced from the tilma, accepted neither the authenticity of the Guadalupan apparitions nor even the historical existence of Juan Diego himself. According to Schulenberg's own words quoted in various publications in 1996, he believed that the Guadalupan phenomenon was more of a myth or symbolic tale than objective historical fact, something "as true as the gospel infancy narratives" of Christ.[2] After a public outcry in the Mexican press, Schulenberg resigned his position a few months later.

Both Tavard and Schulenberg, of course, are part of a long history of intellectual skepticism regarding the historicity of the origins and development of the Virgin of Guadalupe within the Roman Catholic Church. As early as September 8, 1556, in a sermon preached at the first *ermita* (hermitage or small chapel) at Tepeyac on the feast of both the Nativity of Mary and Our Lady of Guadalupe from Estremadura, Spain,[3] Franciscan provincial Fray Francisco de Bustamente claimed that the image already enshrined there was not of miraculous origin but had been painted by an indigenous person (possibly someone named Marcos) and that the devotions practiced there were detrimental to Christian faith, especially because, according to him, many of the indigenes considered the Virgin of Guadalupe to be not the Blessed Virgin Mary but a goddess.[4] Bustamante's sermon was, in large part, a critical response to another sermon preached at Tepeyac, on September 6, 1556, by the Franciscan archbishop of Mexico City, Fray Bernardino de Sahagún, who had been slightly more positive in his approach to the devotion as well as to various miracles beginning to be associated with it. Sahagún himself was devoted to the ermita at Tepeyac. Nevertheless, it was Sahagún, in his *Historía general de las cosas de Nueva España* (written between 1558 and 1569), who criticized strongly what he perceived to be various associations made with Tonantzin and the goddess Cihuacoatl ("Serpent Mother") connected with *indigenous* devotion to Mary at Tepeyac.[5] Sahagún's fear was the that the indigenes were continuing to worship Tonantzin and had no real veneration for Mary. Hence, the first reactions on the part of the church to the Mexican Virgin of Guadalupe in the New World in the sixteenth century, especially with regard to how devotion to her was taking shape among the indigenous population, was either outright rejection or some toleration mixed with strong caution because of perceived Aztec religious-syncretistic associations.

Other critical approaches to the origins of the cult of the Virgin of Guadalupe must also be noted, especially Joaquín García Icazbalceta's 1883 "Carta acerca del origen de la imagen de Nuestra Señora de Guadalupe de México," and the 1976 study by Jacques Lafaye, *Quetzalcóatl and Guadalupe: The Formation of Mexican National Consciousness, 1531–1813*.[6] But by far the best example of what is sometimes called "the anti-apparitionist approach" in the literature on Guadalupe is certainly the 1995 historical study by Stafford Poole, *Our Lady of Guadalupe: The Origins and Sources of Mexican National Symbol, 1531–1797*.[7] Indeed, there is no question but that Poole has produced here a work of incredible erudition and detailed documentation, a work that is now absolutely essential reading for anyone trying to come to an understanding of the origins and development of the Guadalupan narrative, image, and devotion on a historical level. Poole subjects to his careful and critical analysis every extant literary document with regard to Guadalupe from the sixteenth through the eighteenth centuries.

Poole's impressive study can be summarized as follows. According to him, there is no doubt that an ermita or shrine to *a* Virgin of Guadalupe, but most likely the *Spanish* Virgin of Guadalupe from Estremadura, existed at Tepeyac from at least as early as 1555, possibly established by Archbishop Montúfar, the successor to Juan Zumárraga (died 1548)—*the* bishop in the standard accounts of the apparitions—and probably enshrining originally both what has been called the "core image" of the Guadalupan "painting," and a silver statue of the Virgin (possibly a replica of the Estremaduran figure) donated by a Spanish official in Mexico City, Don Alonso de Villaseca. But, notes Poole, there are no *literary* sources that refer to an account of apparitions or even to Juan Diego prior to the 1648 work of Miguel Sánchez *(Imagen de la Virgen María)* or the 1649 *Nican Mopohua* by Luis Lasso de la Vega. According to Poole, "the overwhelming difficulty with the account of the apparitions of Our Lady of Guadalupe is, and always has been, the lack of documentary evidence or unequivocal references between 1531 and 1648."[8] Central to Poole's approach is that there is no mention whatsoever of either the apparitions or the image in the extant writings of Bishop Zumárraga, a rather curious omission if Zumárraga played the key episcopal role in the Guadalupan events assigned to him by the accounts of both Sánchez and Lasso de la Vega.

Furthermore, according to Poole's reading of the tradition, what evidence there is prior to 1648 suggests that Tepeyac was the center, not of a widespread indigenous devotion, but of the transplanted Spanish devotion to the Estremaduran Virgin of Guadalupe, a devotion near and dear to the hearts of Hernando Cortés and his fellow conquistadores and early missionaries. If the favored Marian devotion of the Spaniards themselves in Mexico would become Nuestra Señora de los Remedios (whose shrine in Mexico City is well documented from the mid–sixteenth century on), eventually the criollos, or Creoles—that is, those inhabitants of Mexico born in Mexico of Spanish rather than mestizo (Spanish and indigenous) parents—would come to favor the Mexican Virgin of Guadalupe as their patroness. Thus, Poole argues, any miracles connected with the shrine before this date are associated not with indigenous peoples but with others, especially with the criollos.[9] Similarly, according to Poole, no record of a feast in honor of Our Lady of Guadalupe celebrated at Tepeyac on December 12—interestingly enough, the date of Zumárraga's original appointment as bishop in 1528—exists before 1662, at which time the cathedral chapter of Mexico City requested approval from Rome for the feast on this date, a request that was delayed until 1667. When the request was finally approved by Rome, the response contained the incorrect date of September 12 rather than December 12, an error that delayed the process even further. An official inquiry demanded by Rome and conducted by the cathedral chapter in Mexico between 1665 and 1666 revealed that among the indigenous witnesses there was, indeed, evidence of an apparition tradition associated with Juan Diego and Tepeyac, a tradition that had been passed from parents to children. But because of historical inaccuracies in their testimonies, Poole dismisses the reliability of the accounts of the indigenous witnesses as having been shaped already by the narratives of 1648 and 1649.[10] Prior to the investigation, it appears that the feast day remained September 8, the feast of both the Nativity of the Blessed Virgin Mary on the general Roman Catholic liturgical calendar and the Estremaduran

Guadalupe on the local liturgical calendar of the Estremadura region in Spain. In fact, it was not until May 25, 1754, that Pope Benedict XIV finally confirmed both the patronage of the Virgin Mary under the title of the Mexican advocation of Our Lady of Guadalupe for "New Spain" and approved officially the propers (i.e., prayers, readings, and chants) for the Mass and office for the December 12 feast on the official calendar,[11] although it is quite clear that the feast had been celebrated in Mexico on December 12 for some time prior to this confirmation and approval.

It is, therefore, not in the early sixteenth century but in the middle of the seventeenth century and later—that is, *after* the publication of the apparition accounts of both Sánchez (1648) and Lasso de la Vega (1649)—that Poole locates the real origins of devotion to the uniquely Mexican Virgin of Guadalupe. In spite of the contemporary popularity of the narrative in the *Nican Mopohua,* a version that several have wanted to trace, with little supporting documentation, to a "lost" document called the *Relación* allegedly composed by Antonio Valeriano (ca. 1520–1605), a Christianized indigenous man who was a chronicler, translator, and mayor of Mexico City, Poole follows the earlier opinion of Jacques Lafaye, who viewed the Sánchez version as the primary witness to, and in fact the major catalyst for, the development of the Virgin of Guadalupe as the national symbol of Mexico.[12] Indeed, the *Nican Mopohua* itself not only contains a letter written to Lasso de la Vega by Sánchez but also seems to have been inspired by Sánchez's work. Hence, according to Poole, the story of the apparitions of the Virgin of Guadalupe *is* the Sánchez version, which was composed precisely for the consumption of the criollos in Mexico in order to advance their cause for equal recognition against their Spanish-born rulers. And, Poole says, it appears that it is only in the late seventeenth and early eighteenth centuries that a devotion among the indigenous peoples becomes widespread.

Sánchez's version, as indicated above, expresses a particular interest in the relationship between the Guadalupan story and image at Tepeyac and the events connected to the "woman clothed with the sun" in Revelation 12. This version, in fact, interprets the entire Guadalupan story as the Mexican, that is, Creole, fulfillment of Revelation 12, a kind of Mexican parallel to the U.S. myth of Manifest Destiny. That is, as Poole writes, Sánchez

> had a messianic view of Mexico City, which he sought to put on a par with the great religious centers of the Catholic world. He compared Zumárraga . . . to Saint John the Evangelist and Mexico to Patmos . . . and he interpreted Revelation 12 in terms of Mexico and the Spanish empire. The woman clothed with the sun was the city of Mexico. Mary, he asserted, had aided the Spanish conquest, she was the "assistant conquistador." New Spain was her

homeland. His emphasis, which took up most of the first part of the work, was that Revelation 12 prefigured Mexico, Guadalupe, and the destiny of the sons of the land. Guadalupe was for him primarily a devotion for those 'born in this land.' . . . His reasoning was often contrived, for example, when he pointed out that Juan Diego was called by Mary, and he was named for John and James, whose mother was named Mary, or when he formulated elaborate relationships based on the name John between Juan Diego, Zumárraga, and Saint John the Evangelist. The eagle whose wings were given to the woman fleeing the dragon was the eagle on the escutcheon of Mexico. The eagle in flight formed a cross and so the eagle that symbolized pre-Christian New Spain was to be Christianized by Mary, giving the gift of the cross.[13]

Consequently, in this version of the Guadalupan events Sánchez subordinates what Poole suggests may have been a localized "indian cult legend" to a criollo agenda in order to demonstrate that it was to the Mexicans themselves, understood as those of "pure" Spanish lineage in the New World, that the Virgin came "into the wilderness" of Mexico (see Rev. 12:6) with the intent of establishing and confirming them in their land. As such, the Virgin of Guadalupe became herself *La Criolla* and *La Conquistadora,* and traditional indigenous religion was seen simply as an idolatrous faith that had been overcome by her appearance in the New World (much like the dragon slain by St. Michael the Archangel in Rev. 12:7 ff.). That such an interpretation was ultimately successful in expanding the base of Guadalupan devotion in Mexico among the criollos is demonstrated by several Guadalupan sermons throughout the seventeenth and eighteenth centuries.[14] But perhaps the best example of how much of a national, cultural, and political symbol the Virgin of Guadalupe was to become is the fact that in the Mexican War of Independence from Spanish rule, under the leadership of Father Miguel Hidalgo in 1810, her image was placed on the banners that the revolutionaries carried into battle, much as the Spanish loyalists bore the Virgin de los Remedios on theirs. Such different loyalties even resulted in the Spanish loyalists once executing the Virgin of Guadalupe in effigy. Poole's concluding summary bears quoting in full:

[T]he ermita was founded about 1555 and dedicated to the Nativity of Mary. An image of the Immaculate Conception, probably painted by an Indian, was placed there from the beginning. That image is the original, unretouched part of the one presently in the basilica. . . . The association with the Nativity and the allied devotion of the Immaculate Conception (which was very popular among Spaniards) remained throughout the colonial period. A reputation for working miracles almost immediately grew up, perhaps because a herdsman claimed to have been cured there or perhaps of some less creditable claims. . . . Almost from the beginning the ermita became associated with the Estremaduran Guadalupe, and the image was retouched to re-semble the secondary image at that shrine.[15] One motive may have been to make Tepeyac more attractive to the peninsular [Spanish] population of Mexico City, such as Alonso de Villaseca, in an effort to get them to patron-ize and support it. This change in emphasis was probably the work of Arch-bishop Montúfar, whose procession and placing of the image was changed by legend into that of Zumárraga of 26 December 1531. . . . In this expla-nation it is possible that an Indian named Juan Diego actually existed and somehow became the protagonist of the legend. If indeed he lived, he never experienced in reality the events narrated in the Nican mopohua. For all the attention given to him in the early accounts, no serious move toward his canonization was made until the twentieth century. The Indian witnesses at the 1665 to 1666 inquiry gave evidence of an incipient cultus: how the In-dians sought Juan Diego's intercession for good harvests and how they re-garded him as a holy and upright man who led a retired and penitential life at Tepeyac. Why was there no move to canonize him? Obviously, because he was an Indian. A native saint would have been a rallying point for the natives that no peninsular or criollo wanted. . . . [I]t would have destroyed the myth of Indian inferiority and hence the economic basis of life in New Spain. . . . Guadalupe still remains the most powerful religious and national symbol in Mexico today. The symbolism, however, does not rest on any objective historical basis. Despite that it will probably endure, if only because it can be interpreted and manipulated by succeeding generations to meet the needs of the Mexican people.[16]

The Image of the Virgin of Guadalupe

Not surprisingly, given Poole's comments above, the history of the image of the Virgin of Guadalupe, enshrined since 1976 in its modern basilica in Mexico City, is marked by almost as much controversy as are the narratives of the apparitions themselves. For devout "apparitionists," of course, the image on Juan Diego's tilma was not made by human hands but appeared miraculously there in the presence of Bishop Juan Zumárraga exactly as re-counted in the *Nican Mopohua*. Consequently, for them the image itself serves as an abiding and present "proof" of the divine origins and histori-cal authenticity of the apparition events.

Art historians and others, however, are quick to point out (1) that var-ious additions appear to have been made to what is considered to be a "core image" of the Virgin on the tilma; (2) that the image of the Virgin corresponds stylistically to other Marian images becoming increasingly popular in late-medieval and Renaissance European art; and (3) that other narratives of "miraculous images" associated with apparitions of the Virgin, including, most notably, the Estremaduran Guadalupe herself, are not un-common. Each of these points calls for expansion, and I am dependent here in part, at least for the first two points, on the best available summary, by medieval art historian Jacqueline Orsini Dunnington in her recent book, *Guadalupe: Our Lady of New Mexico.*[17]

First, with regard to various additions to a core image, Dunnington notes, on the basis of various scientific tests made in 1979, that among art historians a consensus is emerging that elements such as the mandorla or rays of the sun surrounding the Virgin, the cinta around her waist, the stars on her turquoise mantle, the black moon at her feet, and the angel, as well as a crown on her head that was later removed, were all added later to an existing image that would have been originally a three-quarter rather than full-length representation of the Virgin Mary. In fact, she notes further, the various pigments used for making these additions have been identified, and it is precisely these additions that have begun to fade on the tilma.[18] At the same time, with regard to what is now being increasingly called the "original" or "core" image, or what Poole refers to as the "original, unretouched part" of the image, no tests have been able to determine its precise origins. Thus, if artists and scientists are not able to claim a "miraculous" origin for it, they *do* say, nevertheless, that its origins remain "inexplicable."

Second, the image of the Virgin of Guadalupe, whether one considers only the core image or the image with the additions, certainly belongs to a style of artistic depiction of the Virgin Mary called the Immaculate Conception, a style that became quite popular in Europe, including Spain, during the late Middle Ages and Renaissance, growing in relationship to the development of theological speculation (particularly strong among the Franciscans) about Mary's own conception. While this theological speculation would not become dogma in Roman Catholicism until the nineteenth century under Pope Pius IX (1854), it is clear that it was already exercising considerable influence in art and devotional practice both in Europe and in the New World. In this style of artistic representation, as reflected in the Guadalupan image itself, Mary is depicted without the Christ Child in her arms and with her head bowed and her hands folded. Occasionally as well, especially with the increasing related popularity in some places of associating Mary with the "woman" in Revelation 12, it was not uncommon to depict her surrounded by the sun and/or standing on a moon (with or without the Christ Child) and crowned. In fact, at the Estremaduran shrine of Our Lady of Guadalupe in Spain, a statue on the choir loft sometimes called the "secondary" image, to distinguish it from the primary one of the Virgin and Child venerated above the high altar at the shrine, depicts Mary with the Christ Child surrounded, as in the Mexican image of Guadalupe, by a mandorla of the sun and standing on the crescent moon. According to Dunnington, even the stars on the mantle of the Mexican Guadalupe and the colors used for her turquoise mantle and red dress are not without parallels in the history of Marian iconography in both East and West. Indeed, the use of similar colors for Mary's clothing (although often reversed, with a reddish mantle covering a bluish dress) is quite common in the Marian iconography of the Christian East. In addition, stars on Mary's mantle and occasionally her veil, often associated with the hymn "Ave maris stella" (Hail, Star of the Sea), are known as early as the ninth century and are again common at least in Byzantine Marian iconography.

Third, stories of miraculous images of the Virgin Mary or miraculous discoveries of lost images of Mary associated with apparitions also have a long history in the church, including in Mexico itself even images of Mary besides Guadalupe. The image of the Virgin de los Remedios, for example, the favored devotion of the *peninsulares* in Mexico, has its own apparition story. Although several versions exist, the basic story is about another indigenous Juan (also referred to in Aztec as Cuauhtlatoatzin), namely, a Juan de Tovar, who either discovered or was directed by the Virgin to discover an image that had originally been brought by Cortés himself and enshrined in the temple in the pyramid of Tenochtitlan but had become lost at some point during the conquest. Poole, in fact, claims that the Mexican narratives of Guadalupe and los Remedios have a common origin.[19]

An obvious parallel to both los Remedios and the Mexican Guadalupe exists in the apparition accounts of the Estremaduran Guadalupe. Similar to that of the Virgin of los Remedios, the narrative of the Estremaduran Guadalupe is about the discovery of a "lost" image, in this case an image said to have been originally crafted by the Evangelist St. Luke, given to Archbishop Leander of Seville by Pope Gregory the Great (590–604), and venerated until it was hidden during the centuries of Islamic (or Moorish) domination in Spain as a result of Islam's strong prohibitions against images. According to the written accounts extant in the mid–fifteenth century at the earliest, a poor farmer at some point during the thirteenth century was searching for a lost cow in the Guadalupe Mountains near Cáceres in the Estremadura region of western Spain. In an apparition the Virgin Mary directed him to have the parish priest and others dig at a spot where her image would be found and to build a shrine to her there, a place where the poor would be helped. After initial skepticism on the part of the local clergy, the image of the Estremaduran Guadalupe was unearthed, and eventually a small shrine was built in Cáceres. A convent was established there by King Alfonso XI in 1340 in gratitude for a victory against the Moors, and from 1389 on, the shrine was expanded as part of a Jeronymite (Order of

St. Jerome) monastery, with the Franciscans ultimately assuming ownership in 1908. Various miracles, such as the raising to life of the farmer's own son, became associated with the Estremaduran Guadalupe, and the shrine itself was to become a national and political-religious symbol of liberation from the Moors. Not only did Christopher Columbus meet King Ferdinand and Queen Isabella at this Estremaduran shrine in 1486 (and subsequently name one of the islands in the West Indies Guadalupe in her honor), but also, as noted previously, Hernando Cortés himself was from this region and professed a strong personal devotion to the Estremaduran Guadalupe.

If there are close parallels here with the story of the Virgin de los Reme-dios in Mexico, however, there are also significant points of contact with the Mexican Guadalupan narrative and image. Contemporary German theolo-gian Richard Nebel, in fact, notes six of these, especially in relationship to the *Nican Mopohua*.[20] First, the faces of both images are of dark complex-ion. and both came to be widely known as La Morena or La Virgen More-na; St. Luke is credited as the creator of the Estremaduran Guadalupe and, of course, divine origins are associated with the Mexican Guadalupe. Sim-ilarly, whereas the image of the Estremaduran Guadalupe had been "mirac-ulously preserved" from the time it was hidden until its rediscovery, the Mexican image is itself seen as a "permanent miracle." Second, both the Es-tremaduran and Mexican accounts are narratives about apparitions to peo-ple who were clearly on the bottom rungs or fringes of society, a farmer or shepherd (Estremadura) and a recently converted indigenous man (Mexi-co). Third, the place of both apparitions was a barren and rocky hill near a running spring. Fourth, in both accounts the Virgin's dialogue with the re-cipients of the apparition is affectionate and and the contents of her mes-sage to them are similar. In the Estremaduran accounts Mary identifies her-self as the "Mother of God" and requests that a sanctuary be built at the place where her image is discovered so that it might be a place where she could help the poor. In the *Nican Mopohua,* as we have seen, the Virgin iden-tifies herself similarly as "the ever-Virgin Mary, Mother of the one true God" and requests the building of a "temple" at the apparition site so that it might be a special place of assistance for the poor. Fifth, the circumstances accompanying both apparitions move in a similar direction. After initial doubt and skepticism on the part of ecclesiastical authorities, the apparitions occur again. This time, however, they are accompanied by other signs or miracles (e.g., the raising of the farmer's son to life in Estremadura, the flow-ers and image on Juan Diego's tilma, and the healing of Juan Bernardino). Eventually, a chapel or ermita is built, and an official procession is organized by the authorities in which the image is placed therein in order to be ven-erated. Finally, Nebel even sees a parallel in both apparitions in the length of time between the supposed date of the apparitions and various events immediately associated with them (veneration on the part of some, a growing tradition of miracles, and national disasters being averted by the Virgin's intercession) and the development of written documentary evidence over one hundred years later, leading ultimately in both cases to the development of her shrine as symbols of national, religious, and cultural identity, though one would be hard-pressed today to say that the Estremaduran Guadalupe functions this way any longer in Spanish Catholicism.

It would appear, then, that both the Guadalupan image and the narrative are to be seen as belonging to specific genres—the Guadalupan image to the genre of Immaculata art, which had taken shape in Europe prior to the conquest, and the narratives of both the *Imagen de la Virgen María* and the *Nican Mopohua* to the genre of apparition narratives—which provide a time-honored pattern for describing such events. With both the image and the narrative the closest parallels appear to be provided by those associated with the Estremaduran Virgin of Guadalupe. And, in spite of attempts that try to explain that the name Guadalupe in Mexico resulted from the Virgin's own Aztec words of self-identification to Juan Bernardino (*Coatallope* or *Tequantlazopueh*), which the Spaniards thought *sounded* like Guadalupe (a term probably of Arabic origins in Spain),[21] it is quite probably the case, given Cortés's own devotion to the Virgin Mary under this title, that, together with an image of the Estremaduran Virgin, the story of her apparition, miraculous image, and Spanish Guadalupan title was brought with the conquistadores into the New World and early on located at Tepeyac, which they later renamed Guadalupe. Subsequently, it would be no surprise at all that the narrative traditionally associated with the Spanish Virgin of Guadalupe would exercise some influence on the development of devotion to the Mexican Virgin of Guadalupe.

Critical Comments and Observations

In spite of the recent historical and artistic work summarized above, it would be incorrect to conclude that all of the questions, historical and otherwise, with regard to the Virgin of Guadalupe have been answered or that one can now conclude automatically, as some have done, that the Virgin of Guadalupe was but a convenient "invention" by Mexican church officials (Sánchez and Lasso de la Vega) in the mid–seventeenth century to further their particular ecclesiastical, social, and political agendas. Indeed, Poole's own work, while widely acclaimed for its painstaking scholarship on extant Guadalupan printed accounts, has not been received uncritically by other

Guadalupan scholars and theologians. Orlando Espín, for example, questions Poole's overall methodology of dismissing "*un*written evidence as unimportant and unacceptable (thereby showing an extraordinary and unjustifiable disregard for much of the evidence that could contradict his conclusions)."[22] He continues:

> [P]erhaps Poole's fascination with colonial Mexican *elites* (and their written texts) made him blind to *popular* pneumatology as the foundational epistemology and hermeneutic of the Guadalupe story. . . . Poole also unexplainably ignores that the Nahua culture (still very much alive, even after the Spanish conquest) would have transmitted its holiest and most fundamental beliefs and wisdom through oral means too; and especially after Nahuatl became alphabetized, orality remained a viable and frequent means of transmission among the majority of Nahuas.[23]

And, building on Espín's critique, Jean-Pierre Ruiz asks:

> What, if anything, is to be made of the 116-year gap between the events at Tepeyac and the publication of the accounts of those events? While scholars struggle with the process of investigating the traditional sources that underlie both works, . . . their appearance *in print* clearly represents a significant development. Without pushing the connection too far, it might be ventured that the move from the (ongoing) oral transmission of popular traditions about the apparitions at Tepeyac to the "canonization" of the accounts in print bears some comparison with the founding dynamics of the gospel, which began with popular traditions in the first century c.e. and only gradually achieved fixed form in texts. At the same time, just as the formation of the New Testament canon by no means put an end to the transmission of the gospel, it must also be recognized that the appearance in print of accounts of the hierophany at Tepeyac . . . surely did not bring the oral traditions about those events to an end. . . . Thus, the distance of 116 years between the events at Tepeyac and the appearance of the first printed accounts of these events may well indicate that the traditions about the Virgin of Guadalupe had reached an important breadth of diffusion throughout the various ethnic and socioeconomic strata of colonial Mexico, ranging from the indigenous Nahuas, to the criollos, to the Spanish born.[24]

Furthermore, it seems to me that one ought to take more seriously the possible evidence supplied by the early critiques of both Fray Francisco de Bustamente and Franciscan archbishop of Mexico City Fray Bernardino de Sahagún. In my own scholarly discipline of the study of early Christian liturgical history, an important methodological principle is that "legislation is better evidence for what it proposes to prohibit than for what it seeks to promote."[25] So, for example, if one reads in an early Christian conciliar decree, such as canon 20 of the First Council of Toledo in 398, that only the bishop and *not* presbyters are to consecrate the oil of chrism to be used in the baptismal anointing, one can be pretty certain that, in fact, fourth-century Spanish presbyters *were* consecrating the chrism themselves and not bothering to obtain it from their bishops.[26] Why should this methodological principle not apply also to the comments of Bustamante and Sahagún? That is, if there was not already in 1556 a growing indigenous tradition about miraculous origins associated with the image of the Virgin of Guadalupe, why would Bustamante feel the need to deny such a claim? And, at the same time, if there was not a correlation between veneration of Mary at Tepeyac and indigenous devotion there to the goddess Tonantzin between 1558 and 1569, then why would Sahagún perceive the need to address this situation critically in his *Historía general de las cosas de Nueva España*? While it is certainly true that neither Bustamante nor Sahagún refers to Juan Diego or to narratives of Guadalupan apparitions in the contexts of their words, the conclusions seem quite reasonable that "something" was going on among the indigenes at Tepeyac in relationship to devotion to Mary-Tonantzin and, at the very least, that a tradition about the miraculous origins of her image (the "painting," *not* a statue) had already developed among some of the indigenous inhabitants within twenty-five years of the traditional date of the apparition.

Shortly before Bustamante and Sahagún, however, the second archbishop of Mexico City, Dominican priest A. Montúfar, had already conducted an investigation on the indigenous devotions taking place at Tepeyac. Elizondo summarizes this investigation:

> During the inquiry, much negative evidence was presented by the missioners. They claimed that the Indians confused her with God and that the confusion was so great, that if an immediate remedy for the situation was not found, they might as well give up the preaching of the Gospel to the natives. A witness stated that the first one to have claimed that the image was capable of miracles should have been given one hundred lashes of the whip. They did not hesitate to state that this event was the ruin of their entire missionary effort. After having carefully investigated the matter the Archbishop reaffirmed his official support and encouragement of the devotion. Actually, he had built the first basilica in 1555, and after the investigation he was all the more convinced of the meaning and impact of the image.[27]

A 1569 catechism on the liturgical year composed in Nahuatl by Sahagún, the *Psalmodia Christiana,* may also be helpful in this regard.[28] Arranged in poetic verse ("psalms") this "catechism" appears to have been intended for use as catechetical sermons on the various feasts and seasons of the liturgical year. Although a feast of the Virgin of Guadalupe does not appear in this catechism, what Sahagún says about Mary in sermons for other feasts certainly has some resonance with how the Virgin of Guadalupe is described in the *Nican Mopohua* and portrayed on the tilma. In his sermon for the Feast of the Nativity of Mary on September 8, also, as noted above, the feast of the Estremaduran Guadalupe, Sahagún says, for example:

> When the dawn appears, when [the sky] now clears, those who have been sleeping then arise [and] start their work. . . . The little birds begin to talk, to fly, and night birds go into their caves. . . . It has become light; day has dawned. It was light when God created for us what was in the earthly paradise. He made a godly brilliance for us. There we would have lived most happily. But our first mother, Eve, brought on us sin's darkness. We lost the godly brilliance. Night fell upon us. . . . When the perfect, virtuous virgin, Saint Mary, was born, the godly daybreak was complete. Then the birds of Heaven began to sing, to speak. The angels said—so greatly did they wonder when the perfect virgin, Saint Mary, was born—Who has now been born so very pure, who shines so brightly? She has risen like the heavenly dawn of day.[29]

He provides a similar description of Mary in his sermon for the August 15 Feast of the Assumption, saying:

> Then her precious body was adorned, attired in heavenly array. She shone brightly; she gleamed brightly. She was very beautiful. She was clothed in heavenly flowers. Then she began; she now ascended. She went shining brightly, gleaming brightly. Many angels went accompanying her. It was truly wondrous how all went in order. The angels, who were watching, who awaited her in Heaven, marveled greatly. They said: She who now comes, comes shining brilliantly, comes gleaming brightly. She is like the godly dawn. She exceeds the moon, the sun, and she comes shining. And the angels who accompanied her said: She is the perfectly wise virgin, God's Mother. No one is like her, no one is her equal, and no one resembles her.[30]

It would be impossible, of course, to conclude from these descriptions that Sahagún has in mind either the image of the Virgin of Guadalupe or an account of the Guadalupan apparitions. But that is really not the point. Rather, what Sahagún's Marian descriptions suggest is that within the overall missionary context of mid-sixteenth-century Mexico, at least, in the region of Tepeyac, if not at Tepeyac itself, and *in Nahuatl,* the language of daybreak, birds, songs, and flowers, together with the imagery of outshining both the sun and the moon, was clearly employed in the catechesis of the indigenous peoples on Mary ("the perfectly wise virgin, God's Mother") and in the inculturation of Marian doctrine and devotion in Mexico. Consequently, whatever Sahagún himself may or may not have known or accepted with regard to the story of apparitions of the Virgin of Guadalupe, and given his highly critical and suspicious attitude toward the development of Guadalupan devotion among the indigenous population, it is difficult not to see at least the descriptions of the Virgin in the narrative of the apparitions in the *Nican Mopohua,* and the image itself, as belonging to the same mid-sixteenth-century worldview. In other words, the portrayal of the Virgin of Guadalupe in the *Nican Mopohua* certainly bears a strong resemblance to Sahagún's own mid-sixteenth-century portrayals of the Virgin Mary in his catechetical sermons and certainly testifies to the fact that Nahuatl religious imagery *(flor y canto)* was being employed with regard to Mary early on in the sixteenth-century evangelization of Mexico.

Another significant element urges further caution with regard to accepting Poole's conclusions uncritically. The recent discovery in Mexico of a sixteenth-century animal-skin codex in Nahuatl, now widely referred to as Codex 1548, may well invite the beginnings of a rewriting and reappraisal of the scholarly history of Guadalupe altogether. This codex, the first folio of a yet-be-identified work, contains several Nahuatl inscriptions referring to the 1531 date of the Guadalupan apparitions, the name and death date (1548) of Juan Diego (Cuauhtlatoatzin), the official seal of Antonio Valeriano with his name, and the signature of Fray Bernardino de Sahagún. In addition, artistic representations both of the Virgin appearing to Juan Diego on the hill of Tepeyac and of Juan wearing the tilma in the presence of the Virgin with her image already imprinted on it are discernible; both representations appear to have inspired and been copied by later Guadalupan artists.[31]

While staunch apparitionists have hailed this discovery as providing incontrovertible "proof" of both the historical reliability of the narrative in the *Nican Mopohua* and the divine origins of the Guadalupan image,[32] probably the most that can be said safely at this time is that if this codex is, indeed, authentic, then it certainly appears to push written and artistic documentation for the Guadalupan events, the existence of Juan Diego, and the image itself (together with what have been called additions to the core image) back to within seventeen years of the traditional date assigned to the apparitions. Further, if the seal of Antonio Valeriano is likewise authentic, then, in spite of Poole's assertion that the attribution of an early version of the *Nican Mopohua* to him (the nonextant *Relación*) is "the single greatest error in the history of the Virgin of Guadalupe,"[33] this codex may suggest that such an attribution of, at least, *a* Guadalupan narrative to him is, significantly, much earlier in the tradition than has been advocated in recent years.

Any firm historical conclusions based on Codex 1548, of course, will have to await further detailed, objective, and historical-critical study. Nevertheless, it would not be unreasonable to conclude at this time that indigenous devotion to the image of the Virgin of Guadalupe in the mid–sixteenth century, although probably much more localized in the region of Tepeyac than widespread among the indigenous people in Mexico, as is often claimed, and at least a core tradition about "some" apparitions to Juan Diego are rather early in the tradition's development. Indeed, together with documented sixteenth-century Franciscan hostility toward the indigenous (potentially syncretistic) devotion at Tepeyac, the oral testimonies of both indigenous and mestizo witnesses gathered in the 1665–66 inquiry, which Poole summarily dismisses as reflecting various historical/chronological inaccuracies or as already having been influenced by details in the apparition narratives of Sánchez or Lasso de la Vega, certainly suggest that oral and familial Guadalupan traditions, including a developing popular devotional cult to Juan Diego, *did* exist and *were* being passed from indigenous and mestizo grandparents to parents and to children. In fact, I wonder if what Poole writes in his conclusion, namely, that "there was no move to canonize [Juan Diego] because he was an Indian . . . [and] a native saint would have been a rallying point for the natives that no peninsular or criollo wanted . . . [because] it would have destroyed the myth of Indian inferiority and hence the economic basis of life in New Spain," does not begin to provide an answer to his own critique and suggest another way altogether to view the development of the Guadalupan traditions. That is, whatever the mid-seventeenth-century ecclesiastical, political, and social agendas and motivations accompanying the publication of the narratives of Sánchez and Lasso de la Vega may have been, if this localized "Indian cult legend" had by this time, in the words Jean-Pierre Ruiz cited above, "reached [such] an important breadth of diffusion throughout the various ethnic and socioeconomic strata of colonial Mexico," then it becomes possible that it could no longer have been conveniently ignored, merely tolerated, or controlled by other means. In other words, given what Poole refers to as the "myth of Indian [and mestizo] inferiority" on the part of those in power, not only in Mexico but throughout Latin America in the sixteenth century and beyond, and given the well-known sixteenth-century debates among the conquistadores and their missionaries on the human identity, civility, and even savability of the indigenous people (including African slaves) in the New World,[34] is it really so surprising that little sixteenth-century written documentation would exist of an indigenous devotional cult or that what does exist would display an attitude of suspicion, critique, caution, or, at times, outright rejection and hostility on the part of (primarily Franciscan) authorities? To give some kind of official credence or recognition to a "Juan Diego" as the recipient of a heavenly visitor or to an "Indian cult legend" associated with Tepeyac, especially in the early to mid sixteenth century, may well have meant similar recognition of the indigenous people themselves, an issue that was by no means yet resolved officially.

I would like to suggest that there may be a motivation behind the publication of both the Sánchez and the Lasso de la Vega versions of the apparition accounts other than mid-seventeenth-century criollo-versus-peninsular politics in Mexico, although I have no doubt that such politics were part of at least Sánchez's motivation. In the history of the relationship between official church practice and teaching and what is called "popular piety" or religion, it has often been the case that in order to control or exercise authority and jurisdiction over a growing devotion or cult, bishops would assume pastoral leadership of it and bring it from the realm of popular practice into the confines of official ecclesiastical structures. In his book *The Cult of the Saints: Its Rise and Function in Latin Christianity*, early-church historian Peter Brown, for example, provides several instances of how in relationship to the developing martyr cult the bodies or other relics of the martyrs, together with local associated devotional practices, were increasingly brought from cemeteries, locally or privately owned tomb-shrines, and other places where the church's official authority had little influence under, into, and around the altars of various basilicas and cathedrals where the authority of the bishop could be exercised decisively.[35] If such moves did not put an end to practices of piety associated with the martyr cult in Christian antiquity (and, indeed, they were not intended to do so), they did try to ensure that such practices would be integrated within the official and public liturgical life of the church where they could be interpreted and promoted in accord with official doctrinal-theological norms.[36] Hence, it becomes possible, if indeed the Guadalupan narrative and image had become widely diffused throughout colonial Mexico by the mid–seventeenth century, that the written narratives of the *Imagen de la Virgen María* by Sánchez and the *Nican Mopohua* by Lasso de la Vega represent a similar attempt on the part of the church in Mexico to ensure that the devotion that had obviously already been developing at Tepeyac and elsewhere for some time would be truly "Christian" in its interpretation and application.

That both the *Imagen de la Virgen María* and the *Nican Mopohua* represent and reflect in written form decidedly orthodox Christian interpretations of the Guadalupan apparitions and image is the thesis of Jean-Pierre Ruiz in his compelling article, already referred to above. While, as we have seen,

Sánchez's version interprets the entire Guadalupan story as the Mexican, that is, criollo, apocalyptic fulfillment of the woman clothed with the sun in Revelation 12, this interpretation, according to Ruiz, was probably due less to Sanchez's own interpretative creativity than to the theological context he had inherited. Ruiz writes:

> As for Sánchez's selection of Revelation 12 as the hermeneutical lexicon through which the hierophany at Tepeyac would be read, that choice may have been more than a matter of Sánchez's personal fascination with the Apocalypse, and more than a matter of his participation in the mood of apocalyptic optimism that accompanied the Spanish conquest of the Americas. . . . [T]here is little doubt that his identification of the Virgin of Guadalupe with the woman of Revelation 12 was strongly influenced by the prescriptive religious aesthetic of the Counter-reformation. Thus, in arguing that the events of Tepeyac were a fulfillment of scripture that confirmed the divine design involved in the Spanish conquest of Mexico, Sánchez simultaneously argued for the hermeneutical sufficiency (and exclusive privilege) of European Christian categories for comprehending and communicating religious experience in the Americas.[37]

But if this kind of hermeneutical approach is easily discernible in Sánchez's *Imagen de la Virgen María,* a similar process of reinterpretation of Guadalupe according to "European Christian categories" may also be discerned in Lasso de la Vega's *Nican Mopohua.* Ruiz continues:

> The books of Sánchez and of Lasso de la Vega . . . represent different directions taken in the same process of recontextualization, of finding a place for the hierophany at Tepeyac in the traditional Nahua religious iconography (Lasso de la Vega) and in traditional Christian biblical language (Sánchez). At the same time, both volumes represent substantial (though divergent) efforts to provide the Guadalupe icon with narrative texts. . . . The incorporation by Lasso de la Vega of the *Nican mopohua* into his Nahuatl account of the events at Tepeyac represents an explicit effort on his part to appeal to familiar language and symbolism in order to encourage Marian devotion among Nahua audiences. . . . Both works explored the intersection of two worldviews, the European worldview of their authors and the Nahua worldview implicit in the events at Tepeyac (and the century of oral tradition that transmitted them). Despite the differences in the traditional symbolic lexica on which they drew, both publications explained the hierophany at Tepeyac in Christian terms.[38]

The interpretation of both of these mid-seventeenth-century works narrating a supposed early-sixteenth-century event as explicit attempts to understand, defend, and further the Guadalupan image and tradition according to Counter-Reformation Marian theological categories is a most helpful perspective. While, of course, it tells us nothing about the Guadalupan oral tradition prior to this date, it does suggest, *pace* Tavard, that the mid–seventeenth century was not the time of the "indigenization" of the cult of the Spanish Virgin of Guadalupe, together with the "Aztec painting" that replaced the former statue, but, rather, was the time in which, whatever the Guadalupan cult may have been prior to this period, the localized but spreading Guadalupan traditions and image were officially accepted, contextualized, and given a kind of official hermeneutical context by well-known European theological categories. Indeed, that in so doing, the available apparition genre, such as the well-known apparition narrative of the Spanish Virgin of Guadalupe, would also be employed to fill out the narrative should come as no surprise. As Sandra L. Zimdars-Swartz has demonstrated in her fascinating study of modern Marian apparitions, not only do apparition narratives themselves belong to a recognizable genre in general but *official* apparition narratives with their "interpretive constructs," together with other devotional and apologetic literature, quickly become an almost indistinguishable part of the apparition itself.[39] That is, whatever the precise historical details of any apparition may have been for the recipient of such a private religious experience, an officially received narrative moves that personal experience from the private to the official public realm and thereafter serves as the canonical vehicle, means, and officially sanctioned interpretation through which others may have access to the the event and its perceived meaning. Consequently, in the absence of other literary remains and because of the de facto inability of oral tradition to leave such remains, the only real access to the Guadalupan events is through the lens of those official narratives. And, to continue Ruiz's analogy to the movement from oral tradition to the writing and canonizing of the New Testament Gospels, one need not expect to find clear objective historical accuracy in the Guadalupan narratives any more than one would expect to find similar historical accuracy in the various details narrated in the Gospels, the intent of which, long recognized by biblical scholarship, was to provide interpretive-theological *portraits* of Jesus for the various communities to which they were written rather than to offer objective biographical accounts.[40] For that matter, even Virgil Elizondo, unquestionably the most ardent defender and promoter of the theological meaning of Guadalupe in our own day, does not shy away from using, even in his earlier writings on the subject, the terminology of "folklore" or "legend" with regard to the narratives themselves. He writes:

The literary genre of the narration *as we have it today* is probably not historical, at least in the popular Western "scientific" understanding of the word historical—it is not based on objective historically verifiable documentation. . . . Yet, today, historians are becoming aware that the valid documentation . . . has been the privilege and domain—for the most part—of the rich and powerful, especially in Latin America. Only the rich and educated have the means to produce "proper" sources of information and subsequently "acceptable" recorded materials. The powerful, through their scientific research and medium of their own defined and accepted categories of thought and value systems, ratify officially their position in the world, so that they can ease their conscience and justify their position as "the good and holy people" of the world. What the conquered, the poor, the oppressed, have to say is quickly dismissed as folklore, losers' rationalizations, pious tales, superstitions, etc. . . . When the powerless tell their story through the medium of their categories of thought and expression it is quickly dismissed and ridiculed as unscientific and automatically false. Thus, the poor will make use of the literary genre of folklore, of the 'fabulous' and legendary in order to keep alive their vision of history and reality.[41]

Hence, for example, if Archbishop Juan Zumárraga (whose own writings, to be fair, have not all survived) did not, in fact, play historically the central episcopal role accorded to him in the official Guadalupan narratives, this does not need to be any more of a problem than the equally problematic worldwide census under Emperor Augustus narrated as part of the birth of Jesus in Luke 2 or other similar questionable historical details throughout the New Testament writings.[42] Indeed, given Zumárraga's reputation as an advocate and defender of the rights of the indigenous in Mexico and his official title as "protector of the Indians" during the 1530s,[43] is it really surprising at all that he would have emerged somewhere in the tradition as an ecclesiastical figure receptive to, and supportive of, such a growing indigenous cult or devotion?

All of this, of course, together with Poole's own critical work, militates against giving a fundamentalist historical interpretation to the *textus recepti* of the Guadalupan events. Like the Gospels themselves, Sánchez's *Imagen de la Virgen María* and Lasso de la Vega's *Nican Mopohua* are not necessarily objective, historically accurate, biographical accounts but *theological* portraits and interpretations of the Virgin of Guadalupe intended for specific audiences in mid-seventeenth-century Mexico and should be read as such. And, if they paint this theological portrait by appealing, in part, to other time-honored apparition narratives, this is precisely what is to be expected in and from such literature.

At the same time, however, to say that the Guadalupan narratives use or correspond to a recognizable genre of apparition accounts does not lead to the conclusion that the Mexican Virgin of Guadalupe is merely an adaptation, indigenization, or inculturation of, perhaps, the Spanish Virgin of Guadalupe. Rather, the parallels noted by Richard Nebel between the Spanish and Mexican narratives can certainly be seen as reflecting the fact that when they put the Guadalupan events into written form, Sánchez and Lasso de la Vega could do so only from within their own theological-interpretive cultural contexts and worldviews, contexts and worldviews shaped in part by a particular literary manner of narrating Marian apparitions. Poole concludes that Guadalupe "will probably endure, if only because it can be interpreted and manipulated by succeeding generations to meet the needs of the Mexican people." Yet, although "manipulate" is a strong and unfortunate word leading, perhaps, to the perception that intentional *deception* was and is a characteristic of Guadalupan interpretation, is it not true that the history of Christianity itself, from the very beginning of the New Testament writings, is precisely the history of "manipulation," or, stated positively, the history of interpretation and reinterpretation, of contextualizing and recontextualizing, for example, the person and work of Christ within and for "succeeding generations" in differing historical and cultural contexts? And, is it not equally true that reinterpretation and recontextualization are precisely the tasks of evangelization, of catechesis, and of theology itself as the church seeks to be faithful to the gospel of Christ in every age and so meet the real needs of people in such differing contexts? Was this not, at least at one level, what the Council of Nicea I (325) was doing in its affirmation of the *homoousios* against Arianism, or what the other great ecumenical councils of Constantinople (381), Ephesus (431), and Chalcedon (451) were attempting to do in relationship to other Trinitarian and Christological issues?

But, for all that, as Nebel himself also notes, identifiable parallels with the Estremaduran account do not explain fully the narratives of Sánchez and Lasso de la Vega. That is, the *Imagen de la Virgen María* and the *Nican Mopohua* are not simply the narratives of the Spanish Virgin of Guadalupe adapted to a Mexican context. Nor is the Mexican Virgin of Guadalupe merely an imported Spanish Marian devotion or image in a Mexican context.[44] The Mexican Virgin of Guadalupe is not simply a foreigner to be interpreted by European theological categories. That is, she cannot be interpreted ultimately as anything other than what resulted from a synthesis between "Old World" and "New World," that is, Mexican categories. As such, whatever the prehistory of the Guadalupan narratives and the image prior to 1648 and 1649 may have actually been, Elizondo is certainly correct when he writes that:

[t]he synthesis of the religious iconography of the Spanish with that of the indigenous Mexican peoples into a single, coherent symbol–image ushered in a new, shared experience....The cultural clash of sixteenth-century Spain and Mexico was resolved and reconciled in the brown Lady of Guadalupe. In her the new mestizo people finds its meaning, its uniqueness, its unity.[45]

This synthesis, resolution, and reconciliation might well have come about historically through a very complex process and a variety of factors. But there is no question that it is the Virgin of Guadalupe herself who emerges from all of this as the one representing both the process and the result of this cultural confrontation. That is, whether already in 1531 or not until much later, the image of the Virgin of Guadalupe and her appearance to Juan Diego *is* what was born in the new "American" synthesis resulting from the racial, social, ethnic, religious, political, artistic, and economic confrontation between Spain and Mexico, a confrontation that began neither in 1531 nor 1648 but already in 1519 with the arrival of Hernando Cortés in Mexico.

Conclusion

While it is a difficult assertion to make for one who is primarily a historian by occupation, it would seem that with regard to the origins and early development of the image and narratives of the Virgin of Guadalupe, historical study actually offers little by way of a definitive answer. The great value of Poole's work is that it provides a detailed analysis of how the Virgin of Guadalupe was to become eventually the great national, religious, and cultural symbol of Mexico that it has been historically and continues to be today. But in the final analysis, with regard to its origins, as to whether or not the Virgin Mary actually appeared to Juan Diego at Tepeyac in December of 1531, the historian cannot offer a conclusive answer. To conclude, then, as some have done, that Mary never appeared at all or that the tradition was merely invented in the seventeenth century is to claim to know far more than historical study and method alone can provide.

It is beyond my own expertise and competence to provide a complete alternative view of the historical development of the Virgin of Guadalupe prior to the narratives of 1648 and 1649. I suspect, however, that Ramón Vásquez y Sanchez, Native American artist and arts program director of the Centro Cultural Aztlan in San Antonio, Texas, is closer to the historical truth in drawing attention to the indigenous roots of the Virgin of Guadalupe when he says:

When I was appointed to the Committee of Peace and Justice [in San Antonio], I got to speak at St. Mary's University [here]. I'm the guy that stood up . . . to talk about [the Virgin of Guadalupe]. I said: "You've got to realize that the Virgin of Guadalupe is not originally Catholic." (And you just don't say that in a room full of priests and nuns). What do you mean by [saying that she isn't "Catholic?"]. And I said: "That you adopted her is well known, and that you crowned her is well known. It's a true thing. But she was [here] before the Catholic Church ever came to the Americas; because when Juan Diego unrolled his cloth, and the flowers came off, and the image was on there, the native peoples said 'Tonantzin! Tonantzin!'" . . . Of course, later Sahagún wrote this down and said, "Well, you know, it is probably Satanic . . . the Devil trying to destroy this holy image of Mary.'"Then I get to Mary, and I look at her and her appearances (e.g., Fatima and Lourdes) and, in any of those, I have never heard her say, "Give me a temple." She says, "I am Mary, Mother of God, Mary, Mother of Jesus," or "Mary, your mother," but never "build me a *temple*." That, to me, stood out. Why would she say, "build me a *temple*"? But then, you keep reading about what happened before she appeared. [The Spanish conquistadores] came in and started destroying the temples. And this lady was looking at this and said, "You know what? I don't like this." And she got someone [of] her own people . . . and said: "Go tell those people to build me a temple here," and that's what they did. . . . And she said to Juan Diego, "I am your mother." Well, Tonantzin was the Mother of Earth, the Mother of Everything to the Aztecs and to the indigenous peoples. They saw the color of her skin and she was not a white person; she was a dark lady, . . . *La Morenita*. And she was Indian, one of us. Right before that apparition . . . the Aztecs had come to the conclusion that "we can whip these guys, we can retake our land." It was in the eve of that insurrection when she appeared. And so, she kind of really stopped the insurrection. . . . Maybe she said, "Too many of my people have already been killed," and "Let's not have any more bloodshed. . . . I am a mother.' And [so] whether we say she is Mother Mary or Mother Mother, she is still Mother [of] Earth [and] Mother of men and women. We've got to respect that.[46]

Indeed, the early Franciscan hostility toward indigenous devotion to the Virgin of Guadalupe at Tepeyac, expressed by both Bustamante and Sahagún, as well as indicated by Montúfar in the 1550s, certainly does suggest that from the very beginning, whatever the peninsulares were or weren't doing with regard to the Spanish Virgin of Guadalupe at Tepeyac, an indigenous cult of the Virgin (Tonantzin) was developing to such an extent that the missionaries found their work seriously threatened. And, given the fact that within Aztec religion deities were conceived of as being dualistic, both male and female,[47] I suspect that the Guadalupan synthesis between indigenous religion and Spanish devotion to the Virgin Mary, later expressed fully in the written narratives and interpretive constructs of the

Sánchez and Lasso de la Vega versions, had already begun.

Furthermore, as we have noted, that the image of the Virgin was seen as having been miraculously produced and acclaimed for miracles by the indigenes is also testified to already by Bustamante and Montúfar. In such a context, and keeping in mind Elizondo's comment that "the poor will make use of the literary genre of folklore, of the 'fabulous' and legendary in order to keep alive their vision of history and reality," it would be quite difficult not to think that some early, oral, indigenous narrative about the Virgin's appearing to a Juan Diego (Cuauhtlatoatzin) had begun to develop very early as well. Indeed, although this is admittedly speculative, it would actually be *more* surprising, within the context of the Spanish conquest of Mexico, a period characterized not only by immense physical violence but also by, what is often more destructive, the kind of spiritual violence wrought through colonial evangelization with its concomitant destruction and replacement of the dominant religious and cultural worldview of the indigenous people,[48] if something like the Guadalupan narrative had not developed orally among the indigenes themselves precisely in order to preserve their own religious and cultural memory and roots. In fact, is not this kind of continuation of an alternative vision of self-preservation, self-identity, even self-defense, and religious worldview exactly what the early Franciscans, seen especially in the comments of Bustamante, Sahagún, and Montúfar, were afraid was taking place in the indigenous devotion at Tepeyac?

Hence, I suspect, but of course cannot prove, that what was to become the final Guadalupan synthesis was developing quite early on in the process of the so-called conversion of the indigenous population in Mexico. And, when the devotion became so widespread that it became clear that continued attempts to discourage and denounce it as diabolical and idolatrous would not work, only then was it given *official* written narrative form and *official* doctrinally sanctioned interpretations such as those permanently enshrined in the versions of Sánchez and Lasso de la Vega. Such an alternative approach to the history of Guadalupe, I would argue, should not be readily dismissed as a mere argument *e silencio* because of the apparent lack of early extensive written documentation any more than Poole's conclusions, based only on later written sources, should be accepted uncritically. Indeed, according to the minimal written documentation in existence, "something" indigenous was happening at Tepeyac very early on in relationship to devotion to the Virgin within Mexican church history and, therefore, there is really no reason to conclude that at least the core of the later versions of Sánchez and Lasso de la Vega is not somehow in continuity with that. The great difficulty, of course, comes in trying to separate what may be the core tradition from the rest of the narratives.

Notes

1. George H. Tavard, *The Thousand Faces of the Virgin Mary* (Collegeville, Minn.: Liturgical Press, 1996), 182–83. On the existence of Juan Diego, see also Fidel González Fernández, Eduardo Chavez Sánchez, and José Luis Guerrero Rosado, *El encuentro de la Virgen de Guadalupe y Juan Diego* (Mexico City: Porrúa, 1999); Javier García, "¿Existió Juan Diego? Comentario a una obra histórica reciente," *Ecclesia* 15, 2 (2001): 287–307; A. Fragoso Castanares, "Vida del Beato Juan Diego," *Histórica: Organo del Centro de Estudios Guadalupanos* 2 (June 1991); and J. Medina Estevez, *El Beato Juan Diego, el indio a quién se apareció la santisima Virgen María bajo la advocación de Guadalupe, es la pequeña historia de uno de los primeros americanos cuya santidad ha sido reconocida por la Iglesia* (Santiago de Chile: Editorial Patris, 1992).

2. See Roberto S. Goizueta, "Resurrection at Tepeyac: The Guadalupan Encounter," *Theology Today* 56, 3 (October 1999): 336.

3. On the Estremaduran devotion to Mary under the title of Our Lady of Guadalupe, see below, 37–39 and 42–45.

4. See Stafford Poole, *Our Lady of Guadalupe: The Origins and Sources of a Mexican National Symbol, 1531–1797* (Tucson: University of Arizona Press, 1997), 62–63.

5. See Bernardino de Sahagún, *Historía general de las cosas de Nueva España,* vol. 1, ed. Angel María Garibay (Mexico City: Editorial Porrúa, 1981), chap. 1.

6. Joaquín García Icazbalceta, "Carta acerca del origen de la imagen de Nuestra Señora de Guadalupe de México" (1883), in *Investigación histórica y documental sobre la aparición de la Virgen de Guadalupe de México* (Mexico City: Ediciones Fuente Cultural, n. d.), 18; and Jacques Lafaye, *Quetzalcóatl and Guadalupe: The Formation of Mexican National Consciousness, 1531–1813* (Chicago: University of Chicago Press, 1976).

7. See Poole, *Our Lady of Guadalupe.*

8. Poole, *Our Lady of Guadalupe,* 219.

9. An engraving of the Mexican Virgin of Guadalupe from 1597 shows her surrounded by ex-votos of seven miracles, none of which have indigenous persons as the subject.

10. See Poole, *Our Lady of Guadalupe,* 128–31.

11. On the development of the feast, see chap. 4, 102–10.

12. See LaFaye, *Quetzalcóatl and Guadalupe,* 251.

13. Poole, *Our Lady of Guadalupe,* 106–7.

14. See the sermons translated and edited by Francisco Schulte in *A Mexican Spirituality of Divine Election for a Mission: Its Sources in Published Guadalupan Sermons, 1661–1821* (Rome: Georgian Pontifical University, 1994).

15. On this image, see below, 41–45.

16. Poole, *Our Lady of Guadalupe,* 224–25.

17. Jacqueline Orsini Dunnington, *Guadalupe: Our Lady of New Mexico* (Santa Fe: Museum of New Mexico Press, 1999).

18. See Dunnington, *Guadalupe,* 13–16.

19. Poole, *Our Lady of Guadalupe,* 24–25.

20. Richard Nebel, *Santa María Tonantzin, Virgen de Guadalupe: Continuidad y*

transformación religiosa en México (Mexico City: Fondo de Culturo Económica, 1995), 55–74, 221–27.

21. See Dunnington, *Guadalupe,* 8.

22. Orlando O. Espín, *The Faith of the People: Theological Reflections on Popular Catholicism* (New York: Orbis, 1997), 7.

23. Espín, *Faith of the People,* 8. On what Espín calls "popular pneumatology," see below, chap. 3, 84–88.

24. Jean-Pierre Ruiz, "The Bible and U.S. Hispanic American Theological Discourse," in *From the Heart of the People,* ed. Orlando O. Espín and Miguel Diaz (New York: Orbis, 1999), 112–13. See also D. A. Brading, *Mexican Phoenix: Our Lady of Guadalupe: Image and Tradition across Five Centuries* (Cambridge: Cambridge University Press, 2001). While in general agreement with Poole that the origins of the *Nican Mopohua* itself are dependent upon Sánchez's 1648 *Imagen de la Virgen María* (see 54–75 and 258–87, Brading's *theological* evaluation (361–68) is quite close to that of the approach suggested above by Ruiz. Unfortunately, Brading's work became known to me only after my own study was completed and so could not be fully integrated, though I have been able to add some references to his work throughout.

25. Paul F. Bradshaw, *The Search for the Origins of Christian Worship* (New York: Oxford University Press, 1992), 68.

26. See E. C. Whitaker, ed., *Documents of the Baptismal Liturgy* (London: SPCK, 1970), 223–24.

27. Virgil Elizondo, *La Morenita: Evangelizer of the Americas* (San Antonio: Mexican American Cultural Center, 1980), 100.

28. Bernardino de Sahagún, *Psalmodia Christiana* (Christian psalmody), trans. A. J. O. Anderson (Salt Lake City: University of Utah Press, 1993). My thanks to Sister Anita de Luna of the Mexican American Cultural Center, San Antonio, Texas, for directing me to this reference.

29. Sahagún, *Psalmodia Christiana,* 275–77.

30. Sahagún, *Psalmodia Christiana,* 250.

31. See Xavier Escalada, *Enciclopedia Guadalupana: Apéndice Códice 1548* (Mexico City: Robles Hermanos, 1997).

32. See, in addition to Escalada, *Enciclopedia Guadalupana,* "The Guadalupan Apparitions: Historical Fact?" Janet Barber Escalada in *A Handbook on Guadalupe,* ed. Francis Mary, F.F.I (San Francisco: Ignatius Press, 1994), 184–191.

33. Poole, *Our Lady of Guadalupe,* 222.

34. On these debates, see the helpful summary provided by Alex García-Rivera in *St. Martín de Porres: The "Little Stories" and the Semiotics of Culture* (Maryknoll, N.Y.: Orbis, 1995), 40–57.

35. Peter Brown, *The Cult of the Saints: Its Rise and Function in Latin Christianity* (Chicago: University of Chicago Press, 1981).

36. This is not to mention that, by so doing, the various offerings of the faithful, monetary and otherwise, often left as votive and thank offerings at the shrines would now also be left at the basilicas and cathedrals and so become a part of diocesan treasuries.

36. Ruiz, "The Bible and Discourse," 107.

37. Ruiz, "The Bible and Discourse," 112–14.

38. Sandra L. Zimdars-Swartz, *Encountering Mary: Visions of Mary from La Salette to Medjugorje* (New York: Avon, 1991), 11–19.

39. Indeed, in spite of the public outcry against him, perhaps Monsignor Guillermo Schulenberg Prado was correct after all in drawing a parallel between the historicity of the Guadalupan events and those of the infancy narratives in the Gospels. See above, 36.

40. See Elizondo, *La Morenita,* 118–19.

41. See Raymond Brown, *An Adult Christ at Christmas* (Collegeville, Minn.: Liturgical Press, 1978), 17n26. See also Brading, *Mexican Phoenix,* 367, who argues in a similar manner that it is the theological purpose of Guadalupe and not the historicity of the Guadalupan events that is most important.

42. See Poole, *Our Lady of Guadalupe,* 34–35.

43. See Nebel, *Santa María Tonantzin,* 82–164.

44. Virgil Elizondo, *Galilean Journey: The Mexican-American Promise* (Maryknoll, N.Y.: Orbis, 1983), 12.

45. Ramón Vásquez y Sanchez, personal interview by author, December 7. 2000, San Antonio, Texas.

46. See Nebel, *Santa María Tonantzin,* 82–92.

47. See Elizondo, *Galilean Journey,* 9–11.

3

Modern Roman Catholic Theological
Interpretations of the Virgin of Guadalupe

Whatever conclusions, pro or con, may be reached on the basis of historical-critical methodology regarding the historicity or authenticity of the Guadalupan events and image, those conclusions actually matter very little in the long run. The narrative, cult, and image of the Virgin of Guadalupe are here to stay and therefore certainly merit theological attention in their own right. As Lutheran theologian Alberto Pereyra has written:

> It is impossible to separate the issue of the historical proofs in the Tepeyac without considering the impact on the Latino people. Whether we have or do not have clear proof of the apparition in the Tepeyac, it will not destroy Our Lady of Guadalupe's influence on Latino spirituality. People can destroy all arguments about the historical presence of the Lady in the Tepeyac, but they cannot destroy the symbol, the devotion to her. This would repeat the actions of the conquerors, destroying the political, educational, and spiritual systems, yet they could not destroy their souls. Latino spirituality is not limited to the Juan Diego experience but is a communal spirituality which comes down through the centuries. It is not an individual experience such as the formula, "receive Jesus Christ as your personal Savior." This spirituality is preserved in the core of the community and its religious celebrations and experiences.[1]

This "communal spirituality" continues to be expressed, as Roberto Piña at the Mexican American Cultural Center, San Antonio, Texas, told me in a recent conversation, in what is passed down from grandparents and parents to children more than through any official ecclesiastical channels. He said:

I know that scholars raise all kinds of questions about the historical events associated with Guadalupe, and some say that she didn't appear. I don't know what happened or what to believe about this. But every day of her life my *abuelita* [grandmother] lit candles in front of her image of Our Lady of Guadalupe on her *altarcito* [little altar] and prayed to her. I know she believed it happened. And I believe my *abuela*.[2]

Therefore, as Pereyra continues, the real Guadalupan challenge is not what historical studies might or might not conclude about her origins and development but, rather, that

[w]e need to be flexible and walk to the Tepeyac of our own spiritual experience. We cannot see the world merely from our own windows or preach the gospel through videos, tapes, or correspondence. The cultural drama is always there. Latinos or other people from different cultures are not a hard disk on our computers where we can erase from their souls all their spirituality and insert a new program. The Roman Catholic Church tried for five hundred years and came to the conclusion that it is impossible to change the Indian spirituality. The challenge to welcome, learn from, and incorporate Indian spirituality is still before us.[3]

Such an invitation and challenge to "walk to the Tepeyac spiritual experience" of, at least, the Mexican and Mexican American spiritual experience is one that has been readily accepted by a number of Roman Catholic scholars in our own day, most notably, of course, by Virgil Elizondo and Jeannette Rodriguez. Including the significant contributions of still others, this chapter provides a summary of their attempts from a variety of methodologies to "welcome, learn from, and incorporate [that] Indian spirituality" as expressed in the Virgin of Guadalupe on behalf of and within the contemporary Roman Catholic Church. It is divided into three subsections: Guadalupe as evangelizer, liberator, and "Mother of the New Creation"; Guadalupe and popular religion; and Guadalupe as the feminine face of God.

Guadalupe as Evangelizer, Liberator, and "Mother of the New Creation"

The leading Roman Catholic defender, proponent, and interpreter of the Virgin of Guadalupe today is clearly Father Virgil Elizondo, who, throughout his pastoral and academic career, has made several significant contributions to Guadalupan topics, in both popular and scholarly journals as well as more highly specialized academic studies. Based primarily in exegetical studies of the *Nican Mopohua* and his own life experiences as a Mexican American Catholic and priest, Elizondo describes his own pilgrimage in Guadalupan study and reflection in the following manner:

> When I first began to explore Guadalupe's theological significance, I saw her as the great evangelizer of the Church and of the Americas. Later I envisioned her as the protector and liberator of the poor, the downtrodden, and the disenfranchised. Today I increasingly see her as the beginning of a new creation, the mother of a new humanity, and the manifestation of the femininity of God—a figure offering unlimited possibilities of creative and liberating reflection. The more I reflect on Guadalupe, however, the more I realize how incompletely we grasp the historical and theological significance of the Guadalupe event.[4]

Since each of these categories remains part of Elizondo's own Guadalupan theological synthesis, it is important that each not be interpreted only as a temporary stage in his developing thought that is subsequently replaced or surpassed by a succeeding stage. Rather, if his theological thought has developed from interpreting Guadalupe as evangelizer to liberator to Mother of the New Creation, each of the previous categories still functions as part of a theological whole, and all three provide an important and unified perspective that needs to be taken seriously in coming to a theological understanding of the Virgin of Guadalupe today.

Guadalupe as Evangelizer

Elizondo's treatment of the Virgin of Guadalupe as evangelizer offers a unique perspective on what might surely be called a process or method of "evangelization through incarnation." On the one hand, this approach can be summarized simply by drawing a parallel between Christ's Incarnation and birth in Bethlehem in first-century Judea and his new "incarnation" in sixteenth-century Mexico in the womb of the pregnant Virgin of Guadalupe. Since in both cases the Virgin Mary is obviously instrumental to the process, Elizondo can write, with specific reference to the image on Juan Diego's tilma:

> [E]ven though this imprint is a Marian image, it is a beautiful Christ-centered presentation of the Incarnation within the American soil. Once again, it is through Mary that God will receive his human face and heart. It will be a woman of this land who will give to the God made man his human characteristics so that He may dwell amongst us. Not as a stranger but truly in every sense of the word as one of our own.[5]

On the other hand, and, perhaps more important, to speak of evangelization through incarnation is far more than attempting to draw a simple parallel between a biblical and sixteenth-century event. For evangelization through incarnation is, precisely, an evangelical process of inculturation and cultural adaptation of Christianity itself. Indeed, what comes to be incarnated in relationship to the Guadalupan event is a new way of being for the church, a way that synthesizes both old and new, both European and Mexican-indigenous, into a new ecclesial reality altogether, a reality concretely expressed in the European-indigenous narrative and iconographic synthesis represented by Guadalupe herself. Elizondo writes elsewhere:

> As at Bethlehem when the Son of God was born as Jesus and signaled the reversal of the power of the Roman empire, so at Tepeyac Christ set foot on the soil of the Americas and signaled the reversal of European domination. Tepeyac symbolized the birth of the Mexican people and the birth of Mexican Christianity. They were no longer an orphaned people and the new religion was no longer that of foreign gods. The power of hope offered by the drama of Guadalupe came from the fact that the unexpected good news of God's presence was offered to all by someone from whom nothing special was expected; the conquered Indian, the lowest of the low. Conversion begins with the poor and marginated; they are the heralds, the prophets, of a new humanity. The new people of the land would now be the *pueblo mestizo, la raza mestiza*. And the new Christianity would be neither a cultural expression of Iberian Catholicism nor a mere continuation of the preconquest religions of the indigenous peoples, but a new incarnation of Christianity in and of the Americas.[6]

To speak of conversion as the goal of evangelization in this context also necessitates asking just who it is that is actually "converted" in and by the Guadalupan event. Certainly the Guadalupan narratives are about the evangelization and conversion of the indigenous peoples of Mexico, represented in those narratives by both Juan Diego and his uncle Juan Bernardino. But, contrary to the then widespread "evangelistic" methods employed by the conquistadores and their missionaries in Mexico and elsewhere, methods based often on logical doctrinal proposition, threats of punishment, and the fear of hell,[7] the evangelizing process reflected in the Nican Mopohua is radically different.

> The method of Guadalupe is based on beauty, recognition and respect for "the other," and friendly dialogue. It is based on the power of attraction, not on threats of any kind. Juan Diego is attracted by the beautiful singing that he hears; he is fascinated by the gentleness and friendliness of the Lady, who by her appearance is evidently an important person; he is uplifted by her respectful and tender treatment of him; he is captivated by her looks. She is so

important, yet she takes time to call him by name and to visit with him in a very friendly way. In her presence, he exhibits no inferiority or fears. Here there is no fear of hell—here, Juan Diego is experiencing heaven. . . . The contrast between the old and the new is sharp. While the church was trying desperately to create vivid imagery of judgment, purgatory, and the eternal fires of hell, Our Lady of Guadalupe is giving Juan Diego a holistic experience of heaven. In her presence, he is transformed. And the final proof of the absolute truth of this experience is not the power and might of God proven in battle by the sword and the gun, but beautiful flowers with a heavenly aroma blooming on the desert hill top—and in the midst of winter! The ultimate sign of God's transforming power is the peaceful and miraculous flowering of new life in the midst of the deserts of human existence, not the destructive power of the growing military might of the modern world. The powerful had crucified Jesus, had executed him unjustly, but God raised him to life. The sign of this power of God has always been the beautiful flowers of Easter. Flowers, not weapons, are the signs of God's ultimate power over unjust executions and death. . . . Juan Diego was re-created through his contacts with the Lady. This was the basis of his enthusiasm, courage, and fervor. He goes hurriedly, with confidence and joy, to the bishop's house. When today's poor experience themselves as recognized, respected, and called by name by the living God, they take on God's cause for humanity with the same joy and conviction as Juan Diego. They are no longer victims and are now survivors. Their fiestas, dances, songs, poetry, and joy make God come alive.[8]

Similarly, with specific regard to the healing and "conversion" of Juan Diego's uncle, Juan Bernardino, Elizondo can say further that:

[t]he restoration to life of the dying uncle on December 12 was nothing less than a historical resurrection of the dying peoples of the Americas who now came to life as the new Christian people of the Americas. Through Our Lady, a collective resurrection of the people would take place. The healing of Juan Bernardino constituted the assurance of survival through the new way of life of the Mother of Tepeyac. The people who had wanted only to die now began to want to live. This was the source of their dancing, feasting, and joy. They were crucified [by the Spanish conquest] but not destroyed, crushed but not held down, for in her they were (and are) alive, risen, and at the beginning of new life. Thus, liturgically, for us in the Americas, December 12 is as important a feast as December 25 and Easter Sunday are for the Christians of the Old World. . . . In the rehabilitation of Juan Bernardino, a totally new chapter in evangelization begins that will not be written about until our own times: evangelization by way of the incarnation. In the healing of Juan Bernardino, the conversion unto life of the people truly begins. In him begins the mestizo Christianity of the Americas.[9]

At the same time, while the Guadalupan narratives are clearly about the

conversion of the indigenous peoples of Mexico to Christianity, "the ultimate point of the narrative," according to Elizondo, is "the conversion of
the bishop and his household—theologians, catechists, liturgists, canonists,
and others." In other words, the Guadalupan narratives are really about the
conversion of the church itself, represented in the narratives by the person
of Bishop Juan Zumárraga. He continues:

> The entire narrative calls them to convert from confident religious ethno-
> centrism to a position of doubt, curiosity, investigation, and finally conver-
> sion. Something new was happening. They were invited into it, but it was
> not within their control. They had been inviting (threatening?) the Indians
> to come to their churches, but now the Indians were requesting a temple
> into which the Spaniards would be invited on an equal footing with all the
> inhabitants of these lands. This was not an uprising. It did not just involve
> new arguments offered by the learned tlamatini (wise men/theologians) of
> the Nahuatl against the presentations of the missioners. Rather it was an in-
> vitation—a demand—for a common enterprise.[10]

Whether one accepts the traditional assumption that all of this actually occurred in December of 1531 or the critical conclusions of Poole and other
scholars that Guadalupe's origins really belong to the overall seventeenth-
century context of the "official" narratives is of little consequence here. In
either case, one cannot fail to note that the method of evangelization by incarnation reflected in those narratives finds its closest parallel only today in
official Roman Catholic teaching on evangelization and missionary work.
The Second Vatican Council's decree on missionary activity of the church
in the modern world, *Ad gentes,* states clearly: "If the Church is to be in a
position to offer all . . . the mystery of salvation and the life brought by God,
then it must implant itself among all these groups in the same way that
Christ by his incarnation committed himself to the particular social and
cultural circumstances of [those] among whom he lived."[11] This decree continues:

> In order to bear witness to Christ, fruitfully, [Christians] should establish re-
> lationships of respect and love, . . . they should acknowledge themselves as
> members of the group in which they live, and through various undertakings
> and affairs of human life they should share in their social and cultural life.
> They should be familiar with their national and religious traditions and un-
> cover with gladness and respect those seeds of the Word which lie hidden
> among them. They must look to the profound transformation which is tak-
> ing place among nations. . . . Just as Christ penetrated to the hearts of [peo-
> ple] and by a truly human dialogue led them to the divine light, so too his
> disciples, profoundly pervaded by the Spirit of Christ, should know and

converse with those among whom they live, that through sincere and patient dialogue these [people] might learn of the riches which a generous God has distributed among the nations. They must at the same time endeavor to illuminate those riches with the light of the Gospel, set them free, and bring them once more under the dominion of God the saviour.[12]

And, finally:

The seed which is the word of God grows out of good soil watered by the divine dew, it absorbs moisture, transforms it, and makes it part of itself, so that eventually it bears much fruit. So too indeed, just as happened in the economy of the incarnation, the young churches . . . take over all the riches of the nations which have been given to Christ as an inheritance (cf. Ps. 2:8). They borrow from the customs, traditions, wisdom, teaching, arts and sciences of their people everything which could be used to praise the glory of the Creator, manifest the grace of the saviour, or contribute to the right ordering of Christian life. To achieve this, it is necessary that in each of the great socio-cultural regions . . . theological investigation should be encouraged and the facts and words revealed by God, contained in sacred Scripture, and explained by the Fathers and Magisterium of the Church, submitted to a new examination in the light of the tradition of the universal Church. In this way it will be more clearly understood by what means the faith can be explained in terms of the philosophy and wisdom of the people, and how their customs, concept of life and social structures can be reconciled with the standard proposed by divine revelation. Thus a way will be opened for a more profound adaptation in the whole sphere of Christian life. This manner of acting will avoid every appearance of syncretism and false exclusiveness; the Christian life will be adapted to the mentality and character of each culture, and local traditions together with the special qualities of each national family, illumined by the light of the Gospel, will be taken up into Catholic unity.[13]

It is difficult not to see this modern focus on evangelization by incarnation, reaffirmed both by Pope Paul VI in his 1975 encyclical, *Evangelii Nuntiandi,* and by the famous Latin American Roman Catholic bishops' Third General Conference at Puebla, Mexico, in 1979, already experientially present centuries before within the Guadalupan narratives themselves.[14] For it is precisely by such means as attraction rather than coercion, respectful dialogue rather than dogmatic pronouncement and threats of punishment, and through affirmation of the "seeds of the Word" present already in indigenous Mexican culture and religion—reflected in the Virgin's self-description as "the Ever-Virgin Holy Mary, Mother of the God of Great Truth, Téotl, of the One through Whom We live, the Creator of Persons, the Owner of What Is Near and Together, of the Lord of

Heaven and Earth"—that Juan Diego is brought to his conversion and, ultimately, Juan Zumárraga to his own. It is certainly not surprising, then, that within his 1999 apostolic exhortation, *Ecclesia in America,* Pope John Paul II can refer to "Blessed Mary of Guadalupe" as "an impressive example of a perfectly inculturated evangelization,"[15] and say that "in America, the *mestiza* face of the Virgin of Guadalupe was from the start a symbol of the inculturation of the Gospel, of which she has been the lodestar and guide."[16] Indeed, it would not be incorrect to conclude from all this that, far from being a mere evangelistic tool or gimmick concocted to make converts to a particular expression of Christianity, whether in the sixteenth century or now, the Virgin of Guadalupe in her image and narratives is precisely revelatory of an evangelical process of conversion and inculturation itself.

One concrete contemporary example of this evangelical process discerned by Elizondo in the *Nican Mopohua* is to be found in the *Encuentro Misionero* retreat designed especially for Mexican immigrants, both documented and undocumented, at the Shrine of Our Lady of Guadalupe in Coachella, California. According to the recent doctoral dissertation on this subject by Daniel Groody, the goal of this *encuentro* (encounter) or retreat is to lead participants, recently arrived Mexican immigrants, separated and cut off as aliens in a strange land from their familiar cultural, linguistic, and religious roots, to a new affirmation, awareness, and appreciation of their own identity and human dignity. Groody writes that this retreat, moving respectfully in stages, like the *Nican Mopohua* itself, from the experiences of darkness and alienation to being healed and uplifted and, ultimately, to celebration

> is a program that comes from the hearts of the team and is offered to the hearts of the participants. All this takes place in a very beautiful and festive atmosphere within their own Mexican cultural setting, in the transposed space of Our Lady of Guadalupe at Tepeyac. In the midst of an alien land, they suddenly find themselves at home, and at home in a very new, attractive and alternative way. The point is that they do not have to leave their home setting, their cultural world, to experience Christian transformation. It is not an abandonment of one world of cultural-religious symbolism and meaning for a totally different cultural-religious world but a transformation within their own world of familiar and beloved cultural-religious symbols. To be explicit, they do not have to cease being Mexican; they do not have to break from the religious traditions of their ancestry and families, to become reborn in Christ.[17]

If the Virgin of Guadalupe in her narratives and image reflects an evangelical process of evangelization through incarnation as a challenge to, and critique of, other evangelistic methods, however, there is a certain sense in which she also reflects, represents, and/or incarnates the very goal of the process itself. Although, to my knowledge, Elizondo does not make this step in his writings, one of the great insights of contemporary Roman Catholic Marian theology is that Mariology itself cannot be separated systematically from ecclesiology (or, for that matter, from Christology and soteriology). For example, the authors of Vatican II's dogmatic constitution on the church, *Lumen gentium,* deliberately included a chapter on the Virgin Mary, contrary to the wishes of those at the council who desired a separate Marian document altogether. An earlier document, the liturgy constitution approved in 1963, *Sacrosanctum concilium,* had paved the way for this approach in its statement that "in [Mary] the Church admires and exalts the most excellent fruit of redemption, and joyfully contemplates, as in a faultless image, that which she herself desires and hopes wholly to be,"[18] an orientation reaffirmed in Paul VI's 1974 significant apostolic exhortation, *Marialis cultus.*[19] In other words, the mestiza Virgin of Guadalupe, the synthesis of European and indigenous cultures and ethnicities, is herself, in some analogous way, the very "church" that came to be incarnated as the result of the sixteenth-century cultural confrontation between Spain and Mexico, and the very multiracial, multiethnic, multicultural, mestizo church that still struggles to be born in our own day. In this sense, then, the Virgin of Guadalupe, in accord with contemporary Roman Catholic thought, might surely be interpreted as the model or image of the process as well as the result and ultimate goal of this evangelization through incarnation. Both the process and the goal are yet to be fully completed but remain as challenge and invitation today for the church to become what the narrative and image of Guadalupe already proclaim. That is, the Virgin of Guadalupe is, *precisely,* the image of that which the church "desires and hopes wholly to be" itself in the modern world, and the narrative of the conversions of Juan Diego, Juan Bernardino, and Juan Zumárraga provides the model of how this kind of church might arise.

Guadalupe as Liberator

The image of Guadalupe as liberator in Elizondo's thought cannot be separated neatly from the image of Guadalupe as evangelizer. This becomes especially clear when it is noted that the very conversions of Juan Diego and Juan Zumárraga in the *Nican Mopohua* were also experiences of profound liberation. For Juan Diego, this liberation came to be expressed in the discovery of his own human dignity and in his being lifted up from his lowly state as an evangelist or herald of the good news to the bishop. And, for Juan Zumárraga, this conversion is expressed in his own liberation from what Elizondo calls his "religious ethnocentrism" in order to embrace the new, emerging incarnation of Christianity taking place within the New World. Thus, both the poor and the powerful together experience liberation in the Guadalupan event.

There is a sense, however, in which the Guadalupan event may be seen to incarnate in a particular way what many Roman Catholic theologians refer to today as the church's "preferential option for the poor," a preference clearly expressed by the leading contemporary liberation theologian, Gustavo Gutiérrez:

> God has a preferential love for the poor not because they are necessarily better than others, morally or religiously, but simply because they are poor and living in an inhuman situation that is contrary to God's will. The ultimate basis for the privileged position of the poor is not in the poor themselves but in God, in the gratuitousness and universality of God's agapeic love.[20]

A similar orientation was underscored in the 1979 Third General Conference of the Latin American Bishops in Puebla, Mexico: "When we draw near to the poor in order to accompany them and serve them, we are doing what Christ taught us to do when he became our brother, poor like us. Hence service to the poor is the privileged, though not exclusive, gauge of our following of Christ."[21] The conference said further:

> Commitment to the poor and oppressed and the rise of grassroots communities have helped the church to discover the evangelizing potential of the poor. For the poor challenge the church constantly, summoning it to conversion; and many of the poor incarnate in their lives the evangelical values of solidarity, service, simplicity, and openness to accepting the gift of God.[22]

And John Paul II himself in *Ecclesia in America,* referring to Puebla directly, can state that:

> "The Church in America must incarnate in her pastoral initiatives the solidarity of the universal Church toward the poor and the outcast of every kind. Her attitude needs to be one of assistance, promotion, liberation and fraternal openness. The goal of the Church is to ensure that no one is marginalized" [no. 306]. The memory of the dark chapters of America's history, involving the practice of slavery and other situations of social discrimination, must awaken a sincere desire for conversion leading to reconciliation and communion. . . . Concern for those most in need springs from a decision to love the poor in a special manner. This is a love which is not exclusive and thus cannot be interpreted as sign of partiality or sectarianism; in loving the poor the Christian imitates the attitude of the Lord, who during his earthly

life devoted himself with special compassion to all those in spiritual and ma-
terial need.[23]

Again, just as the Guadalupan image and narratives might be interpreted as prefiguring the modern Roman Catholic emphasis on evangelization
through incarnation, so also might they be viewed as pointing, somewhat
prophetically, to this contemporary Catholic theological and pastoral emphasis on the liberation of the poor. Elizondo writes that "Our Lady of
Guadalupe is about the liberation of the gospel so that it might appear in
all its salvific grandeur to the peoples who were encountering it for the first
time and, even more so, to the people who thought they already had it."[24]
And in a recent article he states:

> The greatest ongoing force of Guadalupe is not her apparition on the tilma
> of Juan Diego or even the healing of the dying uncle Juan Bernardino and
> the many subsequent healing miracles down to our own days. Rather, it is
> the "uplifting of the downtrodden" (Luke 1.52) as Juan Diego and millions
> after him are transformed from crushed, self-defacing and silenced persons
> into confident, self-assured and joyful messengers and artisans of God's plan
> for America. Out of the Guadalupe–Juan Diego–Bishop Zumárraga en-
> counter, the new church is born—not a mere continuation of the old church
> of Europe or merely a Christian veneer over old native religious practices,
> but a new church born of the biological, cultural, linguistic and religious en-
> counter of the so-called old world and new world. Through her, opposing
> differences are brought together and synthesized into a new and fascinating
> unity.[25]

The New Testament account of Mary's visitation to Elizabeth, together
with her Magnificat of praise (Luke 1:39–56), the Gospel reading assigned
to the liturgical feast on December 12, is frequently invoked in reference
to this theological focus on Guadalupe as liberator. Elizondo notes:

> For millions of Mexicans and Mexican Americans of the United States, Our
> Lady of Guadalupe is the temple in whom and through whom Christ's sav-
> ing presence is continually incarnated in the soil of the Americas and it is
> through her mediation that: "He shows strength with his arm, He scatters the
> proud in the imagination of their hearts. He puts down the mighty from
> their thrones, and exalts the oppressed. He fills the hungry with good things,
> and the rich he sends away empty handed." (Luke1:51–52).[26]

But among Roman Catholic scholars Elizondo is certainly not alone in this
approach. More than twenty years ago leading Roman Catholic New Testament scholar, the late Raymond E. Brown, noted a close parallel between

the Virgin of Guadalupe and the portrayal of the Virgin Mary especially in the Lukan infancy narratives. Brown, in fact, argued that Guadalupe itself was "an authentic development" in terms of Mary's model discipleship portrayed in the Gospel of Luke, writing:

> The symbolism [of the image or the narrative] does not depend on the exact historicity of the vision. In the Indian portrait of the Lady there was a sense in which the Indian people could say to themselves: "We have not been annihilated. Although we have been reduced to slavery, this new religion preserves old religious symbolism and gives us some continuity and survival." . . . [F]or a people downtrodden and oppressed, the devotion made it possible to see the significance that the Christian Gospel was meant to have. In the Indian tradition, when Mary appears in the ancient garb of the mother of the Indian gods, she promises to show forth love and compassion, defense and help to all the inhabitants of the land. Ten years before, the whole Indian nation, their gods and their tradition had been torn down. She hears their lamentations and remedies their miseries, their pains and their sufferings. In the devotion to the Lady, the Christian Gospel proclaims hope for the oppressed. When one looks at the first chapter of Luke one realizes how authentic a Gospel hope that is. . . . Mary's understanding of the Christian message, as Luke presents it, is extremely radical. The angelic message to Mary identifies Jesus as Son of David, Son of God; but then she goes forth and explains her interpretation of it in a hymn, the "Magnificat." She does not proclaim the good news by saying that the Son of David and the Son of God is here. Rather, her soul magnifies the Lord and her spirit rejoices in God her savior because He has regarded the low estate of His slave woman. (We translate the word more politely as "handmaiden," but Mary speaks of the female slave. When Pliny, the Roman governor, went looking for Christians to find out what this strange group was, he turned to slave women because among such lowly creatures one would find Christians.) For Mary, the news about Jesus means that God has put down the mighty, and He has exalted the lowly. . . . The Gospel of God's Son means salvation for those who have nothing. That is the way Jesus translates it, and that is the way Mary translates it. . . . Luke presents Mary as a disciple not only because she said, "Be it done unto me according to your word," but because she understood what the word meant in terms of the life of the poor and the slaves of whom she is the representative. I think that is exactly what happened in the case of Our Lady of Guadalupe. She gave the hope of the Gospel to a whole people who had no other reason to see good news in what came from Spain. In their lives the devotion to Our Lady constituted an authentic development of the Gospel of discipleship.[27]

When compared to modern popular apparitions of the Virgin Mary, whether approved or otherwise (e.g., LaSalette, Fatima, Garabandal, or Medjugorje), the message of the Virgin of Guadalupe is quite distinct and unique in its emphasis on human liberation. Sandra L. Zimdars-Swartz summarizes the overall message of these other apparitions, often containing various "secrets" imparted to the visionaries, and the worldview behind them:

> In this schema, God is portrayed as angry with the world because the sins of humanity have overturned or disrupted the established order, and indeed, he is portrayed as so angry that his justice demands immediate chastisement. . . . In this worldview and in the apparition messages on which it is based, God is portrayed as most offended by sins of a particular kind. In the LaSalette messages, the sins which were said to be particularly offensive to Mary's son were working on Sunday, swearing in her son's name, neglecting to attend Mass, mocking religion, and eating meat during Lent—all transgressions against *a ritually defined sacred order.* In the Fatima messages too, the epitome of sin and evil is a kind of violation of such a sacred order. In the warning about Russia in the second part of the secret, the great calamity threatening the world is seen as the spread of atheism, i.e., the collapse of the ritual of confession of faith in God. There is also offered here, however, *a prescribed ritual which would restore something of the sacred order.* According to Lucia, the Virgin told her that she had come to ask for the consecration of Russia to her Immaculate Heart and the Communion of Reparation on the First Saturdays. If her requests were heeded, Russia would be converted and there would be peace. . . . Future chastisements are not, however, seen in this worldview as inevitable. Indeed, the major purpose of the Virgin's latter-day appearances is to give the world a last opportunity to restore the disrupted sacred order and the divine-human relationship which this order represents—through repentance or conversion, *a return to appropriate devotional practices,* and submission to the ordinances of the Church.[28]

But, while the Virgin of Guadalupe does ask for a "temple" to be built at Tepeyac, nowhere in the *Nican Mopohua* is there any indication of divine anger, fear, retribution, or chastisement directed at the world as the result of a ritually disrupted sacred order that can be appeased by the mere recovery of, or by adopting a newly established, prescribed explicit pattern of ritual or devotional behavior. Nor is there is any sense within the worldview behind the *Nican Mopohua* that the Virgin herself is to be interpreted according to the customary late-medieval (or modern apparitionist) sense as the one who somehow "holds back" the arm of her offended and angry Son from inflicting chastisement on the world. Rather, the temple she requests is no mere ritual solution to a ritual infraction; it is to be a place, a "home," "hermitage," or "temple," where all peoples might find love, compassion, help, and protection, and where the laments of all people would be heard and all their miseries, misfortunes, and sorrows would find remedy and cure.[29] Apart from her instructions to Juan Diego to go to the bishop for

the realization of her request, the Virgin of Guadalupe proclaims no apocalyptic secrets about impending cataclysmic doom and makes no statement
that devotion to her is the only way to escape such doom. In fact, apart
from the building of the temple itself, she doesn't tell anyone to do anything other than to receive divine love, compassion, help, and protection.
Indeed, it is difficult not to see in the Guadalupe narrative a close parallel
here with the burning-bush theophany in Exod. 3:7–8a, where God says to
Moses: "I have observed the misery of my people who are in Egypt; I have
heard their cry on account of their taskmasters. Indeed, I know their sufferings, and I have come down to deliver them." Hence, it might surely be
said that the Guadalupan experience points to and is itself also a type of Exodus experience.

The Virgin of Guadalupe as liberator, of course, has been invoked often
in support of various causes associated with justice and the end of oppression, even within the United States. Elizondo notes, with reference both to
her image and to her widespread "presence" in this image:

> In her eyes, we find recognition, acceptance, respect, and confidence. She is
> always present in the Tepeyacs of the world—the barrios, the slums, the pub-
> lic housing projects, the ghettos, and other such places. She will never leave
> us because she has been woven into the cloth of our suffering-resurrection
> existence. . . . Her compassionate *rostro y corazón* (countenance and heart) are
> alive not only on the *tilma* of Juan Diego but also in the faces and hearts of
> all who see her, call upon her, and believe in her. She is here among us
> where and when we need her; she is always present to rehabilitate the bro-
> ken, uplift the downtrodden, console the afflicted, accompany the lonely, and
> give life to the dying. She has been a source of energy and inspiration for
> many who have struggled for liberty and justice in the Americas: for Father
> Miguel Hildalgo, César Chávez, Dolores Huerta, Adelita Navarro, Samuel
> Ruiz, and for many others who have found their heroic strength for survival
> within her.[30]

At the same time, however, some have been highly critical of the
Guadalupan story and image with regard to questions about the role, dignity, and liberation, specifically, of women. Not only have some contemporary
authors urged caution about modern women appealing to the image of
Mary in general because "she has been invented by misogynist males," but
others, more clearly within a Hispanic-Latino context, have argued that, frequently, the various images of Mary in those contexts, including Guadalupe,
are but the other side of male "machismo," a way to keep women locked in
roles of subservience, bondage, poverty, and, in some cases, even physical
abuse, situations sometimes justified by appealing to the passivity and docil-
ity of Mary herself as the model par excellence of what it means to be a

woman in a patriarchally constituted world.[31] Since these issues will be dealt with later in this chapter under the heading of "Guadalupe as the 'Feminine Face of God,'" it must suffice at this point simply to note that, according to Elizondo's thought, such a use of the Virgin of Guadalupe, while certainly identifiable and present, actually constitutes a misuse or misappropriation of the significance of Guadalupe, a "co-opting" or "domesticating" of Guadalupe by others, including even at times by the church, in support of a repressive Marian ideology.[32] Indeed, as we shall see, in spite of such misuse or abuse, the Virgin of Guadalupe has also been a source of liberation and empowerment of and for contemporary women.

Guadalupe as "Mother of the New Creation"

Just as Guadalupe as evangelizer and liberator cannot be separated from each other in Elizondo's thought, neither can they be systematically separated from his thoughts on the Virgin of Guadalupe as "Mother of the New Creation." If under the subheading of Guadalupe as evangelizer the converted themselves (both indigenous and Spanish) are to be seen as constituting "a new incarnation of Christianity in and of the Americas"; and if under Guadalupe as liberator the poor, especially in the persons of Juan Diego and Juan Bernardino, are to be seen as those who "are transformed from crushed, self-defacing and silenced persons into confident, self-assured and joyful messengers and artisans," then it is precisely under this subheading of Guadalupe as "Mother of the New Creation" that Elizondo points most directly to the new mestizo humanity that is engendered from the Tepeyac event. While this focus is certainly present already within his earlier Guadalupan writings, it is offered in a more developed form in his 1997 book, *Guadalupe: Mother of the New Creation*. Consistent with his overall incarnational or Christological Guadalupan focus, Elizondo concludes:

> The innermost core of the apparition, even though La Virgen never mentions it as such, is what she carries within her womb: the new source and center of the new humanity that is about to be born. And that source and center is Christ as the light and life of the world. . . . The image is both the sign and the announcement of the truly new creation of the Americas—not a "new" world that would simply rebuild the old ways of conquest, greed, avarice, subjugation, and wars in a new space, but a new world that would be authentically new because of its inclusion of all the peoples of all the Americas as children of the one Mother. This image offers a condemnation of the "Christian" societies of the New World that would be based on racial segregation, classism, racism, sexism, enslavement, and exploitation. In asking

for a temple where she can give all her love and compassion, the Lady is in effect speaking about the reign of God that was the core of the life and message of Jesus. Guadalupe is thus a good Nahuatl translation of the New Testament reality of the reign of God as revealed by Jesus. Our Lady is calling for a new temple that will be sacred precisely because segregation and discrimination will have no place there. The unity of all peoples will make it sacred, and that is what her presence as loving and compassionate Mother wants to bring about. If she is the one who attracts, it is through the power of her Son that this will come about.[33]

And, further:

As primitive evangelical Christianity was at the heart of a balance between unifying the tribes and nations of the Old World while still allowing for their diversity, so Guadalupe is the very center and starting point of the synthesis of peoples of the Americas that will become the deepest ingredient and chief characteristic of the new humanity of the New World. . . . Guadalupe did what European Christianity could not do for itself: it transformed conquering Christianity into evangelical Christianity. Out of the ranks of the dying but reborn Christians would begin the new spiritual/Christian mestizaje, the new and all inclusive soul of the Americas. It begins as the child that Our Lady carries within her womb, recognized by Juan Diego as Jesus Christ, becomes alive in us and equally becomes the new center of all life—of all the cosmos.[34]

For Elizondo, then, the narrative of the *Nican Mopohua* is precisely about the beginnings of a new creation, and the Virgin of Guadalupe as mother is the one who gives birth to this new creation. Beginning with the darkness of night in the *Nican Mopohua,* this new creation is heralded at early dawn with the songs of all kinds of birds and comes to its full expression, ultimately, with the blossoming of numerous flowers growing on the barren hillside from within the context of the death of winter. "On the feast of Our Lady of Guadalupe," Elizondo writes elsewhere, "the people come together early in the morning to celebrate the irruption of new life—the dawn of a new humanity. This is the Easter sunrise service of the people. Before the first rays of the sun, they come together to sing *Las Mañanitas* which is our proclamation of new life. It is the roses of Tepeyac that take the place of the Easter lilies of Western Christianity."[35] But if the Guadalupan celebration is about a resurrected *Easter* life, it may also be seen as a *Pentecost* event, a birthing of a new humanity in Christ by the Holy Spirit, a racially, culturally, and ethnically mixed, or mestizo, humanity still in the process of being born, a new creation in which diversity and the distinctive characteristics, traditions (cultural, religious, and other), and contributions of distinct cultural groups are not merely melted down into an unrecognizable homogeneous whole but affirmed and recognized within the context of, and for the sake of, a greater human unity in which such diversity is affirmed and valued. "The tragedy of the Americas," notes Elizondo,

> has not been racial mixture (in fact that has been the source of the America's deepest and most creative newness) but the shame inflicted upon the children of this mixture and their "inferior" parent, most usually the mother. Since the beginning of the European invasion of the Americas, the white European—the northern European Protestant in North America and the Iberian Catholic in Latin America—has been installed as the norm of trueness, goodness, and beauty. Segregation was imposed by the white Europeans with a biological rationale. For many white people, their own interiorized self-image of superiority remains unquestioned even today.[36]

But, like the biblical Pentecost itself, Guadalupe represents a distinctive reversal of this process as now a new "common Mother," who, by reflecting in her mestiza face and appearance the characteristics of both the European and the indigenous people, provides a symbol of unity and coherence in which distinctive cultures could be fused together respectfully to form something new. Hence, if in the mestiza face and appearance of the Virgin of Guadalupe is to be found the image of what the church "desires and hopes wholly to be," it can also be said that this same Guadalupan face and appearance are revelatory of what humanity itself is to become (La Morena), and is already increasingly becoming, in our own day. And in this sense, according to Elizondo, Mount Tepeyac joins the other great symbolic mountains of the biblical/Christian tradition—Sinai (Exod. 20), the place of the Sermon on the Mount (Matt. 5), the mountain of the Transfiguration (cf. Mark 10), and the mount of the Ascension (Acts 1)—and becomes in the Americas the symbolic "womb" from which this new creation in the making begins to arise.[37]

Concerning the Virgin of Guadalupe herself as the mother of this new creation, Elizondo makes a further step in his theological investigations by reflecting on her as a feminine revelation or manifestation of even a mestizo God. While Guadalupe as the feminine face of God will be considered later, it is important to note Elizondo's contribution to this topic briefly here because it is so intimately connected to the notion of new creation in his thought. With reference to the Virgin of Guadalupe's self description in the *Nican Mopohua* as "the Ever-Virgin Holy Mary, Mother of the God of Great Truth, Téotl, of the One through Whom We live, the Creator of Persons, the Owner of What Is Near and Together, of the Lord of Heaven and Earth," Elizondo states:

By using the names of the Gods of the ancient Nahuatl pantheon, Our Lady is affirming that she is their mother too. (Her litany of names is in some ways equivalent to saying, "the God of Abraham, Isaac, Jacob, Moses, David, and Jesus.") She is the mother of their ancestors, who are thus to be revered and venerated, as it was through them that they had been advancing in their pilgrimage of faith. Furthermore, to balance the emphasis on the fatherhood of God, she emphasizes the motherhood of God—after all, only a Father-Mother God could adequately image the origins of all life. The one-sided emphasis of the missioners is thus corrected and enhanced by the Virgin Mother of God. The male Father God of militaristic and patriarchal Christianity is united to the female Mother God (Tonantzin), which allows the original heart and face of Christianity to shine forth: compassion, understanding, tenderness, and healing. The harsh and punishing "God of judgment" of the West is tempered with the listening and healing "companion," while the all-powerful conquering God is transformed into a loving and caring Parent. The distant God of dogmatic formula and abstraction is dissolved into a friendly and intimate presence.[38]

And on this basis, he can write that:

Guadalupe brings about what even the best and most sensitive missioners would not have wanted or even suspected as salutary: the mutually enriching dialogue of the Christian notions of God with the Nahuatl notions of God. In this Guadalupan synthesis, the good news of life breaks through. This is not a juxtaposition or a coexistence of opposing notions of God but the real birth of something new. . . . This new mestizo understanding of God is not a restricted and closed notion that will justify opposition between peoples; rather, it is an open notion that will allow for growth and expansion and a gradual appreciation of the infinite that is ultimately beyond our best understanding and formulation.[39]

Further, from this Guadalupan synthesis, Elizondo can suggest that the *Nican Mopohua* might even provide a "new world way" of reimaging the Christian doctrine of the Trinity as the "Mother" who sends the "Son" (Juan Diego) to the "Father" (Juan Zumárraga) to become a builder of the new "temple" or home. "God will be fully imaged in the Americas," he writes,

when the harmony of Mother-children-Father comes about and there is an end to abused women, abandoned children, and runaway fathers; when there is an end to patriarchal/hierarchical societies that put some down while elevating others to positions of power and prestige; when there is an end to the various structures of the Americas that keep people apart or excluded. The new temple . . . will be a humanity that reflects and images the likeness of the triune God—Mother-child-Father. In the name of the Mother who sends the child to call the Father to build a home for all, a new humanity has been born, and a new appreciation of the mystery of God has been initiated.[40]

If, then, for Elizondo, the Virgin of Guadalupe is about evangelization, liberation, and new creation, she is also, ultimately, revelatory of God and about how the divine-human image of God may be reimaged today.

Elizondo's various contributions on the Virgin of Guadalupe, especially some of his earlier writings, were sharply critiqued by Stafford Poole in the introduction to his recent study as "flawed" because they are reflective of "hyperbole" and "historical inaccuracies" and constitute a "reinvention" or "manipulation" of Guadalupe "to meet the demands of a new orthodoxy" increasingly associated closely with liberation theology. Poole writes:

> Many of the interpretations . . . are flawed precisely because they rely on an inadequate or erroneous historical base. Divorced from that base they lose their credibility. Hence the essential question is that of the historical reality of the apparition account and its message. Are these indeed factual events or are they legends and pious invention? Is there an authentic tradition that connects the modern devotion with its manifold meanings to events that actually occurred in 1531?[41]

Having already dealt with Poole's own attempt to rewrite the history of the origins and development of the Virgin of Guadalupe in the previous chapter, here I can only state that Elizondo's *theological* interpretation of Guadalupe does not appear to stand or fall in relationship to what "Guadalupan events" may or may not have actually occurred in 1531. While all of his conclusions may not be above scholarly and theological critique, and although he does tend to interpret the Guadalupan image and narratives (somewhat uncritically) within the assumed early-sixteenth-century historical context of the Spanish conquest of Mexico, the credibility (or not) of his theological interpretation of the *Nican Mopohua* does not really depend on whether the events in that document are "factual" or "legendary." As also noted in the previous chapter, Elizondo himself can use the terminology of legend or folklore to refer to the written Guadalupan narratives. Hence, bearing in mind the unclear prehistory of Guadalupe before the "official" written narratives of 1648 and 1649, even if Elizondo were to accept uncritically Poole's thesis of a mid-seventeenth rather than mid-sixteenth-century "origin," his theological emphases gleaned from the *Nican Mopohua* on Guadalupe as evangelizer, liberator, Mother of the New Creation would not, I suspect, be much different at all. For, in either case, the fact remains that the Guadalupan image and narratives, as reflective of the particular historical incarnation of Christianity in Mexico and of her widespread and increasing presence and devotion throughout the Americas—even if it *could* be demonstrated conclusively that it did not begin until the mid–seventeenth century—still make such theological interpretations of the religious and cultural phenomenon of Guadalupe an absolute necessity. Nor, in my opinion, should Elizondo be critiqued because he brings to this task a particular "perspective" or "bias" from his own life experience, theological formation, and work. No work of scholarship, including that of historians, is unbiased, and no scholarly work proceeds anywhere, Poole's own included, without some kind of overall operating perspective or hypothesis.

Guadalupe and "Popular Religion"

Apart from the fact that the Virgin of Guadalupe is now an official Roman Catholic liturgical celebration and feast on December 12 throughout the Americas, the subject of the next chapter, she plays a central role among Latino-Hispanics, especially Mexicans and Mexican Americans, in what is commonly referred to, somewhat pejoratively by some, as *religiosidad popular* (popular religion or popular piety) in distinction to "official" or "institutionalized faith." And certainly another of Elizondo's significant contributions to contemporary theological thought has been the invitation to do what he does himself, that is, to take seriously such religiosidad popular as an important, even central, theological locus. While in the past theologians and historians tended to denigrate or even dismiss popular religion as but "superstition," vestiges of "paganism," or as reflecting, somehow, a much "lower" form of belief and practice among the "unenlightened," and while the writing of church history itself has often been centered primarily on the contributions of the intellectually "elite" (bishops and theologians) in the Christian tradition, modern scholarship has been more willing to embrace a much broader view of the whole, including the religious lives of the poor, women, and others. Peter Brown's important 1981 work, *The Cult of the Saints: Its Rise and Function in Latin Christianity,* referred to already in the previous chapter, represents a significant scholarly shift in this regard. Here, in particular, Brown argues convincingly that the *real* history of the early church is to be read precisely in the development of the popular practices and beliefs associated with the cult of the martyrs and later saints at their shrines in the overall shaping of late antique culture, religion, and society, practices shared by both the intellectually elite and others in the church, in spite of their differing intellectual faculties.[42] Similarly, especially among Latino-Hispanic theologians today, such practices of religiosidad popular have increasingly moved from the periphery to the center of theological thought and reflection.

Some of the familiar *practices* often associated with this phenomenon of popular religion today (e.g., rosaries, scapulars, pilgrimages, novenas, eucharistic adoration, devotions to Mary and to particular saints) have been, throughout the past two or three decades, making a definite comeback among Roman Catholics in general.[43] But popular religion itself among Hispanic-Latinos, while appearing to share many of the same devotional *expressions* or *forms,* is often quite distinctive in both substance and orientation. Mark Francis notes that

> while many of these practices appear similar, it would be a pastoral error to assume that they always "mean" exactly the same thing. The popular religion of many Hispanics, for example, while based in part on the same medieval matrix as Euro-American devotionalism, includes elements indigenous to the "New World." These elements express deeply held convictions about one's place in the universe, access to the sacred, and how human beings experience time. These convictions were formed from experiences of life that are different from those of Europeans.[44]

Consequently, as Orlando Espín notes in the introduction to his compelling book, *The Faith of the People: Theological Reflections on Popular Catholicism,* if Euro-American Catholic "liberals" often fail in their attempts to be in real solidarity with Hispanic-Latinos because they tend to dismiss the role and value of popular religion altogether, Euro-American Catholic "conservatives" also fail because they tend to see

> Latino] popular Catholicism from the perspective of [their] own ecclesiastical, political agenda and wrongly assume that our religion agrees . . . or at least can be recruited to appear to be in agreement. Latino popular Catholicism, although not necessarily subversive, can (and quite often has) surprise the conservative with confrontation and opposition. Catholic conservatives suspect that they can separate our holy symbols (especially Marian ones) from the lives and suffering of our people (thereby forgetting that much of the pain inflicted on Latinos is often the direct result of the conservative political agenda). They do not understand how much they offend our faith and our holy symbols![45]

In other words, although devotion to the Virgin of Guadalupe (and other Hispanic-Latino devotions to the Virgin Mary under another of her many advocations) might *look* the same in terms of outward manifestation, and *appear,* at the same time, to be but the common expression of a similar shared worldview or devotional and ecclesiastical milieu, they are not *necessarily* the same at all.

Popular religion, therefore, especially related to a Hispanic-Latino context,

> can be defined as the set of experiences, beliefs and rituals which more-or-less peripheral human groups create, assume and develop (within concrete socio-cultural and historical contexts, and as a response to these contexts) and which to a greater or lesser degree distance themselves from what is recognized as normative by church and society, striving (through rituals, experiences and beliefs) to find an access to God and salvation which they feel they cannot find in what the church and society present as normative.[46]

More concretely, in the words of Roberto Goizueta: "the adjective 'popular' does not primarily mean 'common,' 'widespread,' or 'well-liked' though popular religion is, indeed, all of these. Rather the adjective refers to the socio-historical fact that these religious symbols, practices, and narratives are *of the people*."[47] And, as he continues, "the Catholicism which . . . lies at the heart of . . . Hispanic culture . . . is not so much the hierarchical Catholicism as the Catholicism which manifests itself in the faith and religious practices of the people. . . . Popular religion is 'popular' because it emerges from and constitutes us as a people."[48] In other words, much more than a collection, cultural expression, or sum total of particular Catholic devotional practices, such popular religion is a religion itself with its own symbols, stories, rituals, and religious worldview. That is, popular religion, especially Latino popular Catholicism, is precisely the way in which Christianity itself was incarnated, inculturated, and came to be expressed in Mexico and Central and South America and how it has survived and been passed down through generations, most often under the leadership of Hispanic-Latina women, its preeminent storytellers, practitioners, or "priests." It is, thus, the very way in which this particular people has made and continues to make Christianity its own faith and way of life, the way in which Christianity became and remains the faith of this particular *populus* or people. That is, popular religion, according to Alex García-Rivera, is, ultimately, that religion "in which faith is challenged, interpreted, and made one's own."[49]

To take popular religion seriously as a theological source, then, surely implies that one must look theologically at those very symbols, rituals, and narratives by which and in which this "faith of the people" has been and continues to be expressed. And this, of course, would include, precisely, the Virgin of Guadalupe herself as the central manifestation of this faith among Mexican and Mexican American Catholics. Such a process, as clearly exemplified in Elizondo's own theological approach, as well as in the work of other scholars in treating other popular Hispanic-Latino religious images and stories today,[50] means to investigate what he refers to as the "little story" in an attempt to discern the presence within it of the "Big Story," namely, the "Christian Story," the gospel itself within particular culturally conditioned expressions. Not surprisingly, then, Elizondo can say that the little story of the Virgin of Guadalupe is *not*

> just another Marian apparition. Guadalupe has to do with the very core of the gospel itself. It is nothing less than an original American Gospel, a narrative of a birth/resurrection experience at the very beginning of the crucifixion of the natives, the Africans, and their mestizo and mulatto children. The condemned and crucified peoples of the Americas were homeless, alone, and without protection. But God would triumph. The final and greatest gift of our Virgin Mother was her miraculous painting in the tilma of Juan Diego, which was given first to the bishop and then to all of us. Her gift of that image—a living gift that would keep her memory alive among the people—was like Jesus' gift of the Spirit.[51]

The little story of Guadalupe is, thus, for Elizondo, revelatory of the Big Story of the gospel itself in a Mexican and Mexican American cultural-religious context.

If, however, his comparisons of the Guadalupan event with Pentecost and the gift of her image on the tilma with the Pentecostal gift of the Holy Spirit would undoubtedly be shocking—even, I suspect, scandalous—to some, theological reflection on Guadalupe in the context of Hispanic-Latino popular Catholicism from the perspective of pneumatology is precisely the approach taken and strongly recommended by other theologians today. Among these, I have found the work of Orlando Espín to be most suggestive and helpful. In particular, Espín questions the traditional connections often made between the Virgin of Guadalupe and either the Virgin Mary or the indigenous goddess Tonantzin (whose own tendencies to inflict cruel punishment and send disease and destruction are entirely absent from Guadalupe), writing that

> [t]he Virgin of Guadalupe cannot be simply identified with Tonantzin—not even at the very beginning. But I do not see either how the natives could have simply identified Guadalupe with the Catholic Mary. From the start, it seems that there was an effort (on the part of the Amerindians) at speaking a religious language through culturally understandable religious categories, that would interpret for them the Christian message about God.[52]

And, with specific regard to the connection between Guadalupe and Mary, he writes elsewhere:

Latino/a devotion to the Virgen of Guadalupe might not always—in fact, probably seldom—have to do with the historical Mary of Nazareth, the mother of Jesus. Furthermore . . . it is time to look again at the Guadalupe apparition story and subsequent devotion from the perspective of pneumatology . . . including the very appropriation of otherwise Spanish Marian symbols and categories in early colonial Mexico and thereafter. Perhaps it is time to seriously question if Guadalupe is (or has ever been) really Marian or is in fact pneumatological for the majority of Latinos/as. I am not suggesting that Mary is the Holy Spirit (a theologically impossible affirmation). I am, however, asking whether the Virgen of Guadalupe is Mary of Nazareth at all.[53]

For Espín, then, the indigenous attempt to interpret the Christian message about God through culturally understandable religious categories, expressed especially in and by the Guadalupan image, narrative, and devotion, is not really Mariology at all, in spite of the official "Marian" interpretations which began with the mid-seventeenth-century narratives of Sánchez and Lasso de la Vega. It is, instead, a form of popular pneumatology. That is, Guadalupe represents, reflects, and incarnates a culturally concrete manifestation of what the orthodox Christian doctrinal and theological tradition would associate explicitly with the person and work of the Holy Spirit. And, with regard to the ways in which Guadalupan devotees actually relate by popular Catholicism to the Virgin of Guadalupe in their lives, Espín continues:

If the majority of Latinos/as . . . relate to Guadalupe in ways that any mainstream Christian pneumatology would expect with respect to the Holy Spirit, and if the people's expectations, "gifts" received, and explanations surrounding the Guadalupan devotion all seem to fit those that mainstream pneumatologies would associate with the Holy Spirit, is it unreasonable to question whether in fact we might not be dealing in the case of Guadalupe with the Holy Spirit? Must the symbols and language traditionally connected with the Spirit only be those of European cultural and philosophical origins? Couldn't the symbols and language associated with Marian devotions, given the historical, cultural, and sociopolitical events that profoundly rocked early colonial Mexico, have been "transferred" by the recently conquered people to the still new (to them) doctrine of the Holy Spirit? Didn't something similar happen in early christology with Wisdom and Logos thought and language which had historically preceded christological reflection? . . . Why couldn't the same process . . . occur again and in connection with the Holy Spirit? I strongly suspect, indeed I am increasingly convinced, that this is what happened in early colonial Mexico, and that once the symbolic "transference" was made from the traditional mariological to the newly inculturated pneumatological, it gained the depth of understanding and familiarity necessary to explain its holding power and resilience among later generations of Mexicans and Latinos/as. The clergy's later efforts at "mariologizing" Guadalupe have not been as successful as the ecclesiastical institution wants to believe.[54]

Espín can make this move to a pneumatological interpretation of Guadalupe because within Latino popular Catholicism, especially among Latinas, it is precisely the Virgin of Guadalupe who functions as the primary symbol or "sacrament" of God's *grace* mediated, experienced, and received. That is:

> in and through Guadalupe they encounter and experience the God-who-is-for-us (and, again not the historical Mary of Nazareth) as mother. . . . [I]n Guadalupe [they] also encounter and experience God-for-us as wisdom and understanding. Put briefly, [they] experience *grace* in and through the *Virgen* of Guadalupe. . . . By engaging Guadalupe and responding to her, Latinos/as participate in the life of God and culturally image the gifts of the Spirit. [They] encounter the pneumatological reality of the divine (the Holy Spirit) in and through the Guadalupe symbol.[55]

In making such claims, claims based neither on the historicity of the Guadalupan events nor on exegetical interpretations of the Guadalupan narratives themselves, but on the very role that the Virgin of Guadalupe and devotion to her continues actually to play in the popular religious experience of Latino-Hispanics, Espín, like Elizondo, is very careful in his terminology. By asserting that the Virgin of Guadalupe is clearly *neither* the Holy Spirit *nor* Mary of Nazareth herself but, rather, can be interpreted as providing a "semantic, cultural (never *ontological*) analogy of some divine attributes . . . a culturally legitimate means to express some content of the Christian gospel,"[56] Espín clearly avoids the potential theological-dogmatic dangers of identifying the Virgin Mary explicitly with the Holy Spirit or of elevating the Virgin Mary herself to the status of divinity. It is thus one thing to say, as Elizondo does, that the Virgin of Guadalupe may assist in a reimaging" of the Trinity today as "Mother-Child-Father," or, as Espín asserts, that in Guadalupe the symbols and language associated with Marian devotions have been transferred to the service of a concrete cultural-religious expression of pneumatology. But it is quite another thing to move from a semantic, cultural analogy to making an ontological claim about Mary and the Holy Spirit themselves.

Unfortunately, however, other theologians have not been as careful or theologically precise as Elizondo and Espín. It is well known, for example, that liberation theologian Leonardo Boff, writing out of the context of his own experiences of widespread Marian devotion within the popular Catholicism of Latin America, offers the following hypothesis: "We maintain the hypothesis that the Virgin Mary, Mother of God and of all men and women, realizes the feminine absolutely and eschatologically, inasmuch as the Holy Spirit has made her his temple, sanctuary, and tabernacle in so real and genuine a way that she is to be regarded as hypostatically united to the Third Person of the Blessed Trinity."[57] For Boff, this is no mere semantic or cultural analogy in the service of popular pneumatology but moves to what might surely be called an ontological divinization of Mary, with the result that just as Jesus Christ was the Incarnation of the Word (understood—incompletely, I would assert—as the assumption of *masculine* human nature), so is Mary the incarnation of the Holy Spirit (understood as the assumption of *feminine* human nature). Consequently, for Boff not only are the traditional transferences of pneumatic attributes to Mary in popular religion perfectly legitimate since she actually does "incarnate" the Holy Spirit "hypostatically," but also officially promulgated definitions of Mary as both "Coredemptrix" and "Mediatrix" of salvation would seem to him to be logical and highly appropriate dogmatic developments.

I suspect that Boff, together with Elizondo and Espín, is quite correct in that the Marian symbols and devotions, including Guadalupe, have *functioned* and do function in a clearly pneumatological manner and that, as such, pneumatology is, perhaps, the best theological category available for their interpretation. And of course, there is early Christian precedent for doing pneumatology within feminine categories. In the early Semitic-based Syrian Christian tradition, centered in Edessa, Seleucia-Ctesiphon, and later in Nisibis, not only is the Syriac word for Spirit, *ruah,* feminine in gender (as in Hebrew), but early Syriac liturgical texts frequently refer to the Holy Spirit as "Mother" and invoke her as such in the context of both the rites of Christian initiation and the eucharistic liturgy.[58] Along similar lines, Joseph Chalassery in his commentary on the modern East Syrian rites of Christian initiation, where this theological understanding remains present within the liturgical texts of this ancient but living Eastern Christian tradition both in Oriental Orthodox (Assyrian) and Eastern Catholic (Syro-Malabar and Assyro-Chaldean) forms, calls attention to what he refers to as an "unusual analogy" between the Holy Spirit and the woman deacon (an office once necessary for administering the full body prebaptismal anointings of female baptismal candidates) in the *Didascalia Apostolorum,* a mid-third-century church order or manual. Quoting the *Didascalia,* he writes:

"the bishop sits for you in the place of God Almighty. But the deacon stands in the place of Christ, and you should love him. The *deaconess*, however, shall be honored by you i*n the place of the Holy Spirit.*" This comparison between the deaconess and the Holy Spirit shows how the ancient Syrian-Christian mind conceived the Holy Spirit as the feminine dimension of God.[59]

And, closely related to these feminine characteristics of the Holy Spirit and women deacons is the fact that within this Syrian tradition as well the baptismal font itself is customarily referred to in a number of different authors as a "womb."

However, Boff's own Trinitarian-incarnational hypothesis about the Holy Spirit and Mary or about the assumption of the feminine in a pneumatic Marian incarnation, including other related questionable dogmatic implications, does not necessarily follow, if, for no other reason than that *the* Incarnation of the Word in Christ himself, is, doctrinally speaking, already the work of the *whole* Trinity and not merely of one or other of the divine Persons. If Marian symbols function this way in popular religion, function is certainly not the same as *identity* or ontological *being*. Nevertheless, along with the approaches of both Elizondo and Espín, centered primarily in how the Virgin of Guadalupe functions within the Latino-Hispanic context of popular religion and what that function might actually reveal about God, Boff's hypothesis clearly raises the question of what I have called Guadalupe as the "feminine face of God."

Guadalupe as the Feminine Face of God

As noted above, some have been highly critical of the Guadalupan story and image, indeed, of the numerous popular advocations of the Virgin Mary within the history of Roman Catholicism, with regard to questions about the role, dignity, and liberation of women. Espín himself notes that if the Virgin of Guadalupe is the best symbol of the experience of grace within a Latino-Hispanic context, she is also, especially for "Latina mature women," symbolic of the experience of sin. He writes:

> Through popular Catholicism's devotions to the Virgen of Guadalupe, Latina mature women have been told that they must endure the abuse, the assaults, and the violence. The call to freedom and to the struggle for justice that many Catholics have heard from Guadalupe is frequently muted here—the call itself being abused and betrayed. These are experiences of sin, even when cloaked under the religious veil of piety. . . . A theological consideration of the Virgen of Guadalupe must not be blind to the fact that this symbol of popu-

lar Catholicism has often been used (and is all too frequently still used) to justify domestic violence against women and children, and all sorts of other oppressive and alienating behavior.[60]

Consequently, like other symbols of popular religion, Marian symbols can
be (and have been) used to reinforce situations of injustice and oppression
with Mary herself functioning as the image par excellence of passive, humble endurance and, hence, of a particular patriarchal view of women's roles
and identities. Instead of inspiring change, empowerment, and liberation in
such contexts, Guadalupe has been used to inspire or enforce pious resig-
nation.[61]

Such criticism of the role of Mary, of course, has often been a focus in
the work of contemporary feminist theologians and other feminist authors
who have seriously questioned and critiqued traditional patriarchal (and
ecclesial) assumptions about the identity and presumed roles of women
often concretized in Marian symbols. Rosemary Radford Reuther summarizes this critique, beginning especially in the late 1960s and early 1970s
in the United States, writing that the

> educational transformation of consciousness among American Catholics in-
> terested in religious studies led many Catholic women to suspect that the
> traditional Marian piety and doctrines were not only historically and theo-
> logically questionable, but were also shaped by a male celibate mentality
> hostile to women. Both the idealization of Mary as the perfect model of
> feminine purity and submission and the subtext of negation of female sex-
> uality as impure and the source of all sinfulness were seen as ways of con-
> trolling and suppressing women, negating their fully embodied and au-
> tonomous humanity. Catholic women examined their earlier Catholic
> socialization and came to believe that their full capacities as female human
> beings had been deeply damaged by a Marian ideal of virginal motherhood
> that was both masochistic and impossible for any woman to exemplify.
> Catholic women began to seek other models of womanhood and relation
> to God.[62]

From a specific Latina perspective, author Sandra Cisneros in an intriguing
short essay, "Guadalupe the Sex Goddess," tells of her own experience with
the implications of the Virgin of Guadalupe in her process of socialization:

> What a culture of denial. Don't get pregnant! But no one tells you how not
> to. This is why I was angry for so many years every time I saw *la Virgen de
> Guadalupe,* my culture's role model for brown women like me. She was damn
> dangerous, an ideal so lofty and unrealistic it was laughable. Did boys have to

aspire to be like Jesus? I never saw evidence of it. They were fornicating like
rabbits while the Church ignored them and pointed us women toward our
destiny—marriage and motherhood. The only other alternative was puta-
hood. . . . As far as I could see, *la Lupe* was nothing but a goody two shoes
meant to doom me to a life of unhappiness.[63]

Cisneros's essay is a highly personal account of how she came to a new
awareness and appreciation of the Virgin of Guadalupe in her life, but *not*
Guadalupe as expressed in and associated with the Christian-Catholic tradition:

When I look at *La Virgen de Guadalupe* now, she is not the Lupe of my childhood, no longer the one in my grandparents' house in Tepeyac, nor is she the
one of the Roman Catholic Church, the one I bolted the door against in my
teens and twenties. Like every woman who matters to me, I have had to
search for her in the rubble of history. And I have found her. She is
Guadalupe the sex goddess, a goddess who makes me feel good about my
sexual power, my sexual energy, who reminds me I must, as Clarissa Pinkola
Estés so aptly put it, "speak from the vulva . . . speak the most basic, honest
truth." . . . In my research of Guadalupe's pre-Columbian antecedents, the
she before the Church desexed her, I found Tonantzin, and inside Tonantzin,
a pantheon of other mother goddesses. I discovered Tlazolteotl, the goddess
of fertility and sex, also referred to as Totzin, Our Beginnings, or Tzinteotl,
goddess of the rump. *Putas,* nymphos, and other loose women were known
as "women of the sex goddess." Tlazolteotl was the patron of sexual passion,
and though she had the power to stir you to sin, she could also forgive you
and cleanse you of your sexual transgressions via her priests who heard confession. . . . To me *La Virgen de Guadalupe* is also Coatlicue, the creative/de-
structive goddess. . . . I think of a woman enraged, a woman as tempest, a
woman *bien berrinchuda,* and I like that. *La Lupe* as *cabrona.* Not silent and passive, but silently gathering force. . . . Coatlicue, Tlazoteotl, Tonantzin, *La Virgen de Guadalupe.* They are each telescoped one into the other, into who I
am. And this is why la Lupe intrigues me—not the Lupe of 1531 who appeared to Juan Diego, but the one of the 1990s who has shaped who we are
as Chicanas/*mexicanas* today, the one inside each Chicana and mexicana.[64]

If Cisneros herself eventually returned "back inside the Church from which
[she'd] fled," her nontraditional comments on the Virgin of Guadalupe are
certainly indicative of an approach that several Hispanic-Latino/a authors
are taking to the Guadalupan image and narrative today. That is, even if traditional Christian interpretations of Guadalupe—including often that of
the church itself—are rejected as misogynist and oppressive, Guadalupe
herself remains and is perceived as a life-giving and liberating image and
force too firmly embedded in the Latino-Hispanic religious and cultural

consciousness to be rejected outright and so is frequently reinterpreted in differing contexts as "goddess" or "Mother" in manners similar to the approach suggested by Cisneros.[65] And, although such deification of the Virgin of Guadalupe is certainly to be rejected from any orthodox Christian theological perspective, operating in a powerful manner within such a shift is what Espín refers to as the frequently muted, abused, and betrayed Guadalupan "call to freedom and to the struggle for justice." In other words, it is Guadalupe as liberator and her call to liberation that are here being expressed and understood in ways that specifically address the situation of the empowerment of women within contemporary culture, albeit in decidedly unorthodox and alternative manners.

At the same time, however, other women certainly cognizant of the ways in which this Guadalupan call to freedom and to the struggle for justice has been often muted, abused, and betrayed have, nonetheless, been able to embrace the liberating and empowering aspects of the Virgin of Guadalupe without rejecting either their Catholic identity or the church itself. I am reminded here of the ongoing work of Laura Sánchez, cofounder and director with her husband, Marcos, of Proyecto Hospitalidad, an independent organization operating in and out of her home in San Antonio, Texas, dedicated to providing transitional care (medical, legal, social, and spiritual) for newly arrived immigrants from Mexico, Central America, and elsewhere who have been injured, often in life-threatening ways (e.g., loss of limbs, paralysis, and frequently comatose when found), during their attempts to cross the Mexico–United States border. When asked how she came to this particular vocation in her life, Sánchez gives a response, rooted in her own childhood experiences in the early 1950s as a migrant worker with her family in California, that is clearly Guadalupan in character:

> I was twelve years old and we were picking the [string bean] fields in California. It must have been the second week of the harvest, and I had noticed that there were a lot of men who were Mexicanos working in the [same] field. They worked extremely hard. I actually thought that they were machines the way they moved their hands and how they ran with their baskets loaded to full capacity. The baskets held thirty pounds, but when they pressed down the beans, you could get almost forty pounds into them. My sisters and I were just learning how to do it, but they were doing it very rapidly. I questioned them because it struck me, at first, how they were different, somehow, from the rest of the pickers, and I asked them, "How come?" And one of them said to me as we were all weighing our full baskets: "Well, we have families back in Mexico. All of us are here under government contract [as Braseros] to work in the fields. And you get paid two cents a pound for the string beans that you pick but we get paid one cent per pound. And then we have to send money home to our families, and, in order to do that, we have

to work *very* hard, because we also have to pay for our own board and we have to eat here at the store, and everything is doubled or tripled in price here for us. You pay twenty-five cents for a pack of cigarettes downtown, but here we pay fifty to fifty-five cents a pack. . . ." It was then that I understood several things at different levels. I understood the message of Our Lady of Guadalupe, how she came to bring the message of salvation, and the message of [our being] God's children to all of us, in terms of liberating us from the oppression of the conquistadores, liberating us from the oppression of anybody that would oppress us and take away from us that which made us unique as a person, as an individual, my family as a family, and the whole of the Mexicanos. And then I understood why the Blessed Mother appeared to Juan Diego, an Indian. I knew the story very well, but I experienced it fully at that moment. . . . And I also understood . . . perfectly well the words of the song, "St. Peter, don't you call me, 'cause I can't go. I owe my soul to the company store." These men, who were my kin, because of blood, because of race, were the oppressed, and they were the ones who owed their soul to the company store. Consequently, so did I. Consequently, so did my family. So did everybody who was Mexicano. And then I understood the struggles of the peoples who were oppressed. . . . I literally cried. . . . All of that happened to me in one moment, in one single experience, when I was twelve years old. I was born in '41.[66]

This experience Sánchez interprets as her "vocational call," a formative experience that was preparing her initially for the direction her life was to take. And when asked further how the Virgin of Guadalupe, whose life-size image hangs to the right side of the altar in their (former garage, now) chapel, continues to inspire and shape her current work, she responds:

The [Virgin of Guadalupe] comes as herself. She comes as a woman from Palestine, a Palestinian, and her skin color is brown, just like ours. And she knew that in all of her authenticity we were going to identify with her instantly because we saw ourselves in her. She mirrored us completely. And that is why in ten years the indigenous people, millions of Indians, were baptized. And when you really learn her story, as I did, from my mother, from my grandmother, from my dad, from what I have read, and from what other people have told me, the Blessed Mother came not only to liberate us as a race, she came to liberate a "totality"—the world, the whole—and to place all of us together in it. That's exactly what the church teaches. And she wants us to be Christ centered. And for me, it is amazing. . . . I see her in every movement [for justice and liberation]. I see her in everybody that has this impetus to find that liberation. Because the moment we find that liberation, we find Christ.[67]

Sánchez's story of hearing and being inspired by the Christian gospel of compassion and liberation in the narrative and image of the Virgin of

Guadalupe is echoed in the stories of countless other Hispanic-Latino women today. And the important contribution of theologian Jeannette Rodriguez has been the collection and interpretation of such stories based on her numerous personal interviews over several years, originally with Mexican American women but more recently with women from diverse cultural and religious (even Jewish-Hispanic) contexts.[68] Like Elizondo, Espín, and others, and certainly inspired by their work, Rodriguez addresses as one of her primary concerns a decidedly theological question: what does the Virgin of Guadalupe, as expressed in the actual experiences of Hispanic-Latino Catholic women devoted to her, ultimately say about the nature and imaging of God within their popular religious experience and life? It is from this perspective that Rodriguez can argue that for countless women Guadalupe reveals, concretizes, and makes present in their lives what can fittingly be called "the feminine face of God."

In arriving at this conclusion Rodriguez's work draws from the recent theological-Mariological analyses of Elizabeth A. Johnson, especially from her significant essays "The Marian Tradition and the Reality of Women" and "Mary and the Female Face of God," on the question of how God has been imaged traditionally and how God may be reimaged within our own day in a more gender-inclusive manner.[69] For Johnson, the goal of her theological pursuit is to retrieve from Mariology and restore to a broader theological understanding of God *in se* precisely those feminine images or attributes of the divine that, in the course of Western Christian history, became transferred from God and concretized explicitly in Mary. That is, according to Johnson, Marian images and devotions, beginning in the late patristic period and coming to their full flowering in the Middle Ages, became the vehicle by which the often distant and transcendent, patriarchally conceived God was made accessible under the images of maternity, divine compassion, liberating power and might, divine immanence or intimate presence, and re-creative energy. While Johnson notes that several of these images could be interpreted stereotypically from the perspective of the "patriarchal feminine," that is, patriarchally based, self-serving ways of defining women, she states that especially the

> characteristics of mothering, compassion, and presence, so particular to the historical experience of women, are being reclaimed, reimagined, and revalued by contemporary analysis in ways that liberate. Realization of this state of affairs undergirds the argument that these themes and symbols should not now be transferred to God via the categories of "dimension" or "trait," for this would merely perpetuate the inherited, basically distorted patriarchal system. Rather, each element . . . represents a missing or underdeveloped piece in our repertoire of references to God and, as shaped by women's

experience, should be allowed to connote and evoke the whole of the divine mystery in tandem with a plethora of other images.[70]

In her essay "Guadalupe: The Feminine Face of God," Rodriguez employs these five revelatory elements identified by Johnson and applies them to the Virgin of Guadalupe in order to investigate how Guadalupe herself might fit into this kind of theological approach from within the experiences of the women she has interviewed. First, as Mother, the Virgin of Guadalupe is seen as "a maternal presence, consoling, nurturing, offering unconditional love, comforting—qualities that tell us mother is an appropriate metaphor for God."[71] Second, as manifesting divine compassion, Rodriguez notes that

> [i]n the interviews with the women in my study, we have seen how they take their troubles to Our Lady of Guadalupe because they experience her as being compassionate and responsive to their needs, in a way which, if present, nevertheless has not been identified in their relationship with God. She will understand them better than the male face of God because she too is female and a mother.[72]

As such, Johnson says, the Virgin of Guadalupe reveals that "God is the Mother of mercy who has compassionate womb-love for all God's children. We need not be afraid to approach. She [i.e., God] is brimming over with gentleness, loving kindness, and forgiveness."[73] Third, as revelatory of God's divine power and might, Guadalupe, according to Rodriguez,

> images power *with,* in a dynamism centered around mutuality, trust, participation, and regard. The power accessed by . . . women in their dialogue with Our Lady of Guadalupe is the power of memory, which she continues to stand for, justice, solidarity with the oppressed, belonging, unconditional love, the power of expressed feelings and sharing (women come to her and share their immediate needs and the feel heard). The power of commitment, the power to endure suffering, the power of caring, the power of risk ("As long as she is beside me, I'm going to keep trying"), the power of naming their fears, the power of knowing that the way things are is not the way things are meant to be, and with her help they are encouraged and given hope. She gives them not the will to suffer injustice, but the will to continue la lucha (the struggle).[74]

Fourth, Rodriguez sees Guadalupe manifesting God's immanence, or intimate presence, in all three of the preceding categories but especially in relationship to the presence and experience of God's unconditional love, compassion, and forgiveness. And, finally, as revealing God as a source of re-creative energy, Rodriguez looks to the religious synthesis of the masculine and feminine principles of God coming together in Guadalupe's self-description from both the European Christian tradition and indigenous Mexican religion as restorative of hope and life among her earliest followers.

Like Elizondo, Espín, and Johnson, Rodriguez, of course, is concerned theologically with how the Virgin of Guadalupe actually functions in popular religion rather than with drawing any kind of ontological analogy between the Virgin Mary and God. But, again, the very question of the Virgin of Guadalupe's mediation of the feminine face of God can only be raised because of the way in which she functions in the lives and experiences of the practitioners of popular religion. As Rodriguez notes elsewhere: "I asked the women I talked to as part of my research, 'Do you think that she's more important than God?' and they say, 'Oh no.' But if you say to them, 'When you pray, whom do you pray to?' they say, 'Guadalupe, Mary.' I say, 'Why would you go to her with things that you would not go to God with?' 'Because she's a woman, she understands.'"[75]

To say, then, that the Virgin of Guadalupe manifests or reveals the feminine face of God is not, for Rodriguez, to say that the Virgin of Guadalupe *is* God or that she somehow *replaces* God, at least on a conceptual level. Rather, the point is that if, in general, as Elizabeth Johnson states, "the Marian tradition is one fruitful source of female imagery of God" that makes available "ultimate metaphors for the divine mystery" that have the "potential to contribute to a new naming and experiencing of the holy mystery,"[76] then the Virgin of Guadalupe is herself potentially quite rich in embodying this imagery and does so precisely among those devoted to her. Such an approach or understanding, of course, strongly underscores Elizondo's conclusion that the Virgin of Guadalupe is "not just another Marian apparition" but "has to do with the very core of the gospel itself," and Espín's conclusion that in Guadalupe is encountered and experienced "the God-who-is-for-us as mother" from the perspective of what he calls "popular pneumatology." In Guadalupe, therefore, in spite of the fact that she is an image, narrative, and devotion framed in *Marian* categories, we are not dealing theologically with Mariology per se but with a particular manifestation of a God for whom the feminine analogies of "maternity with its creativity, nurturing, and warmth; unbounded compassion; sovereign power that protects, heals, and liberates; all embracing immanence; [and] re-creative energy" are highly appropriate.[77] The Virgin of Guadalupe thus has to do with the way in which countless people in our own day relate to the God of Jesus as Mother on a personal, intimate level. And since within Latino-Hispanic popular Catholicism the chief practitioners and leaders are, and have always been, women, the Virgin of Guadalupe as revelatory of the feminine face of

God takes on an added significance in terms of issues related to their being, self-identity, self-worth, human liberation, and the ongoing struggle for justice in the world. Even if, then, one were to grant that Marian symbols in the West, including the Virgin of Guadalupe, were merely invented historically by misogynist males operating from within a perspective of oppressive social, ecclesial, and political ideologies, this "invention" has tended to backfire against them.

Conclusion

Within contemporary Roman Catholic theological thought, the Virgin of Guadalupe clearly functions on several levels at the same time. Rodriguez herself summarizes these different functional levels, saying:

> I like to look at Guadalupe as a prism. For those who look at her and come to her as Mary, no problem. There will be other people who will come to her as the maternal face of God, and still others—like a Jewish woman I interviewed who claims to be a Guadalupe devotee—for whom Guadalupe comes through the Spirit. . . . Instead of putting Guadalupe in a box, I would put her in the category of an unconditional and grace-filled gift to the people.[78]

But whether seen through the prism of evangelization and inculturation, liberation, the divine maternity of God and new creation, iconography, popular religion and popular pneumatology, or as the vehicle through which God's unconditional grace is mediated and experienced, the Virgin of Guadalupe clearly cannot be written off theologically as merely a quaint or colorful "Marian" devotion somewhere on the periphery of Mexican and Mexican American religious and cultural life, a popular devotion to be dismissed after further catechesis, formation, and theological education. Rather, the Virgin of Guadalupe is at the very heart of this religious-cultural life. She is so central, in fact, that she remains present even for those who reject any or all associations between her and Roman Catholicism specifically or with Christianity in general. Such is the abiding and intimate power of Guadalupe that calls for and invites serious theological reflection within the increasing Hispanic-Latino context of Roman Catholicism in the Americas. One, of course, may lament as inadequate the traditional Western patriarchal conceptions of God that contributed to the transference of maternal divine imagery from God (or from the Holy Spirit especially) to the figure of Mary in the tradition. And one might certainly critique the sort of deification of Mary herself that has on occasion resulted from such transference. But even if the theological goal, such as Johnson's, is to restore such imagery properly back to God from Mary, and thereby open other avenues for a more biblically based Mariology as well,[79] one can neither reimagine the events and developments of history nor ignore the fact that it is precisely in the figure of the Virgin Mary in her Guadalupan and other advocations, especially as she functions in the life and spirituality of a people, that this encounter with the divine feminine is located and most concretely expressed.

For the ultimate goal of this study, however, the question to be addressed is whether, and, if so, how, the Virgin of Guadalupe, her narrative, and image, especially as reflected in the theological analyses of Elizondo, Espín, and Rodriguez, might also function as challenge and invitation within a Protestant worldview and theological approach. That is, does the Mother of the Americas, as she is called in one of her many titles, have anything to say to Protestant Christians in the Americas, Hispanic-Latino or otherwise, or are Guadalupe and her message so necessarily Roman Catholic in their formulation, and her temple and new creation so exclusively Roman Catholic in membership, that a Protestant theological approach, while affirming potentially some elements discerned from the narratives, is bound by doctrinal necessity to an ultimate rejection of the image and its overall theological implications? This, of course, is the topic for the final chapter in this study. But first it is necessary to look more directly at the December 12 liturgical feast and other celebrations of the Virgin of Guadalupe, since it is precisely by means of such celebrations that the boundaries between popular and official religion and between private devotion and prayer and public liturgy and liturgical prayer are transcended. It is to this that the following chapter is devoted.

Notes

1. Alberto Pereyra, "The Virgin of Guadalupe, History, Myth, and Spirituality," *Currents in Theology and Mission* 24, 4 (August 1997): 353.

2. Roberto Piña, private conversation with the author, August 2000, San Antonio, Texas.

3. Pereyra, "Virgin of Guadalupe," 354.

4. Virgil Elizondo, "Guadalupe: An Endless Source of Reflection," *Journal of Hispanic/Latino Theology* 5, 1 (1997): 65.

5. Virgil Elizondo, *La Morenita: Evangelizer of the Americas* (San Antonio: Mexican American Cultural Center, 1980), 86. Parallels between the biblical Incarnation of Christ and the Guadalupan incarnation of Christ and the church in Mexico are the subject of several of the eighteenth- and nineteenth-century Guadalupan sermons studied by Schulte. See Francisco Schulte, *A Mexican Spirituality of Divine*

Election for a Mission: Its Sources in Published Guadalupan Sermons, 1661–1821 (Rome: Georgian Pontifical University, 1994), esp. 77–110.

6. Virgil Elizondo, *Galilean Journey,* (New York: Orbis Books, 1983), 11–12. See also on the whole relationship between Guadalupe and evangelization Clodomiro. L. Siller Acuña, "El método de evangelización en el Nican Mopohua," *Servir* 17 (1981): 93–94.

7. To be fair and to avoid oversimplification, however, not all Spanish missioners can be accused of employing this kind of "evangelistic" method. Jaime Lara, for example, has shown that in Mexico as early as 1540 a *Manual for Adults* was published that actually attempted to restore an adult prebaptismal catechumenate, beginning either in mid-Lent for Easter baptism or in the middle of the Easter season for baptism at Pentecost. An early attempt at liturgical inculturation and liturgical catechesis, this manual also directed that the parts of the various rites directed to the catechumens, including the profession of faith, be done in Nahuatl. See Jaime Lara, "'Precious Green Jade Water': A Sixteenth-Century Adult Catechumenate in the New World," *Worship* 71, 5 (1997): 415–28. Certainly the catechism of Sahagún, the *Psalmodia Christiana* referred to in the previous chapter (Bernardino de Sahagún, *Psalmodia Christiana* [Christian psalmody], trans. A. J. O. Anderson [Salt Lake City: University of Utah Press, 1993]), is another example of a more culturally sensitive approach. See above, 47–49.

8. Virgil Elizondo, *Guadalupe: Mother of the New Creation,* (Maryknoll, N.Y.: Orbis, 1997), 119–20.

9. Elizondo, *Guadalupe: Mother of the New Creation,* 93.

10. Elizondo, *Guadalupe: Mother of the New Creation,* 94–95.

11. *Ad gentes* II.10. English translation adapted from Austin Flannery, *Vatican Collection,* vol. 1, *Vatican Council II: The Conciliar and Post Conciliar Documents,* new rev. ed. (Collegeville, Minn.: Liturgical Press, 1975), 824–25.

12. *Ad gentes,* 2, article II.11.

13. *Ad gentes,* III.22.

14. On the relationship between the process of evangelization in the *Nican Mopohua* and contemporary Roman Catholic documents on Christian mission in the modern world, see Richard Nebel, *Santa María Tonantzin, Virgen de Guadalupe: Continuidad y transformación religiosa en México* (Mexico City: Fondo de Culturo Económica, 1995), 322–39.

15. John Paul II, *Ecclesia in America* (Boston: St. Paul Books and Media, 1999), 11.

16. John Paul II, *Ecclesia in America,* 70.

17. Daniel Groody, CSC, "Corazón y Conversión: The Dynamics of Mexican Immigration, Christian Spirituality, and Human Transformation" (Ph.D. diss., Graduate Theological Union, September 2000), 221–22; forthcoming also from Rowman & Littlefield.

18. *Sacrosanctum concilium* V.103. English translation from Austin Flannery, *Vatican Council II,* 29.

19. See Paul VI, *Marialis cultus,* 22. See also D. A. Brading, *Mexican Phoenix: Our Lady of Guadalupe: Image and Tradition across Five Centuries.* (Cambridge: Cambridge University Press, 2001), 361–68.

20. Gustavo Gutiérrez, *On Job* (New York: Orbis Books, 1987), 94.

21. Third General Conference of the Latin American Bishops, *Puebla* (Washington, D.C.: National Conference of Catholic Bishops, 1979), para. 1145, p. 179.

22. Third General Conference, *Puebla,* para. 1147.

23. John Paul II, *Ecclesia in America,* 58.

24. Elizondo, *Guadalupe: Mother of the New Creation,* 132.

25. Virgil Elizondo, "Guadalupe: Mother and Patroness of all America," *Celebrate!* 39, 6 (2000): 21.

26. Virgil Elizondo, "Our Lady of Guadalupe as a Cultural Symbol," in *Liturgy and Cultural Religious Traditions,* ed. H. Schmidt and D. Power (New York: Seabury, 1977), 33. Also in Virgil Elizondo and Timothy Matovina, *Mestizo Worship: A Pastoral Approach to Liturgical Ministry* (Collegeville, Minn.: Liturgical Press, 1998), 45.

27. Raymond E. Brown, "Mary in the New Testament and in Catholic Life," *America,* May 15, 1982, 378–79.

28. Sandra L. Zimdars-Swartz, *Encountering Mary: Visions of Mary from LaSalette to Medjugorje.* (New York: Avon, 1991), 247–49; emphasis added. Other Hispanic-Latino advocations of Mary also seem to fall outside of these categories identified by Zimdars-Swartz. The popular Cuban Marian advocation Our Lady of Charity of El Cobre, for example, has often been interpreted along lines similar to Guadalupe in terms of liberation and national identity. For a recent study of this particular devotion see Thomas A. Tweed, *Our Lady of the Exile: Diasporic Religion at a Cuban Catholic Shrine in Miami* (New York: Oxford University Press, 1997).

29. See the text of the *Nican Mopohua,* para. 23–25, above, 21–22.

30. Elizondo, *Guadalupe: Mother of the New Creation,* 135.

31. Cf. Evelyn Stevens, "Marianismo: The Other Face of Machismo in Latin America," in *Male and Female in Latin America,* ed. A. Pescatello (Pittsburgh: University of Pittsburgh Press, 1973), 90–100. See also Ena Campbell, "The Virgin of Guadalupe and the Female Self-Image: A Mexican Case History," in Mother Worship: Theme and Variations, ed. James J. Preston (Chapel Hill: University of North Carolina Press, 1982), 5–24; and George L. Scheper, "Guadalupe: Image of Submission or Solidarity?" *Religion and the Arts* 3, 3/4 (1999): 333–84.

32. See Elizondo, *Guadalupe: Mother of the New Creation,* 113–14.

33. Elizondo, *Guadalupe: Mother of the New Creation,* 128–29.

34. Elizondo, *Guadalupe: Mother of the New Creation,* 114.

35. Virgil Elizondo, "Living Faith: Resistance and Survival," in *Mestizo Worship,* Elizondo and Matovina, 19.

36. Elizondo, *Guadalupe: Mother of the New Creation,* 104.

37. See Elizondo, *Guadalupe: Mother of the New Creation,* 38–48.

38. Elizondo, *Guadalupe: Mother of the New Creation,* 126.

39. Elizondo, *Guadalupe: Mother of the New Creation,* 127.

40. Elizondo, *Guadalupe: Mother of the New Creation,* 131.

41. Stafford Poole, *Our Lady of Guadalupe: The Origins and Sources of a Mexican National Symbol, 1531–1797* (Tucson: University of Arizona Press, 1997), 14.

42. Peter Brown, *The Cult of the Saints: Its Rise and Function in Latin Christianity,* (Chicago: University of Chicago Press, 1981), 12–22.

43. See Patrick Malloy, "The Re-emergence of Popular Religion among

Non-Hispanic American Catholics," *Worship* 72, 1 (1998): 2–25; and Michael Driscoll, "Liturgy and Devotions: Back to the Future?" in *The Renewal That Awaits Us*, ed. Eleanor Bernstein and Martin Connell (Chicago: Liturgy Training Publications, 1997), 68–90.

44. Mark R. Francis, "Building Bridges between Liturgy, Devotionalism, and Popular Religion," *Assembly* 20, 2 (1994): 636.

45. Orlando O. Espín, *The Faith of the People: Theological Reflections on Popular Catholicism* (Maryknoll, N.Y.: Orbis Books, 1997), 5.

46. Sixto García and Orlando O. Espín, "Hispanic-American Theology," *Proceedings of the Catholic Theological Society of America* 42 (1987): 115.

47. Roberto S. Goizueta, *Caminemos con Jesús: Toward a Hispanic/Latino Theology of Accompaniment* (Maryknoll, N.Y.: Orbis Books, 1995), 21.

48. Goizueta, *Caminemos con Jesús,* 22–23.

49. Alex García-Rivera, *St. Martín de Porres: The "Little Stories" and the Semiotics of Culture* (Maryknoll, N.Y.: Orbis Books, 1995), 20.

50. Cf. García-Rivera, *St. Martín de Porres* for a use of this same methodology to explore the significance and meaning of St. Martín de Porres in a Peruvian context.

51. Elizondo, *Guadalupe: Mother of the New Creation,* 134.

52. Orlando O. Espín, "Popular Catholicism among Latinos," in *Hispanic Catholic Culture in the U.S.: Issues and Concerns,* ed. Jay Dolan and A. Figueroa Deck (Notre Dame: University of Notre Dame Press, 1994), 329.

53. Orlando O. Espín, "An Exploration into the Theology of Grace and Sin," in *From the Heart of the People,* ed. Orlando Espín and Miguel Diaz (Maryknoll, N.Y.: Orbis Books, 1999), 138. See also Espín, *Faith of the People,* 6–10.

54. Espín, "Exploration into Grace and Sin," 138.

55. Espín, "Exploration into Grace and Sin," 139.

56. Espín, *Faith of the People,* 76; emphasis added.

57. Leonard Boff, *The Maternal Face of God: The Feminine and Its Religious Expressions* (San Francisco: Harper & Row, 1987), 93. See also, in this context, Elizabeth A. Johnson, "Mary and the Female Face of God," *Theological Studies* 50 (1989): 501–26, esp. 515–17.

58. For texts, see E. C. Whitaker, ed., *Documents of the Baptismal Liturgy* (London: SPCK, 1970), 12–23. For other texts, see Gabriele Winkler, "Nochmals zu den Anfängen der Epiklese und des Sanctus im Eucharistischen Hochgebet," *Theologisches Quartalschrift* 74, 3 (1994): 214–31. See also Gabriele Winkler, "Der Heilige Geist, die Mutter: Anmerkungen zu neuen Veröffentlichungen," *Theologische Revue* 93 (1997): 207–12; and Johnson, "Mary and the Female Face of God," 512–13.

59. Joseph Chalassery, *The Holy Spirit and Christian Initiation in the East Syrian Tradition,* Mar Thoma Yogam (Rome: Pontifical Oriental Institute, 1995), 22.

60. Espín, "Exploration into Grace and Sin," 141.

61. A parallel might surely be drawn here to the work of Robert Orsi on the way in which devotion to St. Jude at his national shrine in Chicago functioned similarly among immigrant women, especially during the early to mid–twentieth century. That is, devotion to St. Jude, as expressed in letters to and responses from the shrine, frequently reflected and fostered a particular view of women, who sought St. Jude's assistance in coping with and often enduring particular problems

brought about by their marital and familial situations. See Robert Orsi, *Thank You, St. Jude: Women's Devotion to the Patron Saint of Hopeless Causes* (New Haven: Yale University Press, 1996).

62. Rosemary Radford Reuther, "Mary in U.S. Catholic Culture," *National Catholic Reporter,* February 10, 1995, 16.

63. Sandra Cisneros, "Guadalupe the Sex Goddess," in *Goddess of the Americas, La Diosa de las Americas* ed., Ana Castillo (New York: Riverhead Books, 1996), 48. For expressions of similar sentiment in modern-day Mexico, see also Eryk Hanut, *The Road to Guadalupe: A Modern Pilgrimage to the Goddess of the Americas* (New York: Tarcher/Putnam, 2001), 49–55.

64. Cisneros, "Guadalupe the Sex Goddess," 49–50.

65. In fact, many of the essays in Castillo's fascinating book, including the title itself, *Goddess of the Americas, La Diosa de las Americas,* point in this direction. Castillo herself has often expressed the hope that this book, "an unorthodox rosary" of essays, now translated into Italian, might attract the negative attention of the Vatican and be condemned.

66. Laura Sánchez, interview with the author, December 9, 2000, San Antonio, Texas.

67. Sánchez interview.

68. See Jeannette Rodriguez, *Our Lady of Guadalupe: Faith and Empowerment among Mexican-American Women* (Austin: University of Texas Press, 1994); Jeannette Rodriguez, *Stories We Live/Cuentos Que Vivimos* (Mahwah, N.J.: Paulist Press, 1996); Jeannette Rodriguez, "Contemporary Encounters with Guadalupe," *Journal of Hispanic/Latino Theology* 5, 1 (1997): 48–60; and Jeannette Rodriguez, "Guadalupe: The Feminine Face of God," in *Goddess of the Americas,* ed. Castillo, 25–31. See also an interview with Rodriguez, "The Gift of Guadalupe," *U.S. Catholic* 64, 12 (1999): 18–22

69. Elizabeth Johnson, "The Marian Tradition and the Reality of Women," in *The Catholic Faith: A Reader,* ed. Lawrence Cunningham (New York: Paulist Press, 1988), 97–123; Johnson, "Mary and the Female Face of God," 501–26.

70. Johnson, "Mary and the Female Face of God," 525–26.

71. Jeannette Rodriguez, "Guadalupe: The Feminine Face of God," 28.

72. Rodriguez, "Guadalupe: The Feminine Face of God," 29.

73. Rodriguez, "Guadalupe: The Feminine Face of God," 29.

74. Rodriguez, "Guadalupe: The Feminine Face of God," 29-30.

75. "The Gift of Guadalupe," *U.S. Catholic* 64, 12 (1999): 22.

76. Johnson, "Mary and the Female Face of God," 525.

77. Johnson, "Mary and the Female Face of God," 525.

78. "The Gift of Guadalupe," 22.

79. See Johnson, "Marian Tradition," 116–21. In particular, with the restoration of this traditional Marian imagery back to God, Johnson proposes that Mary herself be resymbolized in terms of "sister," "type of the Church," and as "proclaimer of liberation."

4

Celebrations of the Virgin of Guadalupe

The Virgin of Guadalupe is more than a narrative about a sixteenth-century apparition, more than an abiding image, and more than a popular devotion of the Mexican and Mexican American people. The celebration of the Virgin of Guadalupe is also an official December 12 liturgical feast on the Roman Catholic Church's calendar occurring almost at the very center of the season of Advent, twelve days before Christmas Eve. As noted earlier, as recently as 1999, the celebration of Guadalupe on December 12—which already, of course, had the rank of a *solemnity* (the highest rank possible on the Roman calendar) in Mexico—was raised in status by Pope John Paul II from an obligatory or optional *memorial* on the liturgical calendars of many dioceses and a *feast* on the liturgical calendars of some (e.g., in the dioceses of the United States since 1987) to the rank of feast for all Roman Catholic dioceses of North, Central, and South America.[1] Since 1999, then, together with several other local Marian advocations and special feasts of the Virgin Mary throughout the Americas, the Virgin of Guadalupe is no longer an optional celebration anywhere for Roman Catholics in the Americas (including the dioceses of Canada) but now has its own specific liturgical propers and lectionary readings.[2] The December 12 feast of the Virgin of Guadalupe is now an official part of the calendar of feasts and is joined in the Americas to the following fifteen other Marian solemnities, feasts, and memorials, or those with Marian connotations (like the Annunciation and the Presentation of the Lord), on the general Roman Catholic liturgical calendar.[3] If no ranking is given for a date, it is an optional memorial.

- January 1: *Solemnity* of Mary, Mother of God

- February 2: The Presentation of Our Lord (Purification of the Blessed Virgin Mary, Candlemas Day)—*Feast*

- February 11: Our Lady of Lourdes

- March 25: *Solemnity* of the Annunciation

- May 31: The Visitation—*Feast*

- May (variable, the Saturday after the second Sunday after Pentecost): The Immaculate Heart of Mary

- July 16: Our Lady of Mount Carmel

- August 5: Dedication of the Basilica of Saint Mary Major (Our Lady of the Snows)

- August 15: *Solemnity* of the Assumption of Mary

- August 22: The Queenship of Mary—*Memorial*

- September 8: The Nativity of Mary—*Feast*

- September 15: Our Lady of Sorrows—*Memorial*

- October 7: Our Lady of the Rosary—*Memorial*

- November 21: Presentation of Mary in the Temple—*Memorial*

- December 8: *Solemnity* of the Immaculate Conception

Hence, the modern *theological* interpretations summarized in the previous chapter cannot really be separated from the fact that the Virgin of Guadalupe is today both an official and, at least for many, also a popular, liturgical festival in the life of the church. In fact, the *celebration* is itself the locus where the overall theological meaning and importance of the Virgin of Guadalupe comes to its concrete expression.

The discipline of liturgical theology often invokes the fifth-century phrase of Prosper of Aquitaine, *ut legem credendi statuat lex supplicandi* ("that the law of prayer might constitute the law of belief"), in support of viewing the liturgy itself—not only its texts but even more its actual performance— as formative of Christian faith, doctrine, and life at the most foundational levels of human experience.[4] Certainly this is true of Guadalupan liturgy as well. For to understand the specific meaning of the Virgin of Guadalupe, one must experience the December 12 liturgical and other associated ritual celebrations in a community for whom she is a living and personal presence and reality. As Roberto Goizueta writes of the function of ritual in general:

> Narratives, or stories, and rituals are the primary ways in which a community generates and identifies with its symbols, by explicitly locating them within the community's ongoing history. Narrative is symbolic discourse; ritual is symbolic action. . . . [T]he image of Guadalupe is not only a static picture but is the birth and ongoing life of the Mexican people and their relationship with God. . . . Like all symbols and rituals, narratives are able to convey the contradictions, ambiguities, and conflicts of life in a way that logical discourse cannot. . . . The most fundamental form in which communities disclose and create meaning is in ritual. Like all relationships, the relationship between God and ourselves which is mediated by symbolic objects (e.g., the crucifix) and narratives (e.g., the gospels) demands more than simply affective participation; it also demands inter-*action,* or performance. It is this interaction which defines and constitutes inter-relationship: e.g., the sacrament (or symbol) of the eucharist is defined and constituted not only by eucharistic bread and wine, and not only by eucharistic narrative, but, first and foremost, by the ritual act of *breaking* the bread together and *sharing* the cup, which is *mediated* by the symbolic objects and narrative. The foundation of symbol and narrative is ritual, just as the foundation of belief, or theory, is praxis, or human action.[5]

Although Goizueta does not refer to Prosper of Aquitaine's phrase in the above quotation, it is, in fact, one meaning of *lex orandi, lex credendi* that he expresses. For, indeed, it is precisely by means of Guadalupan liturgical and other ritual "interaction or performance" that a Guadalupano/a is actually constituted. In other words, it is not through logical discourse or "information" about the Virgin of Guadalupe but through the celebration of the feast, liturgical processions, pilgrimages, *las Mañanitas* sung in a crowded church before her image in the early morning of December 12, *flor y canto,* the communal fiestas, the continual presence of her image in homes and places of business, dramatic reenactments of the events of the *Nican Mopohua* itself, *Matachines* (indigenous and richly costumed dances), countless candles lighted and prayers recited before her image, and stories passed from one generation to the next that what might be called a foundational Guadalupan lex orandi is formed from an early age in the lives of so many. To understand fully how the Virgin of Guadalupe functions, one must attend, then, to her liturgical and other ritual expressions.

This chapter, then, is concerned with the contents and celebration of the December 12 feast of the Virgin of Guadalupe. It focuses not only on the evolution and liturgical-textual contents of the feast but also, and more specifically, on the relationship of this feast to the orientation and context of the Advent season in which it annually occurs. Here special attention is given to what often appears to be a tension between the official Western Christian celebration and theology of Advent, as it is expressed in the liturgical books, and the way the season of Advent itself is celebrated and understood in the popular religion of Hispanic-Latinos. Some attention is also given to "unofficial" Guadalupan celebrations connected to, or outside of, the official liturgical context. Finally, the fact that there are also Guadalupan celebrations within some United States Protestant communities is also discussed. Attention to this will help provide the particular theological focus of the final chapter in this study, which is concerned with locating the Virgin of Guadalupe within an ecumenical perspective.

The Liturgical Celebration of the December 12 Feast

Historical Development and Content of the Feast

As we saw in chapter 2, the origins and development of the feast of the Virgin of Guadalupe on December 12 are as difficult to discern as are the precise origins of the Guadalupan narratives and image themselves. No written record of a feast of Guadalupe celebrated at Tepeyac on December 12 exists before 1662, at which time the cathedral chapter of Mexico City requested approval from Rome for the feast on this date, a request that was delayed until 1667. When finally approved by Rome, the response contained the incorrect date of September rather than December 12, an error that delayed the process even further. Earlier, the feast day was apparently September 8, the feast of both the Nativity of the Blessed Virgin Mary on the general Roman Catholic liturgical calendar and of the Estremaduran Guadalupe on the local liturgical calendar of the Estremadura region in Spain. In fact, it was not until May 25, 1754, that Pope Benedict XIV finally both confirmed the patronage of the Virgin Mary under the title of the Mexican advocation of Our Lady of Guadalupe for New Spain and officially approved the liturgical propers (i.e., prayers, readings, and chants) for the Mass and Divine Office for the December 12 feast on the official, local calendar of Mexico.[6] Nevertheless, it is obvious that the feast had been celebrated in Mexico on December 12 for some time prior to this confirmation and approval, *at least* from 1662.

Stafford Poole takes this late acceptance of the December 12 date for the feast as further confirmation of his thesis that, directly inspired by the written narratives of Miguel Sánchez (1648) and Luis Lasso de la Vega (1649), the origins of Guadalupan devotion itself belong to an overall seventeenth-, and not early-sixteenth-, century context. But the lateness of the "official" recognition of the December 12 date for the *feast* only confirms either that the choice of this particular date, associated in other narratives with the fourth and final apparition, was possibly inspired by the official written Guadalupan narratives or, alternatively, that the date in the narratives was itself possibly inspired by the growing Guadalupan oral tradition. Indeed, in the history especially of Marian feasts in Western Christianity, the time from the origins of a particular feast in a local church or religious community to its official recognition or incorporation into the general liturgical calendar can span several centuries. This does not mean that the feast is not already being celebrated by some communities during this period of development but only that official recognition, approval, or incorporation into the official calendar is not the same thing as the "origins" of its celebration. To give but one example, the December 8 Solemnity of the Immaculate Conception of Mary has its origins in an eighth-century Byzantine Christian feast observed on December 9, the Conception of St. Anne, a feast still celebrated today in the Christian East.[7] This entered the West, via monastic usage in England, in the eleventh century. From England it spread throughout Western Europe especially within various religious orders and communities, most notably the Franciscans, whose own itinerant lifestyle contributed to its wide dissemination. Together with growing theological speculation about Mary's immaculate conception (her preservation, or "redemption by exemption," from original sin), primarily among Franciscan theologians from the thirteenth century on, the feast was accepted for Rome itself by a Franciscan pope (Sixtus IV) only in 1477, and it became a universal feast for the entire Roman Catholic Church only in 1708. Even so, the particular title of this feast today, "the *Immaculate* Conception of Mary," did not become its official title until after the promulgation of the dogma of Mary's immaculate conception by Pope Pius IX in 1854.[8] From its eighth-century origins in the Christian East, then, it took almost *ten* centuries for it to become a universal feast in the West and *eleven* centuries for it to develop into its current form. Hence, that a local feast like the Virgin of Guadalupe might take from 1531 until 1662 or 1754 to evolve—actually a relatively short period of time in the historical development of liturgical feasts—is not surprising.

At the same time, the fact that September 8 may well have been the original date of the feast, corresponding to both the feast of the Nativity of Mary and the Estremaduran Guadalupe celebrated at Tepeyac, is, again, really no indication whatsoever, pro or con, of the historicity of devotion to the Mexican Guadalupe herself. Indeed, not only do dates of feasts periodically change throughout history, but if the September 8 feast of the Nativity of Mary was already the titular feast of the chapel of Tepeyac—that is, if the feast for the Estremaduran Virgin of Guadalupe at Tepeyac was the Nativity of Mary[9]—there is really no reason to expect an alternate date to be sought or established for a separate feast day in honor of the Mexican Guadalupe. The Guadalupan narratives themselves nowhere call for the establishment of a new liturgical feast in her honor, and, in fact, there was really no need for a separate Marian feast. Had there, in fact, been a call for establishing such a feast, it would have undoubtedly been resisted by the early Franciscan ecclesiastical authorities, who were already highly suspicious and critical of the indigenous Guadalupan devotion itself.

Furthermore, there is early-sixteenth-century evidence for the celebration of the feast of the Immaculate Conception of Mary on December 8 in Mexico. If this feast was not yet a universal Roman Catholic feast in the early sixteenth century, it was certainly already being celebrated in the region of Tepeyac, as the existence of a poetic homily of Bernardino de Sahagún for the feast (called by him simply "The Conception of the Blessed Virgin Mary") clearly demonstrates.[10] Even if, then, there had been some kind of early indigenous push for an additional Marian feast in close association to December 8, one can only imagine that it would have been met with similar resistance and rejection for the simple reason that there already was a Marian feast close to the date. At the same time, the fact that the liturgical propers of the September 8 feast of the Nativity of Mary would have been used to celebrate the Virgin of Guadalupe, whether in her Spanish or her Mexican advocation, proves nothing about the existence of the feast itself. It only means that, as in the case of the Estremaduran Guadalupe, the liturgical propers of the Nativity of Mary came to be used for the Mexican Guadalupe and that both were associated originally with September 8 in Mexico. Indeed, there is some evidence to suggest that in this time period the prayers and readings in the Common of Feasts of the Blessed Virgin Mary—that is, the collection of prayer texts and readings to be used for feasts not having their own assigned propers—were identical to those assigned to the September 8 feast of the Nativity of Mary. Further confirmation of this is supplied by the fact that even when Pope Benedict XIV in 1754 finally approved the specific liturgical propers for the Guadalupe feast on December 12, the Mass for the feast remained essentially that of the Nativity of Mary.[11]

As I have attempted to argue earlier is possibly the case with the official Guadalupan narratives of Sanchéz and Lasso de la Vega in the mid-seventeenth century, I suspect that the *official* establishment of the feast of the Virgin of Guadalupe on December 12 is also the response of local (Mexican) ecclesiastical authorities to the increasing popularity of Guadalupan devotion. Indeed, as long as that devotion was localized at Tepeyac and associated primarily with the indigenous peoples, there was no perceived need for a "national" feast. But what Jean-Pierre Ruiz has suggested with regard to how the official narratives appear to reflect the canonization of the Guadalupan events might also well be related to the development of the feast itself. That is, if by this time "the Virgin of Guadalupe had reached an important breadth of diffusion throughout the various ethnic and socioeconomic strata of colonial Mexico, ranging from the indigenous Nahuas, to the *criollos,* to the Spanish born,"[12] the establishment of an official feast in her honor may well have been but another concrete expression and confirmation of this widespread development and acceptance. This kind of development and acceptance, in fact, has continued well up to our own day with a revision of the 1754 liturgy by Pope Leo XIII in 1894,[13] and, more importantly, with new propers for the Solemnity of the Virgin of Guadalupe appearing for Mexico in 1974,[14] and for the Feast of the Virgin of Guadalupe for the dioceses of the United States appearing in 1987.[15] Prior to this development, the December 12 feast had been permitted for United States dioceses only since 1962 as the equivalent of an optional memorial.[16]

In the current Roman Catholic liturgical books for Mexico the propers for the eucharistic liturgy for the December 12 Solemnity of Our Lady of Guadalupe are:[17]

Entrance Antiphon: A great sign appeared in the sky, a woman clothed with the sun, with the moon under her feet, and on her head a crown of twelve stars. (Revelation 12:1)

The Glory to God *is said.*

Opening Prayer: Father of mercy, who has placed this your people under the special protection of the ever-Virgin Mary of Guadalupe, Mother of your Son. Grant us, by her intercession, that our faith may be deepened and that we may seek the progress of our nation through the way of justice and peace. Through our Lord Jesus Christ.[18]

Reading 1: Sirach 24:23–31

Responsorial Psalm: Psalm 66

Reading 2: Galatians 4:4–7

Gospel Acclamation: My spirit rejoices in God my Savior. (Luke 1:47)

Gospel: Luke 1:39–47

The Creed *is said.*

Prayer over the Offerings: Lord, accept the gifts we present to you on this solemnity ["feast" in the United States] of Our Lady of Guadalupe, and grant that this sacrifice will strengthen us to fulfill your commandments as true sons and daughters of the Virgin Mary. We ask this through Christ our Lord.

Communion Antiphon: God has not acted thus for any other nation; to no other people has he shown his love so clearly. (See Psalm 147:20)

Prayer after Communion: Lord, may the Body and Blood of your Son, which we receive in this sacrament, reconcile us always in your love. May we who rejoice in the holy Mother of Guadalupe live united and at peace in this world until the day of the Lord dawns in glory. We ask this through Christ our Lord.

While most of the above is identical in the 1987 propers for the feast of Our Lady of Guadalupe in the United States, there are within the United States propers some differences and subtle nuances or shifts. An optional communion antiphon is provided along with the one based on Psalm 147:20, namely, "The Lord has cast down the mighty from their thrones and has lifted up the lowly" (Luke 1:52). In addition, there are no assigned—but only suggested—lectionary readings for the feast to be selected from those available in the Common of the Blessed Virgin Mary. But, while the suggested Gospel reading is the same (Luke 1:39–47), in place of Sir. 24:23–31 (in praise of Lady Wisdom) and Gal. 4:4–7 ("God sent his son, born of a woman . . ." 4:4), the suggested appropriate readings are Zech. 2:14–17 (verses 10–12 in the New Revised Standard Version) and/or Rev. 11:19; 12:1–6, 10 (the "woman clothed with the sun"). Similarly, the opening prayer, while it contains common themes and is based, obviously, on the same prayer in the Mexican *Misal Romano,* is rather distinct in its formulation or adaptation: "God of power and mercy, you blessed the Americas at Tepeyac with the presence of the Virgin Mary of Guadalupe. May her prayers help all men and women to accept each other as brothers and sisters. Through your justice present in our hearts may your peace reign in the world. We ask this through our Lord Jesus Christ."[19]

These differences between the liturgical propers for Mexico and the United States are rather striking. Apart from the entrance antiphon from Rev. 12:1, which is identical to the first option for the Solemnity of Mary's Assumption on August 15, the rest of the Mass in the Mexican propers makes no allusion to any association between the Virgin of Guadalupe and the "woman clothed with the sun." Rather, the assigned readings, especially in the combination of Gal. 4:4–7 with Luke 1:39–47 (the Gospel account of Mary's Visitation to Elizabeth and, at least, the beginnings of her

Magnificat) might be interpreted as shifting attention away somewhat from the Guadalupan apparition itself to the *biblical* role of Mary in the Incarnation. In other words, that the presumably expected text from Rev. 11:19; 12:1–6, 10 is not a lectionary reading for the Solemnity of the Virgin of Guadalupe in *Mexico* is, at least, interesting in this context. Similarly, the different opening prayer for the Mexican solemnity is also somewhat suggestive when compared to its United States counterpart. While the Mexican prayer certainly refers to Guadalupe's self-identification in the *Nican Mopohua* ("the ever-Virgin Mary of Guadalupe, Mother of your Son"), it makes no explicit statement that can be taken as referring unambiguously to the historical reliability of the apparitions at Tepeyac. But the prayer for use in the United States appears to go beyond this. Not only does the United States version make no reference to the "Mother of your Son" in referring to the identity of the "Virgin Mary of Guadalupe," but what it does say can be taken as suggesting a kind of liturgical recognition or acceptance of the authenticity of the event itself: "you blessed the Americas at Tepeyac with the presence of the Virgin Mary of Guadalupe."[20] Indeed, together with the suggested reading of Rev. 11:19; 12:1–6, 10, the propers for use in the United States feast thus *can* be interpreted as being oriented more toward the Guadalupan apparition itself than are the propers even for the solemnity in Mexico. While one might surely ask of those who created the propers for the feast in the United States whether even the implicit acceptance or rejection of an apparition is the role of liturgical texts at all,[21] one must wonder further why for United States usage the opening prayer and lectionary readings, like the entrance antiphon, communion antiphon, prayer over the gifts, and prayer after Communion, were not simply taken directly from the Mexican *Misal Romano* itself. Indeed, if liturgy always celebrates the centrality of the Paschal Mystery of *Christ's* life, death, resurrection, and gift of the Holy Spirit, then surely the Mexican propers, especially with the clear identity of the "ever-Virgin Mary of Guadalupe, Mother of your Son" proclaimed in the opening prayer and the combination of Gal. 4:4–7 with Luke 1:39–47 in the lectionary readings, are more clearly oriented to that Paschal Mystery. Thus, it would appear that the propers for the solemnity in Mexico are possibly oriented more toward *Advent* preparation for the celebration of the Incarnation of Christ at Christmas.

The Feast of the Virgin of Guadalupe and the Season of Advent

However it was that the feast of the Virgin of Guadalupe came to be celebrated ultimately on December 12, this feast, together with the Solemnity of the Immaculate Conception of Mary four days before it, tends to provide an overall "Marian" focus, especially among Mexicans and Mexican Americans, for the liturgical season of Advent. That is, the popular observance of Advent among Mexican and Mexican American Catholics is organized as follows:

December 3–11: Novena to the Virgin of Guadalupe (nine days of special prayer, devotion, and preparation for the December 12 celebration)[22]

December 8: Solemnity of the Immaculate Conception

December 12: Solemnity or Feast of the Virgin of Guadalupe

December 16-24: Las Posadas ("lodging") Novena (nine days of special prayer, devotion, and preparation, often celebrated in neighborhoods or in parish communities, consisting especially of festive processions, songs, and ceremonies re-enacting the search of Mary and Joseph for lodging in Bethlehem, followed by joyful celebrations with food and singing at the final designated home or place in the search)[23]

On the popular religious level, then, the first part of Advent is oriented to, and concerned with, prayerful preparation for the December 12 appearance of the pregnant Virgin of Guadalupe. And after she appears, the rest of the season is devoted to accompanying her and Joseph to Bethlehem for the birth of Christ, an accompaniment often with profound implications for many Hispanic-Latinos, especially immigrants, in the United States. As Virgil Elizondo notes:

The *posada* is easily a *cultic* reminder and reenactment as well, for Mexican Americans who have walked, often at night and through snake infested deserts, to the United States in the hope of finding work. What they have found instead was rejection after rejection. But, like Joseph and Mary, they did not give up; they followed their star. . . . The *posada* is a living symbol of a living faith.[24]

Particularly as the Virgin of Guadalupe, Mary becomes, then, on the popular religious level the image par excellence of Advent expectation and preparation, and Advent itself becomes a rather "Marian" season in overall emphasis, although, of course, it remains oriented Christologically to Christmas.

The question, however, is whether or not such an obvious Marian focus is what the liturgical season of Advent itself is really about. On the official Roman Catholic (and contemporary Protestant) liturgical level, the focus of Advent is not Marian but primarily eschatological and only secondarily incarnational. That is, within the current three-year lectionary used by Roman Catholics and adapted by several contemporary Protestant liturgical traditions today, the lectionary readings assigned to the first three Sundays of this season are all oriented toward the Parousia, or Second Coming of Christ in glory, and not to his first coming in Bethlehem at Christmas. The Advent call to "prepare the way of the Lord," then, is a call more related to the church's own eschatological stance in the world as oriented in hope toward ultimate fulfillment in Christ when "he will come to judge the living and the dead" than it is to preparing for Jesus' "birthday." Christmas becomes less a celebration of a past historical event (Christ's birth) and more a kind of anticipated celebration of the *Parousia* itself, a celebration of the fullness of redemption and *our* new birth by baptism in the one whom the late Raymond Brown referred to as the "adult Christ at Christmas."[25] In fact, it is only on the fourth Sunday in Advent that the current lectionary readings shift from a clearly eschatological to an incarnational or Christmas focus, with the Gospel pericopes of the Annunciation to Joseph (Matt. 1:18–24), the Annunciation to Mary (Luke 1:26–38), and the Visitation of Mary to Elizabeth (Luke 1:39–45), read respectively in year A, B, and C of the three-year cycle. Such a shift to an incarnational focus is supported also by the use of the famous "O Antiphons" connected to the Gospel canticle of the Magnificat at evening prayer beginning on December 17.

It is because of both the strong eschatological character of Advent (assuming its final and current form in the Roman liturgy under Pope Gregory I at the beginning of the seventh century) and its actual location within the classic Roman liturgical books at the *end*—and not at the beginning—of the liturgical year that some contemporary liturgical scholars are asserting that the eschatological season of Advent has more to do with the conclusion of the liturgical year than with its annual beginning. Historically, its proximity to Christmas, therefore, would have been more accidental than deliberate in Rome, although today it is certainly constructed both as the beginning of the year and as a season of preparation for Christmas.[26] But whatever the historical case, the overall eschatological orientation of Advent toward the Parousia in the liturgical books today certainly suggests that there is a tension between the official Advent liturgy and the Marian focus of the season in Mexican and Mexican American popular religion. Elizondo refers to this tension when he describes the conversion of Bishop Juan Zumárraga in the *Nican Mopohua:*

> The entire complex of events at Tepeyac was as mysterious as it was ultimately real. The bishop was disconcerted and his household was disturbed,

as theologians, liturgists, and catechists usually are with the ways of God's poor. To this day, liturgists do not want to accept the feast of Our Lady of Guadalupe as the major feast of Advent. For them, it seems that God made a mistake in placing the feast of Guadalupe during Advent.[27]

Indeed, related to this, the liturgical color of royal or "Sarum" blue, becoming increasingly (and ecumenically) popular as an alternative to the traditional purple or violet Advent color for vestments and paraments, is actually resisted today in several Roman Catholic dioceses precisely *because* blue has traditional Roman Catholic associations with Mary (the "lovely Lady dressed in blue"). That is, while several contemporary Protestant liturgical traditions have embraced blue as an alternative color for the season, presumably reflecting Advent "hope," Roman Catholics have tended to resist and, in some cases, not even permit its use because Advent is *not*—and is not to be construed as—a Marian season.

But if there is a tension between the official eschatological Advent of modern Western Christianity and the popular Marian Advent of Hispanic-Latino piety, a more Marian-focused Advent does appear to have some affinities to the pre-Christmas seasons of preparation in some of the Eastern Christian liturgical rites, to other early non-Roman Western liturgical traditions, and even to some characteristics within the earlier Roman Advent itself. In the Byzantine Rite, for example, beginning with the November 21 feast of the Presentation of Mary in the Temple, multiple Marian images associated with the "Ark of the Covenant," the "Tabernacle," and even as the "heavenly Temple" appear in the various *troparia* (hymns) and prayers throughout the season.[28] And two Sundays before Christmas the Byzantine Rite commemorates "the Holy Ancestors of Christ," culminating, of course, in Mary, and on the Sunday before Christmas are celebrated "all the Fathers who down the centuries have been pleasing to God, from Adam to Joseph, husband of the Most Holy Mother of God."[29] Among the Syrian Christian traditions, both West Syrian (i.e., Syrian and/or Antiochene Orthodox and Maronite) and East Syrian (i.e., Assyrian, Chaldean, and Syro-Malabar), the assigned Gospel readings on the Sundays for the season of Christmas preparation, called "Weeks of Annunciations," include, in order, the Annunciation to Zechariah, the Annunciation to Mary, the Visitation, the Nativity of John the Baptist, and, finally, the Annunciation to Joseph. Indeed, for these reasons, Eastern Advent is often referred to as a Marian season.

In the historic liturgies of the non-Roman West there is also some correspondence here. While the precise origins of the March 25 celebration of the Annunciation of Our Lord are obscure, the feast on this date is known to have been celebrated in the East by the beginning of the sixth century.[30] Before that shift to a calendrical date, the Annunciation appears to have been celebrated on the Sunday before Christmas. Interestingly enough, the date of the feast of the Annunciation varied in the calendars of other Western liturgical traditions throughout the Middle Ages. In Spain it was celebrated on December 18, and today, within the recently reformed post–Vatican II liturgical books of the Spanish or "Mozarabic" Rite, December 18 has remained a solemnity of Mary called simply *Sancta Maria* ("Holy" or "Saint Mary") where the primary focus is still on the Annunciation, even though the Annunciation itself is celebrated on March 25.[31] And in Milan, within the Ambrosian Rite the Annunciation was and still is celebrated on the last of the *six* Sundays of Advent. Even in the liturgical tradition of Rome, a similar correlation between, at least, the Annunciation and Christmas was also true of the more eschatologically oriented Roman Advent itself, although Rome had clearly accepted the March 25 date of the feast by the time of Pope Sergius I (687–701). Prior to the post–Vatican II liturgical reform of the calendar, in fact, the Gospel pericopes of both the Annunciation and the Visitation were read, respectively, on the Wednesday and Friday of the third week of Advent, formerly known as the Advent Ember Days, one of four annual seasons of special prayer and fasting throughout the liturgical year.[32] Hence, even with the acceptance of the March 25 date for the feast in the West, proximity between the celebration of the Annunciation (and the Visitation) and Christmas remained a traditional characteristic of Western liturgical history in general.

Because in Mary, according to *Sacrosanctum concilium,* "the Church admires and exalts the most excellent fruit of redemption, and joyfully contemplates, as in a faultless image, that which she herself desires and hopes wholly to be,"[33] some today have begun to call for a reevaluation not only of the current ranking of Marian festivals on the liturgical calendar but also of their particular dates in relationship to the central mysteries of Christ at the obvious core of the liturgical year. Shawn Madigan, for example, writes:

> The ranking of present festivals gives non-scriptural imagination as great a place, and occasionally, a greater place, than scriptural imagination. When Mary, Mother of God [Jan. 1], the most traditional scriptural festival is not transferred but dispensed with as a "holy day of obligation" because the clergy are too tired, there is need for liturgical critique. Why not cancel the Immaculate Conception instead? Why are scriptural festivals, such as Visitation and Lady of Sorrows, almost invisible?[34]

And, with particular regard to the appropriateness of Marian festivals and images during Advent, she calls for a kind of rethinking and restructuring of the season itself, asking:

What if the festivals of Annunciation and Visitation were placed early in the Advent season? If the Annunciation were celebrated on the first Sunday of Advent and the Visitation during that week, look at what could be accomplished. Christ the King readings of the end time could stand conclusively as end of the liturgical year without beginning with another set of end times. The present Annunciation festival (March 25) could be relieved from its non-liturgical presence in the midst of Christ imaging related to passiontide. This would also lessen the confusion about whether liturgical calendars are planned according to seasons or biological rhythms. Another accomplishment is that the readings for both festivals are appropriate advent reflections about the church (Annunciation: Is. 7:1–14; Heb. 10:4–10; Lk. 1:26–38; Visitation: Zeph. 3:14–19; Rom 12:9–16; Lk. 1:39–56). If the Visitation were placed on a weekday of the first week of Advent, there is logic to John the Baptist appearing on the second Sunday of Advent. Similar to the Annunciation, the present placement of the Visitation has little relationship to the Christ cycle. If the Annunciation and Visitation festivals occurred in early Advent, fitting gospel readings for the last Sunday of Advent could be found by liturgists and exegetes.[35]

If Madigan's proposal, and others like hers,[36] are certainly consistent with the Advent orientations of the Christian East and various historic traditions in the West, they also make both liturgical and Christological sense by intentionally integrating Marian images and festivals into this season of incarnational preparation. December as the "month of Mary" certainly makes a lot more sense than May! But why limit the festival of the Visitation to a weekday? Indeed, if such a suggestion for restructuring Western Advent is desirable or feasible at all, why not make Advent, as it is in the Syrian East, the celebration of the various "Annunciations" from the opening chapters of Matthew and Luke? That is, why not celebrate the Annunciation to Zechariah and/or the Birth of John the Baptist on the first Sunday of Advent, the Annunciation to Mary on the second, the Visitation on the third, and the Annunciation to Joseph on the fourth?

It is amazing how the overall Marian focus of Advent especially among Mexicans and Mexican Americans already tends to have some affinity to what has been described above both with regard to the focus of Advent within various Christian traditions and to recent proposals for rethinking the season of Advent itself. Such a restructuring of Advent, as suggested by Madigan, might offer the added advantage of bringing official and popular religion closer together within an Advent synthesis. For, indeed, I suspect that within most forms of popular religion and piety, whether Catholic or Protestant, Advent has always been, and will continue to be, decidedly incarnational in focus and closely related to the people and events surrounding the impending birth of Christ, in spite of what we liturgists and the official liturgy say about eschatology. But whether such a restructuring of Advent were ever to take place or not, is it not significant that the Gospels for the December 8 solemnity of the Immaculate Conception and now for the solemnity/feast of the Virgin of Guadalupe are, respectively, the Gospel readings of *precisely* both the Annunciation and the Visitation in annual proximity to the second and third Sundays of Advent? If the titles of the solemnities/feasts are different, the biblical content of both is highly congruent with at least one traditional Advent characteristic even in the Roman West. In other words, the Advent liturgy does not really have to change in order to accommodate either the Annunciation or the Visitation. For Roman Catholics, at least, both emphases have remained within the season under different names and, thus, both already integrate Mary and the principal biblical texts associated with her into Advent.

While certainly sympathetic to a rethinking and restructuring of Advent, I am not yet prepared to give up either the season's overall eschatological focus or the calls to "prepare the way of the Lord," associated especially with the second and third Sundays of the season. But the December 12 festival of the Virgin of Guadalupe, of course, need not be viewed as inconsistent with this Advent eschatological focus. Such an eschatological orientation, in fact, certainly appears already in the prayer after Communion in the propers for the feast: "May we who rejoice in the holy Mother of Guadalupe live united and at peace in this world *until the day of the Lord dawns in glory.*" Similarly, in spite of the fact that modern biblical scholarship would rightly challenge the late-medieval Marian exegesis of Rev. 12,[37] an exegesis certainly presumed in the United States's suggestion that Rev. 11:19; 12:1–6, 10 be one of the readings for the feast, the obvious visual correlation between the Guadalupan image and this apocalyptic biblical text does make some kind of, at least symbolic, connection possible. That is, even if the woman of Rev. 12 is best understood as personifying both ancient Israel and the New Testament people of God, such personification has certainly come to be embodied symbolically as well in the person of Mary as *the* image par excellence of the church itself, an image of "that which she [the Church] herself desires and hopes wholly to be." At the same time, the "woman clothed with the sun" in Rev. 12 and the Virgin of Guadalupe are similarly eschatological in orientation, directing attention to the new life and new creation present in the one to whom both give birth. Consequently, if the biblical "woman clothed with the sun" is not really intended to be Mary, she is nonetheless, like the Virgin of Guadalupe herself, symbolic of the overall Advent stance of the church in the world, living in hope of the ultimate eschatological victory of the fullness of the reign of God over all forms of injustice, oppression, and evil, a victory already revealed in the life, death, and resurrection of Christ. If both the pregnant biblical "woman clothed with the sun" and the pregnant Virgin of Guadalupe give birth to the Messiah, both also simultaneously represent the church. Whether the liturgical season of Advent, then, is conceived of primarily in incarnational or eschatological ways, it is easy to understand why for Mexican and Mexican American Catholics "the feast of Our Lady of Guadalupe [is] the *major feast of Advent.*" Both traditional orientations associated with the season are expressed in her, and so, properly understood, there is no real need for there to be a tension between the official liturgy of Advent and popular faith expressions. The Virgin of Guadalupe and the liturgical season of Advent, thus, can certainly be viewed as belonging together.

The December 12 Feast as a Popular Celebration

The feast of the Virgin of Guadalupe, of course, is more than a December 12 liturgical feast on the Roman Catholic liturgical calendar in the middle of Advent with its own proper prayers and readings. In several places it is a celebration that spills over from and into life itself in powerful and dramatic ways. Indeed, the actual *liturgical* celebration of the feast is only part of the overall celebration and, for many, not necessarily even the most important part. In an essay entitled "The Undocumented Virgin," poet and author Rubén Martínez describes his own experience at the basilica of Guadalupe in Mexico City on December 12, 1994:

> The pilgrims come from all over the republic to celebrate her feast day on December 12, but the party begins the night before. They come as they've come for a thousand years to the Cerro del Tepeyac. The pilgrims come by bus, car, or bicycle. Yet others come jogging or walking from distances greater than the Greek marathon, carrying banners and picture frames and heavy ornate wooden altars, all bearing her image. . . . A mostly brown nation of Indian and mixed-race heritage assembles on the lava stone before the basilica. Their hair is neo-hippie long or punk short—mestizo kids from the city, *indígenas* from the provinces. I came expecting to see a lot of grandmothers with crinkled faces and long white braids, but mostly the pilgrims are young: teenage rocker types in leather jackets carrying ghetto blasters with stickers of Metallica and Nirvana right next to *La Virgen*'s. . . . It's a Catholic Woodstock attended, according to official crowd estimates, by some four million faithful every year. The biking pilgrims park tens of thousands of machines on top of one another, ceremonial piles of aluminum and rubber. The pilgrims drink, a little rum or brandy to ward off the chill of the night and—why not?—to toast *La Virgencita*. The pilgrims smoke, too.

A crew of rockero youth at the top of Tepeyac pass the pipe around and listen to Pink Floyd on a battered box. La Virgen doesn't suffer from any generation gap. . . . It's the biggest party I've ever been to. My street paranoia fades as I realize that this is probably the safest place on the planet to be: who would dare diss Lupe by committing the sin of robbery? . . . There is virtually no security, except for a few Red Cross crews with stretchers and ambulances at the ready for those who pass out in the crush of the crowd. The few cops are in an uncharacteristically jovial mood (cops are hated in Mexico City as much as they are in the barrios of Rodney King's L.A.). . . . After two in the morning, the chill grows bitter and the party energy flags. The thousands of faithful turn in for the night: the marathon runners from Hidalgo, the Marian devotees from Morelos, the Indian dancers from Oaxaca, the young former drug addicts–turned–missionaries from Tijuana. They lay out their blankets and huddle together against the cold. It's as if the entire country is in one huge embrace; Mexico hugs itself through the night to keep warm. . . . This is the greatness of mestizo culture, I think to myself. Everyone's welcome, we can all get along. Because of her. Because She is both Indian and Spanish. A rocker and an Aztec dancer. She's olive skinned, a blend of indigenous copper brown and Iberian white. She's the woman that puts the Mexican macho in his place—no matter how much he beats his chest, she's the origin of All Things, the serpent-woman Tonantzin. . . . She is the protector of Family, and lashes out at anyone who would endanger a child's well being. She is, after all, the Savior's Mother and sees her Son's visage in the face of every Mexican son or daughter. Perhaps that's why most of the pilgrims are so young. It is young Mexico that stares into a bleak future, a violent world, that is looking for itself today in the jungles of Chiapas, along the endless asphalt of Mexico City and in the cold cities of the United States. Young Mexico desperately needs to believe. . . . Beginning at dawn on the twelfth, thousands of Indian dancers pound the lava stone of the plaza with their bare feet amid clouds of incense. The fierce beat of the drums melds with the church hymns emanating from the cathedral. Pilgrims painfully approach the entryway on their knees, rosaries swinging from their hands, sweat streaming from their brows. I watch one man inch his way toward *La Virgen*'s birthplace carrying his sick child in his arms. Mexico comes to Her to heal itself. . . . We come to pay Her tribute, and to petition her as well, the tradition of the *mandas*. I speak to a family that's come all the way from East Los Angeles to honor Her. "I want to ask Her for better luck with work in the North," the teenage son, a longhaired rocker, tells me. "And for Her to accompany all Latinos in California now that they passed 187," adds the father. . . . I have faith that Mexico will survive this turbulent time with its essence intact. That essence is the festival of *La Virgen,* where all of Mexico's children come together to admit that the very pain of our history—the racism against the Indian, the diaspora and conflict of immigration—is what offers us the path toward redemption. It is a hope that brings with it a tremendous responsibility: to live up to *La Virgen*'s own faith in us. . . . As the sun sinks into the coppery hues of the smoggy horizon of the most populous city on earth, the festivities of Mexico's most important holiday draw to a close. The Indian elders leave the cathedral, chanting in the Spanish of *La Virgen* and in the dialects of Tonantzin: *"Adiós, Madre de Cielo."* Good-bye, Mother of Heaven. They walk backwards, their eyes never leaving the doorway to the cathedral, as if to say that Mexico will never turn her back on Her faith.[38]

What Martínez describes for the celebration of this feast in Mexico is by no means limited geographically to that country. He continues later in the same essay to describe how his Mexican experiences of December 12, 1994, were duplicated the next year in Los Angeles. While similar examples from around the United States could surely be given, the celebration of December 12 at the Cathedral of San Fernando, San Antonio, Texas, a cathedral in the very center of the city long known for its grand and public rituals related to the liturgical year (especially the celebration of Las Posadas in later December and the solemn public Passion play or Way of the Cross each year on Good Friday)[39] is certainly worthy of special note here. Roberto Goizueta writes:

Like the gospel narratives, this story [Guadalupe] is not past history; it is taking place today and is relived each year, especially on December 12. This is true of the San Fernando community and many others throughout the United States, where the annual celebration, like the Guadalupe story itself, begins with beautiful music. The night before the feast, the community gathers to serenade Our Lady, usually led by some of the most popular musicians and singers from the Mexican-American community. Shortly before midnight, the Mariachi choirs and all the members of the community gather around Our Lady for the *serenata* (serenade). The next morning, the community gathers before sunrise for the singing of *Las Mañanitas,* the traditional Mexican song that, recalling the encounter on Tepeyac, celebrates the birth of new life. The Lady's mantle has been covered with ribbons, which are now tossed into the crowd so that each person will be holding a part of the mantle. This, "the Easter sunrise service of the people," is a spectacular scene that proclaims in glorious music, the dawn of a new day—in many more ways than one. . . . The rest of the day the church is abuzz with activity. People stream into church all day long, as individuals but, especially, as families to visit Our Lady, often touching her tenderly, kissing her feet, and presenting her with flowers from their homes. At the end of the day, the children of the parish take turns in leading the entire community in praying a "living rosary." Once again, the people walk up to Our Lady to present flowers to her, this time in between the mysteries of the rosary. And again, the people kiss, touch, and caress Our Lady. Some have gentle smiles on their faces, others a tear in their eye—though, their facial expression indicates, probably from joy rather than sorrow.[40]

The celebration of the feast of the Virgin of Guadalupe on December 12, therefore, is clearly much more than a liturgical feast celebrated in church. And this, of course, speaks strongly about the very nature of festivity itself. For a real feast is never confined to the liturgical expressions of that feast. Nor does one really feast or celebrate because one has been mandated by another to do so. As my Notre Dame colleague Professor James F. White likes to say, "A holy day of *obligation* is an oxymoron." Rather, as the great Byzantine liturgiologist Juan Mateos once wrote, festivity is "an exuberant manifestation of life itself standing out in contrast to the background rhythm of daily life. . . . [T]he feast [is] the communitarian, ritual and joyful expression of common experiences and longings, centered around a historical fact, past or contemporary."[41] And in an important essay, "On Feasting the Saints," Jesuit liturgiologist John Baldovin comments on feasts of Mary and the saints:

> The most important factor is that feasts are extraordinary. They lift people out of ordinary chronological time. . . . But since feasts are not merely collective visible events but also "total social facts," the Eucharist alone is probably not sufficient for a celebration of a genuine feast. Pulling all the stops out for a celebration means having it in a larger social context, something that the entire community can celebrate meaningfully.[42]

Elsewhere Baldovin refers specifically to the feast of the Virgin of Guadalupe as embodying powerfully both hope and Christian identity:

> No doubt the popularity of various saints will wax and wane according to cultural and historical circumstances, but to abandon the saints for a rationalized Christo-monistic approach to Christian faith is to impoverish not only the liturgical calendar but Christian faith itself. . . . That devotion to the saints has at times in the history of Christianity been perverted does not negate its usefulness. . . . One need not look only to the medieval period to find examples of individuals who provide a powerful focus for the liturgical expression of Christian faith. In our own time the Virgin of Guadalupe has served as an effective rallying point for a whole people's hopes for liberation and justice as well as an anchor for their Christian identity.[43]

As an "exuberant manifestation of life" itself, as an extraordinary occasion lifting "people out of ordinary chronological time," and as providing a firm "anchor for their Christian identity," the feast of the Virgin of Guadalupe is perhaps best understood in light of the Spanish word *fiesta*. Indeed, the concept of fiesta is an important key to understanding Hispanic-Latino identity and life. Again, it is Virgil Elizondo who notes:

The joy of Mexican-Americans is one of their most obvious characteristics. They love their fiestas and everyone is welcome to participate. Neither destitution nor wars can dampen their festive spirit. Even in the midst of suffering, there is a spontaneous joy that is not easily found elsewhere. Outsiders notice it and comment upon it. It is obvious in liturgical gatherings, spontaneous in home life, and carefully planned into commemorations of historical events. In their sorrows, disappointments, reverses, and struggles there is joy. It is evident in the eyes and smiles of their children, in the playfulness of their youth, and in the inner peace and tranquility of their elderly. In the midst of whatever happens—triumph or tragedy—they rise above it to celebrate life.[44]

That such a spirit of fiesta is often associated explicitly with the poor is also significant. Elizondo continues:

The new creation today begins not as a result of logical thinking or planning, but as the consequence of the new joy of being, experienced above all else in the fiestas of the poor and rejected. . . . If the poor can celebrate as no one else, it is precisely because, being deprived of the goods of this world, they are very aware of the one gift that alone counts—awareness that God lives among us and has especially chosen us to be the bearers of the good news of salvation. Everyone else might reject us but it makes little difference when we know that God has chosen us to be his messengers. . . . The fiestas of the poor are truly celebrations: the poor have a *reason* to celebrate. Hence their celebrations are joyful, free, and spontaneous, whereas the celebrations of the rich tend to be more of a tedious chore than a spontaneous joy. . . . [I]t is out of the celebrations of the poor, which will always be a scandal to the rich who are not capable of truly liberative celebrations, that God's universal and barrier-destroying love will erupt for all to experience and enjoy. Participants will rise above what enslaves them and will experience the full liberation of the children of God. They can truly be themselves because they are "at home" in the household of the father—no mask to put on, no "higher ups" to impress, no jealousies to worry about. In this joy we have a foretaste of a final result of the plenary fellowship of humanity. Having experienced the end, we will begin working to make it more of a reality in today's world.[45]

More than a solemnity or feast on the liturgical calendar, the December 12 celebration of the Virgin of Guadalupe is a true fiesta of birth, identity, and life itself for a particular people within a particular social and cultural context. Indeed, perhaps the greatest gift that the Mexican and Mexican American celebration of the Virgin of Guadalupe can offer to the rest of the church is the gift of truly embracing and celebrating the very meaning of life itself as the gracious gift of God. For is it not in their fiestas that the poor themselves can teach the rest of us how truly to celebrate the God who has "brought down the powerful from their thrones, and lifted up the lowly" and who "has filled the hungry with good things, and sent the rich away empty" (Luke 1:52–53)?

Guadalupan Celebrations among Protestants

Although, as we have seen, not included on the calendars of the *Lutheran Book of Worship,* the Lutheran *Libro de Liturgia y Cántico,* or the Episcopal *Book of Common Prayer* (in either the English or Spanish editions), the Virgin of Guadalupe *is* celebrated on December 12 in some Protestant churches in the United States. The recently developed Lutheran liturgical planning series from Augsburg Fortress Press, *Sundays and Seasons,* in its 1997–98 volume for year C, for example, contains the following entry for December 12, called, interestingly enough, the "Day of Our Lady of Guadalupe":

> Many Mexican and Mexican-American Christians, as well as others of Central and South America, commemorate Mary, mother of our Lord on this day. In a famous painting, found on the cloak of Juan Diego, a sixteenth-century Mexican Christian, Mary is depicted as a dark-skinned indigenous native, head bowed in prayer, and pregnant with the Word of God. As a sign of the blending of Aztec and European culture, as a sign of God's identification with the poor and powerless, and as an evangelical sign of the coming of the gospel to the new world, *La Virgen Morenita* ("the little brown Virgin") can be a powerful symbol of Advent longing for the Word of God among the poor in this hemisphere. Images for preaching or prayer on this day might arise from Rev. 12, Luke 1:39–56, or Luther's *Commentary on the Magnificat.*[46]

And *Sundays and Seasons* for year A, 1998–99, continues to point to the possibility of a Lutheran Guadalupan celebration on December 12, still listed as "Day of Our Lady of Guadalupe," by noting that

> this feast is especially observed in Mexico where Our Lady of Guadalupe is their patron saint. In 1531, Juan Diego saw a vision of Mary and told the bishop that she wanted a church to be built on that spot where the cries of the poor and oppressed would be heard. The hopes of the Aztec people were stirred by Mary appearing clothed like one of them. . . . In Mexico people rise early today to offer a morning serenade to Mary, followed by Mass and a festive breakfast. This day provides an opportunity to celebrate the importance of Mary in the church around the world, especially in our Advent observance.[47]

Hence, somewhat through the back door, so to speak, the Virgin of Guadalupe has, in fact, managed to appear on at least one version of the liturgical calendar of the ELCA, in spite of the contrary approach exemplified in *Libro de Liturgia y Cántico*.

More importantly, however, celebrations of the Virgin of Guadalupe on or near December 12, as well as images of her, are present within some Protestant churches in the United States today. Among ELCA Lutherans, one can find examples of this in parishes at least in southern California, three I know of in the greater metropolitan region of Chicago, in Pennsylvania, in Texas, and, one suspects, elsewhere in the United States. Pastor Antonio Cabello of La Iglesia Luterana de San Estéban, Martír, Carpentersville, Illinois, writes of her presence in his parish:

> In our church, which is comprised of both Hispanic (largely Mexican-American and Salvadoran) and Anglo members, there are two statues of Our Lady of Guadalupe, one to the right of the altar in our worship space and another located in a narthex chapel, where people enter the church building. Parishioners often bring flowers and light candles and leave them burning in front of one of these. The feast of Our Lady of Guadalupe on December 12 (including *Las Mañanitas* and the Eucharist) is, with *Las Posadas,* the celebration in our community that brings alive the spirit of Advent and Christmas to our parishioners. The Incarnation of Christ is celebrated not only in light of the theological understanding of the feast of Guadalupe, but on the practical side, it is the color of the Virgin's skin and her prayerful spirituality that lets us call her "blessed among women." The feast of Guadalupe is one of the ways in which we at San Estéban express both our "catholic" heritage and our Hispanic culture.[48]

And one of the ELCA's own four-year liberal arts colleges, Gustavus Adolphus College, in St. Peter, Minnesota, a college with a strong *Swedish American* Lutheran heritage, chose the Virgin of Guadalupe as the overall focus for its annual Advent-Christmas Vespers in December 1994.[49] The program guide for this celebration, including a wide variety of choral music and readings from both European (Latin and Spanish) and indigenous Mexican (even Nahuatl) sources, indicates that the service commenced with "The Virgin of Guadalupe begins in Old Spain" and concluded with "The Virgin of Guadalupe comes to Minnesota." In an introductory note, campus chaplain and ELCA pastor the Reverend Richard Q. Elvee writes:

> The power of the pregnant Virgin asking Native Americans in a native tongue to become bearers of the Good News of Jesus Christ to the Americas was a powerful experience. Native peoples, who were being exterminated by

foreign disease and decimated by oppression and war, became the bearers of the news that Jesus Christ was waiting to be born in the Americas. The oppression of the conquistadors would not destroy the people. God's messenger, the mother of Jesus, came to give hope and strength to a people wandering in despair. These conquered people were to teach their European conquerors the meaning of God's call of faith. These seemingly hopeless people were to become the hope of a hemisphere. With Jesus waiting to be born in the Americas, the Mexican people were to give him a home.[50]

At least among Episcopalians involved with Hispanic-Latino ministries in the United States the situation appears to be similar and is undoubtedly even more pronounced in some areas of the country. In California alone, for example, images of the Virgin of Guadalupe are present within some parishes in San Francisco, in at least two parishes in Oakland, many throughout the Episcopal diocese of El Camino Real, and several in the "cathedral center" of Los Angeles. Professor Lizette Larson-Miller, who teaches liturgy at the Church Divinity School of the Pacific in Berkeley offers the following description of her own 1998 experience of a Guadalupan celebration at an Episcopal parish, Pueblo Nuevo, in Los Angeles:

Pueblo Nuevo is a small mission church of the diocese of Los Angeles (Episcopal), founded in 1985 by the Rev. Philip Lance, who remains as rector. It began as a training center and secondhand store where recent immigrants (primarily from Central America) and those who for several reasons may have had great difficulty getting a job, could receive job-training and a recommendation for a permanent job. The liturgical life consisted of a Sunday "Mass in the Grass"—a eucharistic liturgy in MacArthur Park in central Los Angeles offered for and with the homeless and others who gravitated to this scrubby opening in an equally gritty urban area. That weekly gathering eventually expanded to include feast days and other celebrations, finally finding a more or less permanent home in a storefront location between the thrift store and the offices of Pueblo Nuevo's janitorial service. All of the Sunday liturgies and the other celebrations of note from the larger liturgical calendar and the cycles of individual members' lives are monolingual (Spanish), often blending the local traditions of several regions of Mexico with traditions from El Salvador, Nicaragua, and Guatemala. On Sundays, the Spanish language *Book of Common Prayer* and lectionary are used. On feast days such as December 12th the written resources give way to oral sources and corporate memory in celebrating the feasts close to the lives of the gathered community. What follows is a description of a single celebration in 1998 (Dec. 12th fell on a Saturday that year), although the pattern remains constant for other years.

    Our Lady of Guadalupe is commemorated in an early morning gathering at Pueblo Nuevo, as it is commonly in many other places. The "congregation" (here three to four times larger than the Sunday gathering and so gathering the regular worshipping community and many others) gathered about 4:00 am in the storefront chapel to rehearse and prepare for the procession. While the priests oversaw some of the preparations (in addition to the Rev. Philip Lance, Pueblo Nuevo also has the Rev. Zoila Manzañeres), particularly in the gathering of things necessary for the later Eucharist, it was more or less individuals or small groups who took responsibility for giving out individual candles and song books (congregational copies of *Flor y Canto* were used by many present, others simply knew the music and words by heart),[51] gathering the donations of flowers from those arriving (the flower of choice is the red rose), preparing and decorating the "float" on which the statue of the Virgin was to be carried, tuning guitars and generally trying to keep warm in the unheated, predawn space. Another group, unseen at the time, had been preparing the breakfast which would follow the liturgy at the park—stored in vans parked around MacArthur Park. Time and ritual flow are both relative concepts at Pueblo Nuevo. When it appeared that enough time had passed and enough people had gathered the group was called to focus with a simple *"Vamos,"* the platform (a decorated board with metal fastenings through which two poles were inserted) was raised and carried by four parishioners (two men and two women) and behind that the musicians (three guitarists) and everyone else fell into place.

The group took a while to form itself into a procession on the somewhat narrow sidewalks of downtown Los Angeles, but this was obscured by the ongoing singing of Cantos de la Virgen, chosen by the guitarists who were assisted by one person calling out the appropriate number in the songbook for those who needed the words. The choices included the most popular for the day: *Buenos Días, Paloma Blanca, Con Guitarras y Trompetas, Ave Luz Mañanera, Las Apariciones Guadalupanas* and of course *Las Mañanitas a la Virgen de Guadalupe.* Although it was close to 5:00 am when the procession actually started, it was still dark on the streets of Los Angeles, so the hand-held candles were necessary to see the words (although most people knew all the verses by heart). MacArthur Park is about five blocks from Pueblo Nuevo, and as the procession made its way to the park, we attracted the attention of everyone who was making their way to work, or waking up on the streets, for the day. Several of the latter group fell into the procession too, so it grew on the way to the park. When we arrived, the statue of La Virgen was placed in a prominent spot on a slight hillside which formed a small natural amphitheater for what followed. The story of Juan Diego and the apparition was told by a group of parishioners who took the part of characters in the story (Juan Diego, Mary, the bishop, a narrator—each of whom knew their part by memory) and the retelling of the story lasted about 15–20 minutes. This was followed by a brief homily or commentary on what the story and the event meant today to two individuals who responded to the invitation from the priest (who stepped forward for the first time at this point) for people to share their sense of the day. He added to their testimonies (which were touching, especially in light of the difficult life which many of the people lived) a weaving together of the story of the apparition with the theology of incarnation in keeping with the Advent and Christmas season. The Eucharist then commenced (*Las Apariciones Guadalupanas* having functioned as the synaxis [service of the Word]), which coincided with the sun rising over the park and the gathering there. Following the eucharistic prayer, communion and a regular conclusion (blessing), we sang a few more songs (including *Adiós, Reina del Cielo*) and broke the morning fast with tamales and hot chocolate which appeared from the parked vans, having been prepared at a number of parishioners' homes over the last week. The gathering began to break up about 7:00–7:30, as people left to go to work or return to their original plans for the day. The statue was returned to Pueblo Nuevo (by van) and remained in the chapel for the Sunday liturgies of Advent the next day (on the platform and adorned with flowers).

It may be worth pointing out that the majority of parishioners at Pueblo Nuevo are very poor, recent and often undocumented immigrants. . . . Only a minority of them are literate (in either Spanish or English) which makes the repetitive quality of the music and texts a necessity for participation. The amount and generosity of food (freely distributed to anyone who asked) was quite astounding and reflected the reality that this feast cost these people dearly. The only other ritual events of the season which came close to matching this in attendance and scope was the celebration of the *Posadas*. The regular Advent and Christmas liturgies were much smaller by comparison and lacked the excitement and expansive participation that this celebration engendered.

The above descriptions certainly suggest that when the Virgin of Guadalupe is celebrated within Protestant Christian communities, there is really nothing to distinguish those "Protestant" celebrations from Roman Catholic ones. They also suggest, even in spite of the lack of Guadalupe's official recognition on the liturgical calendars or within the liturgical books of Episcopalians and ELCA Lutherans, that where pastors and priests are sensitive to, and embracing of, the cultural-religious roots of their people, the Virgin of Guadalupe can be integrated and received into an overall Protestant liturgical context.

Conclusion

This chapter has provided a brief overview of the December 12 celebrations—both liturgical and popular—of the Virgin of Guadalupe. If the origins and development of the liturgical feast on December 12, rather than September 8, are rather obscure before the mid–seventeenth century, there is no question that the feast itself rapidly became and remains the central Marian feast—if not *the* central feast—on the liturgical calendar for Mexican and Mexican American Catholics, a feast properly understood as a true fiesta of life and identity. In addition, even though the mid-Advent location of the feast, together with its preparatory novena among Mexicans and Mexican Americans, tends to shift the emphasis away from the eschatologically oriented official Advent to a more Marian-centered season, within several other Christian liturgical traditions, both past and present, Advent or its equivalent does have a kind of overall Marian character. And, as increased attention is given to the ranking and placement of Marian feasts on the Roman calendar, and especially their relationship to Scripture and Christology, proposals for reintegrating the Annunciation and the Visitation into a reconceived Advent, somewhat consistent with the earlier Roman practice of the Advent Ember Days, correspond rather closely to the emphasis already present within the Advent of Hispanic-Latino popular religion. If I am not yet willing to abandon the eschatological Advent of the current liturgy of both Roman Catholics and Protestants, I do think that the *sensus fidelium* about Advent and Mary expressed in this popular religion just might be trying to tell us something even biblical about the proper location of a Marian emphasis in the liturgical life of the church, an emphasis clearly subordinated to Christology!

The Virgin of Guadalupe is also beginning to appear more frequently within the changing cultural context of Protestantism in the United States, where her image is present and her feast day celebrated in some, primarily Episcopalian and Lutheran, communities. While some, probably many, would see such Protestant attempts at Guadalupan integration and reception negatively, as either a way to "appease former Catholics"[52] or even as a way to do "evangelism" or to proselytize among Hispanic-Latino Catholics, the issue may really be whether American Protestantism itself is able to embrace critically and integrate into itself Hispanic-Latino popular religion with its decidedly distinct spirituality and culturally conditioned forms of faith expression. Obviously, at least in some places, there are those who believe that Protestantism *can* do so.

The question here, however, is a decidedly *theological* one. That is, are the image, the narrative, and the feast of the Virgin of Guadalupe compatible with an evangelical or Protestant theology and worldview, in which Mariology and Mary herself have not played much of a role since the early sixteenth century? In other words, can and does the Virgin of Guadalupe speak to Protestant Christianity in the Americas as well? It is to this we turn in the final chapter of this study.

Notes

1. John Paul II, *Ecclesia in America* (Boston: St. Paul Books and Media, 1999), para. 11.

2. Various advocations of Mary, complete with feast days, for example, are popular throughout Mexico and Central and South America. Together with the Virgin of Guadalupe in Mexico, the following are to be noted in other countries: Our Lady of Luján (Argentina); Our Lady of Copacabana (Bolivia); Our Lady "Aparecida" (Brazil); Our Lady of Carmel of the Maipú (Chile); Our Lady of Chiquinquirá (Colombia); Our Lady of the Angels (Costa Rica); Our Lady of Charity of El Cobre (Cuba); Our Lady of "La Altagracia" (Dominican Republic); Our Lady of Quinche (Ecuador); Our Lady of Peace (El Salvador); Our Lady of the Rosary (Guatemala); Our Lady of Suyapa (Honduras); Our Lady of the Immaculate Conception of El Viejo (Nicaragua); The Immaculate Conception (Panama); Our Lady of the Miracles of Caacupé (Paraguay); Our Lady of Mercy (Peru); Our Lady of Divine Providence (Puerto Rico); Our Lady of the Thirty-Three (Uruguay); and Our Lady of Coromoto (Venezuela). For brief descriptions of each, see Oficina regional del sureste para el ministerio hispano, *Las advocationes marianas en la religiosidad popular latinoamericana, Documentaciones sureste* 5 (Feb. 2, 1996). But even this should only be taken as a representative and not a comprehensive list, since cities and villages throughout the Americas, even in Mexico (e.g., Our Lady of El Pueblocito del Querétaro in Querétaro, and Our Lady of San Juan de los Lagos in Jalisco, Guadalajara, with a major national shrine, Our Lady of San Juan del Valle, in San Juan, Texas) have their own individual Marian images, feast days, and devotions in addition to those that are recognized and celebrated nationally. For the Guadalupan feast in Canada, see the essays in *Celebrate!* 39, 6 (2000). This particular issue is entitled *Guadalupe: Mother and Patroness of All America.*

3. On the historical development of Marian feasts in general, see Kilian McDonnell, "The Marian Liturgical Tradition," in *Between Memory and Hope: Readings on the Liturgical Year,* ed. Maxwell E. Johnson (Collegeville, Minn.: Liturgical Press, Pueblo, 2000), 385–400; and Pierre Jounel, "The Veneration of Mary," in *The Church at Prayer,* vol. 4, *The Liturgy and Time,* ed. A. G. Martimort (Collegeville, Minn.: Liturgical Press, 1986), 130–50. For a theological interpretation of the development of Marian feasts and Marian theology in relationship to Trinitarian and Christological issues, see esp. the classic study of Joseph Jungmann, "The Defeat of Teutonic Arianism and the Revolution in Religious Culture in the Early Middle Ages," in *Pastoral Liturgy* (New York: Herder & Herder, 1962), 1–101.

4. See Aidan Kavanagh, *On Liturgical Theology* (Collegeville, Minn.: Liturgical Press, Pueblo, 1984), 73–95.

5. Roberto Goizueta, *Caminemos con Jesús: Toward a Hispanic/Latino Theology of Accompaniment* (Maryknoll, N.Y.: Orbis Books, 1995), 27–28 n. 26.

6. See the detailed doctoral dissertation of J. J. Salazar, "'¿No estoy yo aqui, que soy tu madre?' Investigación Teológica-Bíblica-Litúrgica acerca de La Nueva Liturgia de Nuestra Señora de Guadalupe," vol. 1 (S.T.D. diss., Pontificio Istituto Liturgico, 1981), 141–202. This dissertation is notoriously difficult to obtain in the

United States, and several attempts to locate it through interlibrary loan proved unsuccessful. I am therefore most grateful to Father Francisco Schulte, OSB, of Saint John's Abbey, Collegeville, Minn., for lending me his personal copy of vol. 1. Two other volumes are available.

7. While the date of December 8 for this feast in the West places it exactly nine months before the September 8 feast of Mary's Nativity, the choice of December 9 in the East was made, it appears, for a theological reason. That is, only with regard to Christ can there be a perfect nine-month interval between his conception (the feast of the Annunciation on March 25) and his birth (December 25). In the East, the intervals between the conceptions and births of others, including Mary, are thus symbolically less than a perfect nine months.

8. On the development of this feast, see Jounel, "Veneration of Mary," 139–40; and McDonnell, "Marian Liturgical Tradition," 390–91.

9. See Fidel de Jesús Chauvet, "Historia del Culto Guadalupano," in *Album Conmemorative del 450 Aniversario de las Apariciones de Nuestra Señora de Guadalupe* (Mexico City: Buena Nueva, 1981), 34. Chauvet refers here to a sixteenth-century journal of a Juan Bautista.

10. See Bernardino de Sahagún, *Psalmodia Christiana* (Christian psalmody), trans. A. J. O. Anderson (Salt Lake City: University of Utah Press, 1993), 353-359.

11. On all of this see Salazar, "¿No estoy yo aqui?" 141–202.

12. Jean-Pierre Ruiz, "The Bible and U.S. Hispanic American Theological Discourse," in *From the Heart of the People,* ed. Orlando O. Espín and Miguel Diaz (New York: Orbis, 1999), 112–13.

13. On this, see Salazar, "¿No estoy yo aqui?" 1: 174–202.

14. *Misal Romano,* 2d ed. (Mexico City: Obra Nacional de la Buena Prensa, 2001), 596–97; and *Leccionario,* vol. 3, *Propio de los Santos y Otras Misas* (Mexico City: Obra Nacional de la Buena Prensa, 2002), 172–74.

15. Bishops' Committee on the Liturgy, *Newsletter 23: Feast of Our Lady of Guadalupe* (Washington, D.C.: National Conference of Catholic Bishops, 1988), 45; and Bishops' Committee on the Liturgy, *Newsletter 24: Feast of Our Lady of Guadalupe and New Liturgical Texts* (Washington, D.C.: National Conference of Catholic Bishops, 1988), 5–6.

16. See Dom Gaspar LeFebvre, OSB, *Saint Andrew Daily Missal* (Bruges, Belgium: Abbey of Saint Andrew, 1958), 1927–30.

17. See *Misal Romano,* 596–97, and *Leccionario,* 3: 172–74. Where the texts are identical in the liturgical books for the United States, I have quoted from the approved English translations presented in the Bishops' Committee on the Liturgy, *Feast of Our Lady of Guadalupe.* Where they are different, I have indicated this either by a footnote or by a parenthetical insertion in the text.

18. This particular opening prayer appears only in the Mexican liturgical books and not in the United States edition. The above is my own translation of "Padre de misericordia, que has puesto a este pueblo tuyo bajo la especial protección de la siempre Virgen María de Guadalupe, Madre de tu Hijo, concédenos, por su intercesión, profundizar en nuestra fe y buscar el progreso de nuestra patria por caminos de justicia y de paz. Por nuestro Señor Jesucristo."

19. Bishops' Committee on the Liturgy, *Feast of Our Lady of Guadalupe,* 45.

20. I realize that this too is rather ambiguous, and one can certainly interpret this phrase as implying no more than that the Virgin Mary is present and venerated in a particular way at Tepeyac. But the problem of interpretation would have been avoided altogether if the allusion to the event had not been made at all.

21. I am reminded here of a comment once made by noted French liturgical scholar Bernard Botte, OSB, with respect to the now optional memorial of Our Lady of Lourdes on February 11. Botte wrote that "the spirit of welcome which the Church has toward some divine manifestations which she wishes to guarantee is here carried to the maximum" (B. Botte, "La liturgie mariale en Occident," in *Maria: Études sur la Sainte Vierge*, ed., D'Hubert du Manoir (Paris: Beauchesne, 1952), 1: 229); English translation in McDonnell, "Marian Liturgical Tradition," 391). In the pre–Vatican II *Missale Romanum,* the missal known to Botte at that time, the opening prayer for this feast made explicit reference to the apparition itself: "O God, by the Immaculate Conception of the Virgin You prepared a worthy habitation for Your Son; we humbly pray You, that we who *celebrate the feast of the Apparition of the same holy Virgin,* may obtain health both of soul and body" (LeFebvre, *Saint Andrew Daily Missal,* 1134), emphasis added. In the current version, however, such references are absent and the prayer has a more general Marian tone: "God of mercy, we celebrate the feast of Mary, the sinless mother of God. May her prayers help us to rise above our human weakness" *The Sacramentary of the Roman Missal* [Collegeville, Minn.: Liturgical Press, 1985], 565).

22. For an example of this novena, see Celestina Castro, MC-M, *Novena a La Santísima Virgen de Guadalupe, Reina de las Américas* (San Antonio, Texas: Mexican American Cultural Center, n.d.).

23. For a brief description, see *Faith Expressions of Hispanics in the Southwest,* rev. ed. (San Antonio, Texas: Mexican American Cultural Center, 1990), 12–13.

24. Virgil Elizondo, "Living Faith: Resistance and Survival," 11–12, in Virgil Elizondo and Timothy Matovina, *Mestizo Worship: A Pastoral Approach to Liturgical Ministry* (Collegeville, Minn.: Liturgical Press, 1998),

25. See Raymond Brown's delightful short commentaries on the infancy narratives of Matthew and Luke in *An Adult Christ at Christmas* (Collegeville, Minn.: Liturgical Press, 1978).

26. On this, see esp. J. Neil Alexander, *Waiting for the Coming: The Liturgical Meaning of Advent, Christmas, and Epiphany* (Washington, D.C.: Pastoral Press, 1993), 7–27. See also Bryan D. Spinks, "Revising the Advent-Christmas-Epiphany Cycle in the Church of England," *Studia Liturgica* 17 (1987): 166–75.

27. Virgil Elizondo, *Guadalupe: Mother of the New Creation,* (Maryknoll, N.Y.: Orbis, 1997), 95; emphasis added.

28. See Mother Mary and Kallistos Ware, *The Festal Menaion* (London: Faber & Faber, 1969), 164–98.

29. Pierre Jounel, "The Christmas Season," in *The Church at Prayer,* vol. 4, *The Liturgy and Time,* ed. A. G. Martimort (Collegeville, Minn.: Liturgical Press, 1986), 93.

30. In early Christianity March 25 was one of two calendrical dates assigned to the historical date of Christ's Passion as the equivalent to 14 Nisan. In some communities April 6 was recognized as the corresponding date.

31. Conferencia Episcopal Española, *Missale Hispano-Mozarabicum* (Barcelona, 1994), 34, 136–42.

32. On Ember Days, see Thomas J. Talley, "The Origins of the Ember Days: An Inconclusive Postscript," in *Rituels: Mélanges offerts à Pierre-Marie Gy, O.P.,* ed. Paul DeClerck and Eric Palazzo (Paris: Éditions du Cerf, 1990), 465–72.

33. *Sacrosanctum concilium* 5 103. English translation from Austin Flannery, *Vatican Collection,* vol. 1, *Vatican Council II: The Conciliar and Post Conciliar Documents,* new rev. ed. (Collegeville, Minn.: Liturgical Press, 1975), 29.

34. Shawn Madigan, "Do Marian Festivals Image 'That Which the Church Hopes to Be?'" *Worship* 65, 3 (1991): 201.

35. Madigan, "Marian Festivals," 202.

36. See also John Samaha, "Mary in the Liturgical Calendar," *Emmanuel* 100, 1 (1994): 45–47. Bryan Spinks also suggests that a couple of Advent Sundays in the West might be devoted to the "Annunciations." See his "Revising the Cycle," 172–73.

37. On the interpretation of Rev. 12, see Raymond Brown, "The Woman in Revelation 12," in *Mary in the New Testament,* ed. Raymond Brown et al. (New York: Paulist Press and Philadelphia: Fortress Press, 1978), 219–39.

38. Rubén Martínez, "The Undocumented Virgin," in *Goddess of the Americas/La Diosa de Las Americas,* ed. Ana Castillo (New York: Riverhead Books, 1996), 106–9. For a description of events at the plaza and basilica on a Sunday outside of December, see Eryk Hanut, *The Road to Guadalupe: A Modern Pilgrimage to the Goddess of the Americas* (New York: Tarcher/Putnam, 2001), 118–26.

39. See the video *Fiesta!* (Mahwah, N.J.: Paulist Press, 1998); and Virgil Elizondo and Timothy Matovina, *San Fernando Cathedral: Soul of the City* (Maryknoll, N.Y.: Orbis, 1998).

40. Goizueta, *Caminemos con Jesús,* 45–46.

41. Juan Mateos, *Beyond Conventional Christianity* (Manila: East Asian Pastoral Institute, 1974), 225, 279, as quoted by John Baldovin, "On Feasting the Saints," in *Between Memory and Hope,* ed. Johnson, 375–76.

42. Baldovin, "On Feasting the Saints," 382–83.

43. John Baldovin, "The Liturgical Year: Calendar for a Just Community," in *Between Memory and Hope,* ed. Johnson, 436–37.

44. Virgil Elizondo, *Galilean Journey: The Mexican-American Promise* (New York: Orbis Books, 2000), 120.

45. Elizondo, *Galilean Journey,* 122.

46. *Sundays and Seasons: Worship Planning Guide. Year of Luke, Cycle C: 1997–1998* (Minneapolis: Augsburg Fortress 1997), 57. In light of the lectionary readings assigned to the festival in the Mexican liturgical books, it is unfortunate that Gal. 4:4–7 is not suggested. Interestingly enough, both Gal. 4 and Luke 2:39–56 are the readings for the August 15 Lesser Festival of Mary, Mother of Our Lord, in the *Lutheran Book of Worship.*

47. *Sundays and Seasons: Worship Planning Guide. Year of Matthew, Cycle A: 1998–1999* (Minneapolis: Augsburg Fortress, 1998), 56. Other volumes of *Sundays and Seasons* for 2000 and 2001 tend to copy either of the above two descriptions

48. The Rev. Antonio Cabello, private conversation, July 2001. For a Lutheran

interpretation of lighting votive candles before images of Mary and the saints in a Hispanic–Latino cultural context, see Ivis LaRiviere-Mestre, "Field Work Manual for Seminarians and Pastors Who Want to Do Outreach with Latino/Hispanic/ Mestizo Families" (October 2000), 14.

49. "Christmas in Christ Chapel, December 2, 3, and 4, 1994" (St. Peter, Minn.: Gustavus Adolphus College, 1994).

50. "Christmas in Christ Chapel," 1.

51. *Flor y Canto* is published by Oregon Catholic Press (OCP) and contains most of the familiar music used at this celebration and on Sunday mornings. Other music is remembered from celebrations representing the various local traditions, and at times newer compositions published by OCP are also used. The majority of traditional Marian songs, however, are available in *Flor y Canto.*

52. According to Margaret Ramirez, religion writer for the *Los Angeles Times,* this is precisely the reaction of at least one Protestant pastor in Los Angeles who is against any adaptation of the Virgin of Guadalupe within a Protestant context. E-mail conversation, July 19, 2000.

5

The Virgin of Guadalupe
in Ecumenical Perspective

In a highly polemical anti-Catholic book from the early 1960s with the rather suggestive title *Romanism in the Light of Scripture,* Dwight L. Pentecost offers the following description and interpretation of what is most likely the famous image on Juan Diego's tilma in the Basilica of Our Lady of Guadalupe in Mexico City:

> Some years ago it was my privilege to travel through the land of Mexico with my brother, who has been a missionary there for some years. We visited a number of the outstanding shrines and edifices erected by the Roman system to the praise and glory of Mary. On one occasion my brother said to me, "If you want to see the theology of Mary in the Roman Church, come with me to a church where over the altar is a scene which, more than volumes could say, reveals their actual belief concerning the position of Mary." He took me downtown and into a rather large church in the center of the old part of the city. We walked forward to the altar where we could look up and see a great painting based upon the twelfth chapter of the Book of the Revelation. . . . The chapter gives a number of cues to let us know that the Apostle John is depicting the nation Israel under the form of a woman. The man child produced by that woman was none other than the Saviour, the Lord Jesus Christ. But there over the altar, as the center of attention in that edifice, was the scene of a great blazing sun, with a picture of the Virgin Mary in the midst of that sun. According to this artist's conception, the woman of Revelation 12 was none other than Mary. Under that blazing sun, in lesser glory and light, was painted a moon and on that moon was the face of the Lord Jesus Christ. Mary was standing in that sun with her feet upon the head of the Lord Jesus Christ and He was bowed in submission and subservience to Mary who stood above Him. . . . Mary was elevated above . . . the Son of God Himself. She was occupying the place of pre-eminence and authority as the sun of the day rules over the moon and the stars of the night.[1]

The fact that in the Guadalupan image it is, of course, not Christ but an angel at her feet[2] notwithstanding, such anti-Catholic interpretations of the Virgin of Guadalupe, and of other popular images of the Virgin Mary within Hispanic-Latino Catholicism and culture, for that matter, have long been characteristic approaches of Latin American Protestantism in general. United Methodist theologian Justo González writes:

> The *Virgen de la Caridad del Cobre* may be very important for Cuban identity, and certainly for Cuban popular Catholicism; for Cuban popular Protestantism, however, she is at best a matter of historical and ethnographic interest, and at worst an idol the devil has produced to lead the Cuban people astray. . . . [I]t is also true that still today for most Protestant Latinos—even those of Mexican origin—rejecting Guadalupe is an essential mark of being truly Christian! Indeed, in some Protestant churches I have heard renderings of the stories of Caridad and Guadalupe that can only be interpreted as counter-myths—stories of how the devil invented these and other national "Virgins" for his own satanic purposes.[3]

Given this historical background of Protestant polemic, it is probably not surprising at all to discover that there was considerable debate among the members of the subcommittees involved in the production of the recent 1997 ELCA Lutheran Hispanic-Latino liturgical resource, *Libro de Liturgia y Cántico,* about whether to include on its liturgical calendar an optional commemoration of the Virgin of Guadalupe on December 12. I am told by a reliable source that including her was initially considered and that some advocated strongly for it because of her traditional importance as a symbol of, at least, Mexican and Central American cultural-religious identity and, not least, as a concrete expression and religious icon of God's identification with the poor and oppressed. But others objected strongly to her inclusion on diverse grounds: some on the basis of its implied "Marian apparition theology" as foreign to, and inconsistent with, Lutheran theology; others because it gave too much preference to what was considered to be a uniquely *Mexican* devotion and symbol with little perceived relevance to the broader Hispanic-Latino community; and still others because it was thought that members of some communities would be so strongly opposed to Guadalupe that they might actually refuse altogether to purchase and use the book if it were to include her.[4] To this may be added what other sources have told me was a controversy in southern California a few years ago over the Virgin of Guadalupe among some Hispanic-Latino Lutheran pastors and congregations. Apparently, some congregations were hanging a banner of Guadalupe in their churches and occasionally processing in the streets behind it. According to one pastor at least, the men in her congregation had actually begun to receive communion after the banner had been brought into and installed in the sanctuary. But during one of the semimonthly meetings of Hispanic-Latino Lutheran clergy in the area, the parish where the group was meeting had a framed picture of the Virgin of Guadalupe leaning at the base of the altar, and because of it, several of the pastors present refused to participate in the liturgy being celebrated or even enter the worship space. Feelings about the Virgin of Guadalupe—pro or con—obviously run quite deep.

But if the Virgin of Guadalupe has been, traditionally, such a sign of division between Catholics and Protestants within the history of Hispanic-Latino Christianity that the mere possibility of an *optional* liturgical commemoration of her on December 12 can cause such debate, and if the presence of her image in a sanctuary can create such a negative response on the part of some, it needs to be asked if this type of division and opposition must remain the case any longer. Justo González himself narrates the following anecdote from his own past experience as a Protestant seminarian, which suggests that a theological reevaluation of Guadalupe within Protestantism might well be in order today:

> When I was growing up, I was taught to think of such things as the Virgin of Guadalupe as pure superstition. Therefore, I remember how surprised I was at the reaction of a Mexican professor in seminary when one of my classmates made some disparaging remarks about Guadalupe. The professor, who was as Protestant as they come and who often stooped because he was then elderly, drew himself up, looked at my friend in the eye, and said: "Young man, in this class you are free to say anything you please. You may say anything about me. You certainly are welcome to say anything you wish about the pope and the priests. *But don't you touch my little Virgin!*" At that time, I took this to be an atavism of an old man who had been fed superstition in his mother's milk. But now I know better. What he was saying was that, in spite of all that our North American friends had told us, in spite of the veneer of superstition, in spite of the horrendous things that took place every Sunday morning as people crawled to the shrine of Guadalupe, there was in there a kernel of truth that was very dear to his heart—and all the dearer, since so much of the religiosity that he knew, both Catholic and Protestant, denied it. For generation upon generation of oppressed Indian people, told by word and deed that they were inferior, the Virgin has been a reminder that there is vindication for the Juan Diegos. And that is indeed part of the gospel message, even if has not always been part of our own message.[5]

The problem, as González notes further, is precisely the relationship of religious faith and culture. Does one need to deny one's very culture in becoming or being Protestant, especially when that culture has been shaped to a large extent by Roman Catholicism? He writes elsewhere that

> there is in much of Latino Protestantism a sense of cultural alienation that is
> very similar to that produced by the much earlier Spanish colonization of the
> Americas. Just as Spanish Roman Catholicism told our native ancestors that
> their religion, and therefore much of their culture, was the work of the devil,
> so has Anglo Protestantism told us that the Catholic religion of our more
> immediate ancestors, and therefore much of our culture, must be rejected.
> . . . Just as native populations can accuse the earlier Catholic "evangelization"
> of undermining their culture and destroying their identity, so do some ac-
> cuse the later Protestant "evangelization" of similar misdeeds. In many ways,
> just as for many natives in the sixteenth century it was necessary to abandon
> much of their cultural traditions in the process of becoming Catholic, so are
> many Latinas and Latinos forced away from their cultural roots as they be-
> come Protestant. And in both cases, this cultural alienation is depicted as
> good news! . . . Yet many Latino/a Protestants refuse to abandon their cul-
> ture and its traditions.[6]

Consequently, he continues: "Caridad, Guadalupe, and novenas are not part
of my more immediate tradition. Yet they are part of my culture. Does that
mean that, like my native ancestors five centuries ago when faced by the
initial Catholic 'evangelization,' I must renounce my cultural heritage in
order to affirm my Christianity? I do not believe so."[7]

In this light, the story told by the pastor who spoke of the men in her
parish beginning to receive communion after a banner of the Virgin of
Guadalupe was installed in their worship space comes as no surprise to me
at all. Within Roman Catholic Hispanic-Latino contexts, for example, the
story is frequently told of a newly arrived priest either removing or refus-
ing to install a typical Latino-style crucifix in the sanctuary. To this priest,
one Mexican American man supposedly responded to the effect, "If you
don't want our *Cristo,* perhaps you don't want us either!" Undoubtedly part
of the dynamic at work in this particular congregation regarding the
Guadalupan banner was that this congregation's willingness to accept the
image of Guadalupe really signified their own willingness to embrace and
welcome these men. In other words, the congregation's worship space had
now become "theirs" because the presence of the image of the Virgin of
Guadalupe identified it as their "home" where they would be welcome.

For Protestantism in general, however, I would like to suggest that the
question is actually much broader than cultural hospitality or multicultural
affirmation. That is, if it is the increasing presence of Hispanic-Latinos
within American Protestantism that may well provide the catalyst or suggest the need for Protestants to investigate the Virgin of Guadalupe theologically, the issue is not simply, or even ultimately, a Hispanic-Latino one

alone related to questions of the relationship between culture and faith. Rather, given the kinds of contemporary Roman Catholic theological analyses summarized in chapter 3, the theological question is whether the narrative and image of the Virgin of Guadalupe has a message for Protestants in general, especially, but not exclusively, for those within those particular Protestant traditions like Lutheranism and Anglicanism that share with Roman Catholicism much of the common liturgical and sacramental heritage of Western Christianity.

As we saw in the previous chapter, images and celebrations of the Virgin of Guadalupe obviously exist in a variety of Protestant congregations in the United States. But how might that phenomenon be interpreted theologically? That is, are the image and narrative of the Virgin of Guadalupe consistent with a Protestant or evangelical theological-confessional perspective, which in its classic Lutheran formulation finds its center in Article IV of the Augsburg Confession of 1530? This article reads:

> Our churches also teach that [human beings] cannot be justified before God by their own strength, merits, or works but are freely justified for Christ's sake through faith when they believe that they are received into favor and that their sins are forgiven on account of Christ, who by his death made satisfaction for our sins. This faith God imputes for righteousness in his sight (Rom. 3.4).[8]

For Protestants, and, increasingly for Roman Catholics as well, especially in light of the 1999 Lutheran–Roman Catholic *Joint Declaration on the Doctrine of Justification by Faith,* are the image and narrative of the Virgin of Guadalupe compatible with this doctrine, a doctrine that now "is to serve" ecumenically "as a criterion which constantly orients all the teaching and practice of our churches to Christ, whom alone we ultimately trust as the one Mediator (1 Tim. 2:5–6) through whom God in the Holy Spirit gives himself and pours out his saving gifts"?[9] In other words, is the Virgin of Guadalupe "of the gospel" and, if so, is it then possible to be both an evangelical Christian, a Protestant centered in the gospel (understood classically in terms of justification by grace alone, through faith alone, on account of Christ alone), and a Guadalupano/a at the same time? It is to this we now turn.

The Virgin of Guadalupe and Protestant Theologians

For a Roman Catholic like Virgil Elizondo there is, not surprisingly, no contradiction whatsoever between being a Guadalupano/a and being simultaneously an evangelical Christian. Elizondo himself refers to this relationship indirectly in writing that "Protestants tell me: 'But Christ alone is necessary for salvation.' And I say to them: 'You are absolutely right. That is precisely what makes Guadalupe so precious. Precisely because she is not necessary, she is so special! She is a gift of God's love.'"[10] And, in his book *Guadalupe: Mother of the New Creation,* he addresses this issue directly, claiming:

> What most people who have not experienced the Guadalupe tradition cannot understand is that to be a Guadalupano/a (one in whose heart Our Lady of Guadalupe reigns) is to be *an evangelical Christian.* It is to say that the Word became flesh in Euro-Native America and began its unifying task—"that all may be one." In Our Lady of Guadalupe, Christ became American. Yet because the gospel through Guadalupe was such a powerful force in the creation and formulation of the national consciousness and identity of the people as expressed, understood, and celebrated through their art, music, poetry, religious expression, preaching, political discourse, and cultural-religious expressions, its original meaning—that is, the original gospel of Jesus expressed in and through native Mexican terms—has become eclipsed. This has led some modern-day Christians—especially those whose Christianity is expressed through U.S. cultural terms—to see Guadalupe as pagan or as something opposed to the gospel. It is certainly true that just as the gospel was co-opted and domesticated by Constantine and subsequent "Christian" powers, so has Guadalupe been co-opted and domesticated by the powerful of Mexico, including the church. Yet neither the initial gospel nor the gospel expressed through Guadalupe has lost its original intent or force, a force that is being rediscovered as the poor, the marginated, and the rejected reclaim these foundational gospels as their chief weapons of liberation and as sources of lifestyles that are different from those engendered by ecclesial and social structures that have marginalized, oppressed, and dehumanized them.[11]

But if a theologian like Elizondo can say this from within a Roman Catholic perspective, can a Protestant theologian make a similar claim today?

Protestant theologians who have written directly on the Virgin of Guadalupe are certainly not numerous. Indeed, no Protestant theologian, to my knowledge, has until now written a book-length treatment of the subject. Those few who have written on or referred to her, however, have tended to be quite positive in their overall assessments. As noted above, Justo González has written that "the Virgin [of Guadalupe] has been a reminder that there is vindication for the Juan Diegos. And that is indeed part of the gospel message, even if has not always been part of our own message." And, as referred to at the beginning of chapter 3, Lutheran Alberto Pereyra has seen in the Guadalupan event and narrative a paradigm for the contemporary Christian spiritual journey, writing that: "People can destroy all arguments about the historical presence of the Lady in the Tepeyac, but they cannot destroy the symbol, the devotion to her.... We need to be flexible and walk to the Tepeyac of our own spiritual experience.... The challenge to welcome, learn from, and incorporate Indian spirituality is still before us."[12]

While others, like former Lutheran (now Eastern Orthodox) Jaroslav Pelikan, make only passing reference to Guadalupe as an example of a "multicultural Mary," with close affinities to the various Black Madonnas of African and European art,[13] still others, like Anglican John Macquarrie, in his ecumenically sensitive book on Mariology, *Mary for All Christians,* see in the continued Mexican devotion to Guadalupe a possible "sign of contradiction" against the values of "the neglect of the personal, the assertiveness and the individualism of the modern world."[14] With specific reference to the modern basilica of Guadalupe in Mexico City, where a moving walkway, behind the main altar and invisible to those present at liturgical celebrations in the main part of the basilica, now moves pilgrims (and tourists) slowly past the image of the Virgin, Macquarrie asks:

> Are those worshippers . . . merely survivors from a past age, unenlightened by the intellectual and social progress of the past two hundred and fifty years? Are they like the old saint whom Nietzsche's Zarathustra met in a secluded valley, and exclaimed: "Can it indeed be possible? This old saint in his forest hath not yet heard that God is dead!" Or is this much too simple an answer to the question? It may be the case that these simple worshippers, even if they are not entirely aware of what is going on, are resisting the encroachment of the modern world *because they know that they possess something very precious in their tradition.* They cannot prevent and may even welcome the transformation of the daily routine by technology, they are forced to accept the demands of industry with its promise of rewards, their minds are besieged and infiltrated by new ideologies ranging from consumerism to Marxism. But they do not want to be wholly engulfed by it all, for there is something alien and threatening in the new ways. So the cult of Mary has continued to flourish in Guadalupe.[15]

And Harvey Cox, in his 1984 *Religion in the Secular City,* pointed explicitly to the Virgin of Guadalupe as having the "potential for a nonsexist, postmodern theology." In words reminiscent of Orlando Espín, Jeannette Rodriguez, and Sandra Cisneros, quoted in chapter 3, Cox reflects on the Virgin of Guadalupe:

What a cosmic paradox it might turn out to be if Mary, perhaps the most male-manipulated Christian symbol of them all, turned out to be a key ingredient in the liberation of women and in the formulation of a post-modern and postsexist theology. . . . .This is not an impossibility. Take Our Lady of Guadalupe . . . as an example, not as she is defined by the hierarchy, but as she actually functions among the people. This symbol which comes "from the bottom" . . . represents the persistence of a female image of the divine in a culture—our own—that has been dominated for nearly two millennia by a religion stemming from a tribal war god, a male Messiah, and an official religious organization created and managed almost exclusively by men. . . . We must be extraordinarily careful not to accept without qualification the present official churchly definition of the Guadalupe as one of the many apparitions of Mary Immaculate. . . . [T]he story of Juan Diego's problems with Bishop Zumárraga and the fierce priestly opposition to *guadalupismo* in its early years reminds us that the energies she generates and represents can escape from their carefully constructed domestication as they did with Hidalgo and Zapata. . . . In a male-dominated religious system like Christianity, in which women have been systematically deprived of leadership, the tug of war between clerical power and popular religious imagination is in part a battle between male and female visions of reality. . . . This perennial contest between the clerical and the popular, the male and female visions of the cosmos, has also become a clash between modern and post-modern perspectives.[16]

He continues:

Guadalupismo is much more than a widespread devotional cult. It preserves and incarnates an awareness of the cosmos, and of mystical time. It does so, not in a theological system but in a religious movement practiced by millions of people, not eons ago but today, not halfway around the world but in a neighboring country and indeed in hundreds of barrios in the United States itself.[17]

But if Cox sees Guadalupe primarily in terms of its contemporary feminist theological potential and implications, other Protestants underscore her biblical connections to the Magnificat in Luke 1:39 ff. Professor José David Rodriguez Jr. of the Lutheran School of Theology in Chicago writes of this connection:

The true intent of the [Guadalupe] story is not to bring people to venerate an image of the Virgin. The purpose of the story is to challenge people then as well as today *to join in an ancient biblical tradition,* a very important and popular tradition, that the early Christian community attributed to the virgin Mary. It is the tradition that is so eloquently presented in the Magnificat. It is the tradition that has a pre-history in the Scriptures with the song of Miriam in Exodus 15, the song of Hannah in 1 Samuel 2, and the song of Deborah in Judges 5. It is a tradition of a God who loves all human beings. But for this love to be actualized, God "scatters the proud, puts down the mighty from their thrones and exalts those of low degree" (Luke 1:51–52). . . . God's liberation of the poor and oppressed also calls for the liberation of the rich and mighty. The oppressed are not called to take vengeance on the powerful but to liberate them from their own violence. The humble are not raised to dominate over others but to get rid of all forms of domination. Slaves are not liberated to put others in bondage but to rid the world of slavery. God became human in the son of Mary to transform us from arrogant and selfish beings to true "humanized" beings. . . . The story of the Virgin of Guadalupe is part of a broader story of the great saving acts of God in history. The good news for us is that we are invited to be a part of that wonderful and meaningful story.[18]

Along similar lines, the Reverend Ivis LaRiviere-Mestre, pastor of San Martín de Porres Evangelical Lutheran Church, in Allentown, Pennsylvania, in her treatment of indigenous piety in her "Field Work Manual for Seminarians and Pastors Who Want to Do Outreach with Latino/Hispanic/Mestizo Families," refers directly to the Guadalupan experience:

What is extraordinary about this [Guadalupan] story is that the Aztec people heard the good news of Jesus Christ and believed in the goodness of God. The powerful witness of this and similar stories is that the *mestizo indigenous popular piety* portrays a passion for hearing and proclaiming the good news of Jesus Christ. Through God's mystery and majesty, the powerful message of the good news is proclaimed to the humble and pure of spirit. When attention is paid to the powerful witness of these stories, the liturgy is complemented with indigenous rituals that are theologically and biblically sound.[19]

And, in reference to the popularity of Marian apparitions in general among Hispanic-Latinos, she continues later on in the manual:

[The] universal (catholic!) value of the apparitions includes, among many other teachings: a call to deeper, more disciplined prayer (a frequent theme of St. Paul); a warning to repent of greed and to share wealth with the poor (as in the tradition of the Old Testament prophets); a petition for renewal of Christian community centered in faithfulness to . . . worship; and a proclamation of the power of Christ for healing, new life, and salvation. . . . The message of the indigenous stories speaks of *God's compassion, God's unconditional love, and God's presence* in the particular moment of peoples' historical events. These messages offer the believer that unique experience of God's mystery and majesty revealed within his or her cultural and historical con-

text. As the believer shares the message of the good news of Jesus Christ, indigenous piety is centered . . . in the biblical and Christ-centered teachings
proclaimed and reinforced by the tradition of apparitions.[20]

The connections made between the Virgin of Guadalupe and the message of the gospel itself, expressed especially in the above-quoted comments
of González, José David Rodriguez, and LaRiviere-Mestre, are remarkably
consistent with the approach taken by the late Roman Catholic biblical
scholar Raymond Brown, who, as we noted previously, viewed the Virgin
of Guadalupe as giving "the hope of the Gospel to a whole people who
had no other reason to see good news in what came from Spain. In their
lives the devotion to Our Lady constituted an authentic development of
the Gospel of discipleship."[21] Similarly, there is an equal consistency here
with the approach of Virgil Elizondo when he writes:

> The greatest ongoing force of Guadalupe is not her apparition on the *tilma*
> of Juan Diego or even the healing of the dying uncle Juan Bernardino and
> the many subsequent healing miracles down to our own days. Rather, it is
> the "uplifting of the downtrodden" (Luke 1.52) as Juan Diego and millions
> after him are transformed from crushed, self-defacing and silenced persons
> into confident, self-assured and joyful messengers and artisans.[22]

To relate the Guadalupan event and narrative with Mary's Magnificat and
the account of her Visitation to Elizabeth in Luke 1: 39–56 is also, of course,
highly consistent with the Mariological emphases in the theologies of the
great sixteenth-century Reformers Martin Luther, Ulrich Zwingli, John
Calvin, and others. With reference to Luther's own 1521 commentary on
the Magnificat,[23] often called "the centerpiece of Luther's Marian views,"
Eric Gritsch summarizes Luther's overall approach, noting that for him

> Mary is the prototype of how God is to be "magnified." He is not to be
> "magnified" or praised for his distant, unchangeable majesty, but for his un-
> conditional, graceful, and ever-present pursuit of his creatures. Thus Mary
> magnifies God for what he does rather than magnifying herself for what was
> done to her. . . . "Being regarded by God" is the truly blessed state of Mary.
> She is the embodiment of God's grace, by which others can see what kind
> of God the Father of Jesus Christ is. . . . Mary is the model for theologians
> who need to properly distinguish between human and divine works. . . .
> Mary sees wisdom, might, and riches on one side and kindness, justice, and
> righteousness on the other. The former reflect human works, the latter the
> works of God. God uses his works to put down the works of [people], who
> are always tempted to deify themselves. God's works are "mercy" [Luke 1:
> 50], "breaking spiritual pride" (v. 51), "putting down the mighty" (v. 52), "ex-

alting the lowly" (v. 53), "filling the hungry with good things," and "sending the rich away empty" (v. 53). . . . [And] Mary is the "Mother of God" who experienced his unmerited grace. Her personal experience of this grace is an example for all humankind that the mighty God cares for the lowly just as he cares for the exalted. . . . Thus she incites the faithful to trust in God's grace when they call on her.[24]

Consequently, according to Gritsch, "to Luther Mary was the prime example of the faithful—a *typus ecclesiae* embodying unmerited grace. Mary is a paradigm for the indefectibility of the church."[25] Gritsch also notes that Luther dedicated to Mary his 1535/45 hymn, "To Me She's Dear, the Worthy Maid," based, significantly, on the "woman clothed with the sun" in Rev. 12:

> To me she's dear, the worthy maid,
> And I cannot forget her;
> Praise, honor, virtue of her are said;
> Then all I love her better.
> I seek her good,
> And if I should
> Right evil fare,
> I do not care,
> She'll make up for it to me,
> With love and truth that will not tire,
> Which she will ever show me;
> And do all my desire.
>
> She wears of purest gold a crown
> Twelve stars their rays are twining;
> Her raiment, glorious as the sun,
> And bright from far is shining.
> Her feet the moon
> Are set upon
> She is the bride
> With the Lord to bide.
> Sore travail is upon her;
> She bringeth forth a noble Son
> Whom all the world must honor,
> Their king, the only one.
>
> That makes the dragon rage and roar,
> He will the child upswallow;
> His raging comes to nothing more;
> No jot of gain will follow.
> The infant high

> Up to the sky
> Away is heft,
> And he is left
> On earth, all mad with murder.
> The mother now alone is she,
> But God will watchful guard her,
> And the right Father be.[26]

Admittedly, the text of this hymn—like Rev. 12 itself—is ambiguous regarding the precise signification of the woman, and Luther appears to be referring here more to the persecuted church of both the first and sixteenth centuries than to Mary directly. But the mere fact that for Luther Mary is herself a *typus ecclesiae* and that he dedicates this hymn to her, in the first place, makes a Mariological-ecclesiological interpretation or connection quite possible.

Luther's approach to Mary, therefore, especially in his commentary on the Magnificat and in this hymn, should be easily applicable to the Virgin of Guadalupe. For clear "Lutheran" theological reasons, it is perfectly understandable why the 1997–98 ELCA liturgical resource, *Sundays and Seasons,* suggests that for a celebration of Guadalupe "images for preaching or prayer on this day might arise from Rev. 12, Luke 1:39–56, or Luther's *Commentary on the Magnificat.*" For, together with the corresponding image of the woman clothed with the sun in Rev. 12, it is precisely the message of Mary's Magnificat that the Guadalupan narrative still embodies and makes concrete in the lives of countless Juan Diegos and Juan Zumárragas.

Such a biblical approach to Guadalupe might also be reflected from within the Reformed Protestant tradition associated originally with the Reformers Ulrich Zwingli and John Calvin.[27] Referring especially to Calvin's approach, Reformed theologian Daniel Migliore identifies several characteristics of how "Mary exemplifies Christian faith and discipleship" from within a contemporary Reformed theological perspective.[28] Among these he includes: "her trustful hearing of the Word of God and . . . her free and glad consent to the electing grace of God"[29] and "her location at the foot of the cross and . . . her call to ministry with and for others."[30] And, although expressing caution about reducing Mary to a mere symbol of the *human* secular and political struggles for liberation, he writes that she certainly "exemplifies Christian faith and discipleship in her praise of God's surprising and unmerited grace and in her fearless announcement of God's righteous concern for the poor,"[31] and that she is a "woman of humble and courageous faith from whom we might learn to praise the sovereign grace of God [and] to cry out against injustice."[32] Interestingly enough, Migliore concludes his essay with an explicit reference to an image of Mary in a Mexican church:

> In a Roman Catholic Church in Cuernavaca, Mexico, renovated after Vatican II, a large crucifix hangs over the main altar. On the left wall—toward the front, yet still clearly in the nave—there is a simple, modest, unadorned figure of Mary. She does not draw special attention to herself. She stands among the people of God, and her eyes are turned to the cross. This is, I would venture to hope, a picture of Mary that Christians of the Reformation heritage, in solidarity with their Roman Catholic sisters and brothers, might happily make their own.[33]

Migliore's reference to an image of the Virgin near a crucifix within a Mexican church indirectly raises a related issue often encountered in Hispanic-Latino contexts where images of Jesus, whose own sufferings and crucifixion, often expressed in very realistic and gory detail, appear frequently in juxtaposition to images of Mary, like that of Guadalupe herself, in which she is lavishly and richly adorned. For many Protestants (but not only Protestants) this presents a particular theological problem because it has often been interpreted as suggesting the persistence of an inadequate Christology among Hispanic-Latinos, one in which Christ regularly appears as the defeated one but Mary as victorious and life-giving. Alberto Pereyra himself undoubtedly reflects the perception of many when he writes that

> Aztecs did not have Christ in their theology and never accepted totally the second person of the Trinity. In their theology they had the god Quetzalcoatl, the Plumed Serpent who died and promised to return. Aztecs believed that Hernán Cortés was Quetzalcoatl and asked him to wear Quetzalcoatl's mask. The Christ figures in Mexico are all baroque and defeated, dead, prostrate, bleeding, whether they are on the cross or laid out in a glass bier. By contrast, the Virgin of Guadalupe is still the Lady of Tepeyac with roses and perfume. One can walk into a church in Mexico and see this difference, a glorious presence of the Mother rather than a triumphant Christology. People can see two different altars in the same church, one dedicated to a defeated Christ and the other to the glorious transformation of Tonantzin, full of flowers and lights. . . . [A]fter the transformation of Quetzalcoatl into Christ, it has been impossible to know who is worshipped at the baroque altars of Puebla, Oaxaca, and Tlaxcala. The same applies to Mary and Tonantzin.[34]

Others, however, would strongly question this widespread perception. Justo González, in fact, argues that the "baroque and defeated, dead, prostrate, [and] bleeding" images of Jesus within Hispanic-Latino piety are to be viewed precisely from within the categories of traditional orthodox Christology because of how this apparently "defeated" Christ actually functions within those cultural-religious contexts. For González, such images are actually representative of a very high Ephesian (Council of Ephesus, 431) and Chalcedonian (Council of Chalcedon, 451) Christology. He writes:

> Nestorianism has never been a temptation for Hispanic Christians. The reason for this is that we feel the need to assert that the broken, oppressed, and crucified Jesus *is God*. A disjunction between divinity and humanity in Christ that denies this would destroy the greatest appeal of Jesus for Hispanics and other groups who must live in suffering. North Atlantic Christians have often criticized Hispanics for representing Jesus and his sufferings in gory detail. This, they claim, is a sign of a defeatist religion, or of a sadomasochistic attitude that delights in pain. But this is not the case. The suffering Christ is important to Hispanics because he is the sign that *God suffers with us*. An emaciated Christ is the sign that God is with those who hunger. A flagellated Christ is the sign that God is with those who bear the stripes of an unjust society. Blood and suffering have long been the lot of the impoverished masses in Latin America. Blood and suffering are the history of Mexican-Americans in the Southwest. Nestorianism denies that God took these up. For this reason, the Nestorian Christ can never be the Lord of our devotion.[35]

Similarly, with regard to the rejection of Monophysite Christology at the Council of Chalcedon and within Hispanic-Latino devotion to Christ, González continues:

> If in Jesus the human is swallowed up in the divine, to such a point that he no longer functions as a human being, his sufferings are sham and are not like ours. He did not bear our sufferings, and therefore we cannot find in him vindication for those who now suffer. The Crucified One must be truly crucified. The gory Hispanic Christ that so offends North Atlantic sentiments must be truly smitten, truly one of us. He must be divine, for otherwise his suffering has no power to redeem, and he must also be human, for otherwise his suffering has nothing to do with ours. And the two must be joined in such a way that his true humanity is neither destroyed nor swallowed up in his divinity.[36]

Such central focus on the cross, with obvious affinities to the centrality of a *theologia crucis* in most of Protestantism, where it is *God* who is revealed precisely as the *crucified God* in the opposites of rejection, suffering, and death, comes to its fullest expression among Hispanic-Latinos in the celebration of Good Friday, a daylong celebration filled with both official liturgical and popular ritual activities, including often-dramatic reenactments of the Agony in the Garden on Holy Thursday and the Way of the Cross, the Seven Last Words from the Cross, and even a service of burial on Good Friday itself. Of these celebrations Roberto Goizueta comments:

> [T]he . . . Hispanic tendency to emphasize Jesus' crucifixion over his resurrection becomes . . . understandable: the resurrection already takes place when, as a community and as individual persons constituted by that community, we accompany Jesus and each other on Calvary. It is then that, in the person of the Crucified, we encounter the powerlessness of death in the face of our common life. Jesus is already resurrected when he dies accompanied by his mother and the other women—by the converted centurion whose words proclaim that Jesus' death is not the end—and by us, who walk with him from Gethsemane to the grave. Easter, then, is but a ratification of what has, in fact, already occurred on Calvary: the victory of life over death. The supremely human crucified Jesus is the resurrected Jesus. . . . And this Jesus permeates Latino culture, from the bloodied images of the *Divino Rostro* found in so many Latino homes to the tortured and scarred Jesus hanging from crosses in Latino churches. . . . This is not a Jesus we can ignore or avoid, either as casual visitors to a Latino community, or, especially, as scholars and pastors seeking to understand and explain in theological language how God is present in that community. . . . Whatever our theology textbooks may tell us about the importance of Christmas and Easter, there is little doubt that, for Latinos and Latinas, religious faith is identified above all with the crucified Jesus. . . . [H]e is a particular, concrete, historical person, with flesh and bones, a body, and a face which reveal the universal, spiritual Christ of faith—and he is made concrete in the performative, ritual act of "walking with." This is a popular religion which, as indistinguishable from life itself, is always embodied and enfleshed: like life itself. If this Jesus bleeds, it is not to sanctify suffering but to sanctify the flesh; and to sanctify the flesh is to see in it a sacrament, or symbol, of the God of Jesus Christ.[37]

It needs to be noted, however, that, as in Migliore's example of the image of the Virgin oriented toward the crucifix in a renovated Cuernavacan church, the Virgin herself is never absent from, at least, Roman Catholic Hispanic-Latino devotion to the crucified Christ, whether generally or in relationship to the specific celebrations of Good Friday. Rather, she plays a central role. Referring to the popular burial-of-Jesus ritual on Good Friday evening, including the *Pésame a la Virgen* (condolences to the Virgin), Goizueta writes:

> Mary too is defined by her relationships. These are not merely incidental to her identity; like Jesus, she does not have an identity *except in relationship*. Mary is never just Mary; she is also our mother, *comadre, compañera,* friend,

and, above all, mother of Jesus. In the Good Friday celebration, Mary is always alongside her son, even after his burial. The last image we see on Good Friday is the image, in the celebration of the Pésames, of Mary, kneeling at the tomb of her son, and the community kneeling beside her. . . . As *la Soledad,* Mary experiences the most profound desolation and dehumanization, that of the abandoned, isolated individual. As the Crucified, Jesus experiences the same: "My God, my God, why have you abandoned me?"[38]

Along similar lines, Virgil Elizondo writes of the close association between Mary as La Soledad or La Virgen de los Dolores (the Virgin of Sorrows) in this context and the all-too-frequent contemporary experience of Hispanic-Latino women:

> Mary's role in the crucifixion of her Son is relived by millions of women in Latin America—grandmothers, mothers, wives, girlfriends. They stand by silently as injustice, violence, is done to their loved ones. They are silent not because they are afraid or because they agree with the civil authorities, but because they are afraid or do not even understand the language. They are silent because they know, through their collective experience with other women who have gone through similar experiences, that they are powerless against the authorities. . . . They are silent not only because they do not have the money to hire a lawyer, but because they probably do not even know about the existence of lawyers. They are silent because if they said something, reprisals might be taken against other members of the family. . . . Thousands of persons watch their loved ones be taken away, accused of some crime, condemned, and sentenced by the "justice of the powerful"—and all they can do is stand silently by them to the very end. . . . The final Good Friday reenactment is the burial service. Some ridicule this popular rite of the burial of Jesus and attribute its popularity to the "morbid" inclinations of the Mexican Americans—"always preoccupied with death." But when it is realized that even in death this people is rejected, the quiet, almost clandestine, burial of Jesus takes on a deeper significance for them. Segregated cemeteries are sill a commonplace, even if not segregated as in the past—along skin-color lines. . . . The Mexican-American people have a very special devotion to *nuestro Diosito en la cruz* [our little God on the cross]. Good Friday is *nuestra fiesta,* the cultic celebration of *nuestra existencia.* It is not an "other-worldly" make believe; it is a celebration of *nuestra vida.*[39]

For many Hispanic-Latinos, quite obviously, to identify with the sufferings of Christ includes an identification with the sufferings of his mother as well in a solidarity of compassion, consolation, and hope. Neither Christology nor Mariology within this cultural context, then, is an abstract formulation but is embodied or incarnated in experience and life. Both Jesus and Mary function as concrete and tangible living persons.

If, then, in spite of widespread perceptions to the contrary, González is correct in asserting that "the gory Hispanic Christ that so offends North Atlantic sentiments" is actually representative of classically formulated orthodox Christology, it is important to note that classic Mariology itself is closely related to these Christological doctrinal positions. That is, while González himself makes no reference to this, it is precisely by means of the Christological title of *Theotokos,* God-bearer or, more popularly, Mother of God) given to Mary at the Council of Ephesus that Nestorianism itself was rejected as a Christological heresy. And, of course, the purpose of the Theotokos doctrine was precisely to safeguard the unity of the personhood of Christ himself as the Incarnate God. For, the one to whom Mary gave birth was not only human but *God* in human flesh! One wonders, then, if one of the reasons "the gory Hispanic Christ" remains Christologically orthodox is that such a high Christology has traditionally been accompanied in Hispanic-Latino contexts by a rather high Mariology. Is it possible, then, that the Virgin of Guadalupe and other popular Hispanic-Latino images of Mary, far from *competing* with a "defeated" Christ for loyalty and allegiance, actually function, like the Theotokos doctrine itself, as ways to safeguard the very identity and personhood of Christ as the one who, by her flesh and the power of the Holy Spirit, has perfectly united divinity and humanity in a personal union within himself? Perhaps in such contexts it is precisely solidarity with Mary at the foot of the cross and in prayerful vigil at the tomb that keeps the community in simultaneous solidarity with Christ.

But just how "high" a Mariology would be acceptable to Protestants? Not *very* high, of course. And, if the Theotokos doctrine itself is certainly accepted doctrinally—at least theoretically and rather abstractly—by some Protestant traditions because of its Christological assertion about the identity and personhood of Christ (Mother of *God* rather than *Mother* of God), Protestants in general will become very cautious and leery of any additional Mariological claims. When, for example, Orlando Espín says that "the majority of Latinos/as . . . relate to Guadalupe in ways that any mainstream Christian pneumatology would expect with respect to the Holy Spirit"[40] or Elizondo suggests that Guadalupe might provide a "new world way" of reimaging the Christian doctrine of the Trinity as the Mother who sends the Son to the Father to become a builder of the new temple, or home,[41] Protestant (and some Catholic) suspicions about the actual place of Mariology in some forms of Roman Catholicism would surely be raised. And when someone like Leonardo Boff can even suggest his hypothesis that Mary might "be regarded as hypostatically united to the Third Person of the Blessed Trinity,"[42] those suspicions would seem to be confirmed. Indeed, a Protestant theologian might claim that there is really nothing very new at all in this line of reasoning because the apparent replacement of the Holy

Spirit by the Virgin Mary is exactly *the* problem of a high Mariology and one that is easily discernible from within the history of Roman Catholicism and is encountered today especially in Hispanic-Latino popular religion. Lutheran theologian Paul Tillich argued several years ago that "the Holy Spirit even now remains an abstraction. . . . In the moment in which he was deified in the same sense that Christ was considered divine, the Spirit was replaced in actual piety by the Holy Virgin. The Virgin who gave birth to God acquired divinity herself to a certain extent, at least for popular piety."[43] In 1959, with reference to the 1950 promulgation of the dogma of Mary's bodily Assumption, Tillich also claimed that

> the Roman Church sticks to it on the basis of its tremendous symbolic power which step by step brings [Mary] nearer to the Trinity itself, especially in the development of the last decade. If this should ever be completed as is now discussed in groups of the Roman Church, Mary would become Co-Saviour with Jesus. Then, whether this is admitted or not, she is actually taken into the divinity itself.[44]

And, in a frequently quoted statement from the mid 1960s, Elsie Gibson referred to a discovery she made in her study of Catholic theology, writing that "every place I expected to find an exposition of the Holy Spirit, I found Mary. What Protestants universally attribute to the action of the Holy Spirit was attributed to Mary."[45]

To be fair, however, with the exception of the particular conclusions and dogmatic implications drawn by Leonardo Boff, none of the contemporary Catholic theologians writing on Guadalupe surveyed in chapter 3 (i.e., Elizondo, Espín, and Jeannette Rodriguez) is arguing for any particular new Catholic dogmatic developments or promulgations regarding Mary herself. Rather, they are more directly concerned with how the Guadalupan event and narrative may be revelatory of the feminine face of *God,* especially "the God-who-is-for-us as mother" (Espín), under the categories or attributes of divine maternity, compassion, liberating power and might, immanence or intimate presence, and re-creative energy. In other words, it is not what the Virgin of Guadalupe says about the identity of *Mary* (other than the narrative's own reaffirmation of the Theotokos doctrine, "I am the Mother of the true God") but what is revealed about the identity and nature of *God* in the narrative and the continuing devotion that is theologically important. And in this, certainly *some* Protestant theologians, like Harvey Cox, concerned with gender-inclusive ways of imaging or reimaging God can find much of benefit both in the Guadalupan narrative and within the history of Marian devotion, where especially in Mariology is to be located the presence and persistence of a classic pneumatology. In one of her articles, in fact, Elizabeth Johnson refers to a study done by a group of Lutherans in Germany during the early 1980s in which it was concluded that "as Mary was the first human being to give a full response to God's word, so too as Mother of God she becomes the 'revelation of the feminine-maternal side of the being of God.'"[46] And, for that matter, Paul Tillich himself, while certainly doubtful as to the possibility of Protestantism ever restoring the symbol of the Virgin to its theological consciousness, claimed that his own theology of God as the "ground of being" transcended gender specificity and, as a symbol, his theology pointed "to the mother-quality of giving birth, carrying, and embracing, and, at the same time, of calling back, resisting independence of the created, and swallowing it."[47]

Nevertheless, although Espín suggests that understanding the Virgin of Guadalupe as the expression of popular pneumatology might be fruitful for "honest intra-Latino ecumenical dialogue (especially with pentecostals!)," [48] the Virgin of Guadalupe—and, for that matter, any theology of Mary—will for Protestants ultimately stand or fall in relationship to the doctrine of justification. How, then, might the doctrine of justification serve "as a criterion that orients" Guadalupan teaching and practice "to Christ, whom alone we ultimately trust as the one Mediator"? If clues to how this might be done have already been provided above, it is important that this question now be addressed more directly.

The Virgin of Guadalupe
and Justification by Grace through Faith

The theological interpretations of the Virgin of Guadalupe expressed by those contemporary Roman Catholic theologians surveyed in chapter 3 would seem to be highly compatible with the doctrine of justification by grace through faith. Indeed, if the God revealed in the Guadalupan narrative is none other than "the God-who-is-for-us" (Espín), characterized by "a maternal presence, consoling, nurturing, offering unconditional love, comforting" and "brimming over with gentleness, loving kindness, and forgiveness" as an "unconditional and grace-filled gift to the people" (Jeannette Rodriguez), then it is precisely a proclamation of the God who justifies "by grace alone." And that this gift is received "through faith" is surely exemplified in the response of Juan Diego, who, like Abraham and countless prophets in the Hebrew Bible before him, interprets this encounter as a call to his own prophetic ministry both to his own people and to the governing (ecclesiastical) authorities to whom he was sent. It must be recalled here that in distinction to several other Marian apparitions throughout history, especially the more modern ones, the Virgin of Guadalupe asks for *nothing* to be done other than the building of the "temple." And this temple is itself to be nothing other than a place or home where all peoples might encounter divine love, compassion, help, and protection and where their laments would be heard and all their miseries, misfortunes, and sorrows would find remedy and cure. In other words, this temple, this Beth-El (House of God) of the Americas, was (and is) to be a place where the God of unconditional love, mercy, compassion, grace, and forgiveness is proclaimed and encountered. Certainly, then, the Guadalupan event *can* be interpreted as "not just another Marian apparition" but as something having "to do with the very core of the gospel itself" (Elizondo) even as that gospel is understood specifically in a Protestant theological context. It might surely be said that the way the Guadalupan image and narrative function in the particular cultural context of Hispanic-Latino popular religion is precisely an inculturation or incarnation of the gospel of justification itself.

Even the implications and call for justice and liberation so often associated with the Guadalupan narrative and continued devotion are also consistent with the doctrine of justification. Again, from within his Reformed theological perspective Daniel Migliore writes of the relationship between the sovereignty of grace and the pursuit of justice exemplified in Mary's Magnificat:

> Neither the biblical portrayal of Mary's passion for justice expressed in the Magnificat nor the classical Reformed emphasis on the sovereignty of grace lead to passivity or complacency. On the contrary, acknowledgment of salvation by grace alone goes hand in hand with a passionate cry for justice and a transformed world. This passion for justice remains anchored in God; trust is not transferred to revolutionary ideologies. Nevertheless, zeal for God's honor and the manifestation of God's justice in all the creation ignites a real rebellion and a spirit of resistance against all forces of injustice and all the powers and principalities that oppose God's redemptive purposes.[49]

If Migliore himself is not concerned specifically with the Virgin of Guadalupe in this context, the parallels should be rather obvious. As in the Magnificat so in Guadalupe is manifested Mary's own "zeal for God's honor," which, perhaps today more than ever, has led to a "real rebellion and a spirit of resistance" against racial, social, and economic injustice in the world. If, at times, that rebellion and resistance may indeed be transferred more to revolutionary ideologies than to the biblical God of justice and/or righteousness, the persistent presence of the Guadalupan image often associated with movements of rebellion and resistance nonetheless keeps open the possibility of hearing what Migliore calls "*God's* righteous concern for

the poor" and its implications expressed so powerfully in Mary's own biblical proclamation, her Magnificat. To be justified by grace alone sets one
free in the name of God to risk oneself and one's identity in the pursuit of
God's own justice and righteousness for the world.

That a Marian symbol like Guadalupe might be a vehicle for the doctrine of justification by grace through faith should not really be all that surprising, even when one considers traditional Roman Catholic Marian
dogma. Although Protestants (and others) have rejected, and will continue
to reject, the explicit dogmatic formulations of Mary's Immaculate Conception (1854 by Pius IX) and bodily Assumption (1950 by Pius XII) as
having no foundation in Scripture and as tied closely to the equally con-
troversial dogma of papal infallibility, there is a theological core in both of
these Marian dogmas that may well be acceptable to Protestant theology
within a contemporary ecumenical context. This might especially be the
case when one considers the close relationship that exists between Mariology and ecclesiology in contemporary Roman Catholic thought. Surely, at
one level at least, the dogma of Mary's Immaculate Conception is nothing
other than the proclamation of justification by grace alone since such redemption by Christ of Mary in the womb (and, according to Catholic
teaching, it *is* a redemption) could come about through no other possible
means. As Berard Marthaler states: "It is the symbol par excellence of 'free
grace'—Mary was justified from the first instant of her existence indepen-
dently of anything she desired or did *(ante praevisa merita)*." Similarly, with
regard to her bodily Assumption, it is important to note the necessary contrast between the technical terms *ascensio* (ascension) and *assumptio* (assumption). If, as John Macquarrie notes, "ascension" implies an active role
assigned to the one ascending (e.g., the *Ascension* of Christ into Heaven),
"assumption" can only be an act of God in which the one assumed (in this
case, Mary) remains passive.[51] Consequently, Mary's Assumption, like the
Immaculate Conception, is dependent solely upon God's grace and Mary
remains a passive recipient of both divine actions. Marthaler continues:

> Mary typifies, in a way that Jesus (who did not need redemption) could not,
> what it means to be redeemed in Christ. While neither the Immaculate
> Conception nor the Assumption are mentioned in Scripture, they nonethe-
> less affirm truths that are clearly implied in the mystery of grace and elec-
> tion. They illustrate once again how church doctrine affirms more about
> human nature and needs than about the Godhead—an axiom that seems es-
> pecially true of the Marian dogmas.[52]

With regard to how contemporary Roman Catholic theology sees in
Marian doctrine and devotion a close relationship to ecclesiology, we have

already noted the words of *Sacrosanctum concilium* V.103 that "in [Mary] the Church admires and exalts the most excellent fruit of redemption, and joyfully contemplates, as in a faultless image, that which she herself desires and hopes wholly to be." Hence, whatever the Immaculate Conception and bodily Assumption might mean for Mary as a historical person, the symbolic importance of these dogmas has to do with what they mean for the nature and identity of the church itself. And if at their core what these dogmas assert has ultimately to do with justification by grace alone, then the image of Mary becomes simultaneously the image of a graciously redeemed humanity and church. Mary thus becomes the prototype and paradigm of how human salvation in Christ takes place. Yes, like Tillich, one can interpret these dogmas as referring to a "triumphalist" Roman Catholic ecclesiology, and one can certainly fear in this context any other Marian dogmatic developments. But one can also read them in light of justification and its implications. I have written elsewhere about the ecclesiological implications of these Marian dogmas even for baptismal theology and practice:

> Given our long Western Augustinian history of interpreting baptism as liberation from original sin, the December 8 solemnity of the Immaculate Conception of Mary provides not only another possible occasion for baptism but for baptismal catechesis and mystagogy. That is, in the womb of baptism the Church itself has been "conceived immaculately" by water and the Holy Spirit and, if mariology is best understood in relationship to ecclesiology, christology, and pneumatology then there is, indeed, a close parallel between what is asserted of Mary's conception in service to her ultimate role as the Theotokos in the Incarnation and the ultimate role of the Church, the community of the baptized, as the "God bearers" of the Incarnate Christ in the world as well. For baptism makes us all Theotokoi! "Like Mary herself," a Roman Catholic homilist might well proclaim on this feast, "so we too in baptism have been 'conceived immaculately' in the watery womb of our baptismal mother." Surely the Solemnity of Mary's Assumption on August 15, by providing a concrete sign of our eschatological hope and future in Christ, for which baptism is itself the downpayment by the gift of the Holy Spirit (see 2 Corinthians 1:21–22, Ephesians 1:13–14), might also suggest itself.[53]

While Protestants might continue to lament the fact that both of these "pious and pleasing thoughts," as they are sometimes called, were elevated from the realm of piety and the Church's *lex orandi* (or liturgical tradition) to the status of *lex credendi* or *de fide* dogmatic definitions in Roman Catholicism,[54] the theological core of what these dogmas imply about the redeemed themselves may well be ecumenically acceptable in light of contemporary ecumenical convergence on the doctrine of justification. Indeed, the wonderful irony of this might just be that, in spite of the church-dividing nature of these dogmatic formulations, they actually affirm *within* Roman Catholicism itself what Protestants have always taught is to be the central focus in proclaiming how God saves humanity. Like Mary, the church is the passive recipient of grace alone. Clearly such an understanding is not far removed from Luther's own Mariological concerns, for whom, as we have seen, Mary herself "was the prime example of the faithful—a *typus ecclesiae* embodying unmerited grace" and "a paradigm for the indefectibility of the church." Is it so surprising, then, that Luther himself, in distinction to many of his own sixteenth-century Roman Catholic contemporaries, even gave a positive evaluation and affirmation of both the Immaculate Conception and the Assumption as long as they were not imposed on people as matters of faith?[55]

If the core of Roman Catholic Marian dogma can be interpreted positively by Protestants in the light of justification by grace through faith, then certainly one is also justified in viewing the Marian symbol of the Virgin of Guadalupe along similar lines. But it is not only that the Guadalupan narrative proclaims the unconditionally gracious, loving, merciful, and compassionate God who justifies the Juan Diegos, Juan Bernardinos, and Juan Zumárragas. In addition, the Guadalupan image itself, as revelatory of the multiracial, multiethnic, multicultural mestiza church that came to be incarnated as the result of the sixteenth-century cultural confrontation between Spain and Mexico, and still struggles to be born in our own day, functions as a typus ecclesiae. That is, if the narrative of the Virgin of Guadalupe can be interpreted correctly as being about justification, then the Guadalupan image—which depicts the typus ecclesiae herself as pregnant with the Incarnate Word—can surely be seen both as an image of Mary as the embodiment of unmerited grace and, as, in a mirror reflection, of what the church itself, thanks to the same unmerited grace, is and is called to be as similarly pregnant with the same Incarnate Word for the life and salvation of the world. And all of this is certainly consistent with a Protestant theological approach even if Marian narratives and images have not been employed or closely attended to historically within Protestantism. Indeed, for those who might object that it is *Christ* who appears to be absent from this narrative and image of justification, the words of Elizondo bear repeating: "The innermost core of the apparition . . . is what she carries within her womb: the new source and center of the new humanity that is about to be born. And that source and center is Christ as the light and life of the world."[56] And in this sense, then, certainly a Protestant can say that the Virgin of Guadalupe *is* "of the gospel" because the narrative and image of Guadalupe is, ultimately, about Christ. Applied to Guadalupe,

then, the criteriological function of the doctrine of justification in orienting the teaching and practices of the churches "to Christ, whom alone we
ultimately trust as the one Mediator," would appear to suggest that it is precisely Christ to whom Guadalupe points and whom the message of
Guadalupe proclaims.

Another theological approach to this might also be valuable for Protestants who would struggle with such an obviously Marian-based approach
to the question of justification. To be sure, the message of the Guadalupan
narrative does not explicitly articulate in identical language the Protestant
doctrinal position of "justification by grace through faith for the sake of
Christ." But for those countless devotees for whom the Virgin of
Guadalupe manifests God-for-us as grace, mercy, forgiveness, and unconditional love, there can be little doubt that we are dealing here theologically
with a concrete experience of what might surely be called justification by
grace alone through faith, even if that experience is mediated through a vehicle not characteristically Protestant in form or expression. And, of course,
the experience of justification, in which people are actually raised to new
life and new creation in Christ, is not dependent upon identical or even
precise theological or doctrinal articulation.

Helpful in this regard may well be the linguistic paradigm of doctrine
proposed in recent years by Yale Lutheran theologian George Lindbeck,
whose "rule theory of doctrine" attempts to explain how doctrines actually function in a religious tradition by employing an analogy drawn from
modern studies of linguistics. According to Lindbeck, it is necessary to distinguish between the particular "grammar" of a religion—its "rules" or
"doctrines," which serve as "communally authoritative teachings regarding
beliefs and practices that are considered essential to the identity or welfare
of the group in question"[57]—and its "vocabulary" (for example, its symbols,
rites, and stories). But if the grammar or grammatical rules stay the same
throughout diverse historical time periods, the vocabulary itself may
change. As Lindbeck writes:

> To the degree that religions are like languages, they can obviously remain the
> same amid vast transformations of affirmation and experience. When put this
> way, it seems almost self-evident that the permanence and unity of doctrines,
> despite changing and diverse formulation, is more easily accounted for if
> they are taken to resemble grammatical rules rather than propositions or ex-
> pressive symbols.[58]

That is, doctrine, like grammar, provides the permanent rules by which
the particular meaning of an ever changing and living vocabulary is to be
discerned and interpreted. In a recent essay on liturgical inculturation and

translation Clare Veronica Johnson states that "Lindbeck's theory suggests that the doctrines (or rules) of a religion (functioning in the same way as the grammar of a language) remain the same throughout history, while the particular vocabulary used to express those doctrines in varied historical time-periods and in various cultural and linguistic contexts may change."[59]

With regard to the Virgin of Guadalupe and the doctrine of justification, Lindbeck's approach appears to provide a most helpful interpretative framework. For it is as a particular Hispanic-Latino cultural vocabulary—expressed in a story (the Guadalupan narrative), an enduring symbol (the image on Juan Diego's tilma), and repeated ritual celebrations (at least the annual December 12 feast)—that what the grammar of justification attempts to safeguard doctrinally is expressed concretely in the lives and experience of Guadalupan devotees. If the vocabulary is different from that of traditional Protestant vocabulary the same grammar may nevertheless be operative.

What Lindbeck's linguistic paradigm of doctrine suggests may also be paralleled in the recent approach to liturgical inculturation adopted in the 1996 Lutheran World Federation's *Nairobi Statement on Worship and Culture: Contemporary Challenges and Opportunities.* This statement outlines four ways that Christian worship may be seen as relating dynamically to culture: "First, it is *transcultural,* the same substance for everyone everywhere, beyond culture. Second, it is *contextual,* varying according to the local situation (both nature and culture). Third, it is *counter-cultural,* challenging what is contrary to the Gospel in a given culture. Fourth, it is *cross-cultural,* making possible sharing between local cultures."[60]

If the liturgical celebration of the Virgin of Guadalupe might naturally seem to belong to the category of cross-cultural worship, which is characterized by ecumenical and multicultural "sharing . . . as a witness to the unity of the Church and the oneness of Baptism,"[61] I suspect that for most Protestants the category of contextual worship might be the more illuminating one to consider in this context. Here especially it is the method of contextualization known as "dynamic equivalence" that suggests itself. Such a method, according to this statement,

> involves re-expressing components of Christian worship with something from a local culture that has an equal meaning, value, and function. Dynamic equivalence goes far beyond mere translation; it involves understanding the fundamental meanings both of elements of worship and of the local culture, and enabling the meanings and actions of worship to be "encoded" and re-expressed in the language of local culture.[62]

While a Roman Catholic might surely argue that such dynamic equivalence is precisely what has already happened with Guadalupe in its history and ongoing development, it is Orlando Espín's (and others') insight that Latino popular Catholicism is a religion itself with its own symbols, stories, rituals, and religious worldview that might make such an approach rather attractive to Protestants. That is, if the Virgin of Guadalupe, as is asserted by several contemporary Roman Catholic authors, actually does function in the Hispanic-Latino *cultural* context of popular *religion* as revelatory of God-for-us in such life-shaping ways, then it would seem highly possible for a Protestantism becoming ever more conscious of its need for a multicultural approach to find much in Guadalupe that is dynamically equivalent to its own traditional theological approach and worldview. In other words, if something like Guadalupanismo was itself a *world* religion, reflecting the indigenous culture, values, ritual practices, and beliefs of its practitioners, but with no discernible relationship whatsoever to the Christian tradition, the method of dynamic equivalence would assert that: (1) "a given culture's values and patterns, insofar as they are consonant with the values of the Gospel, can be used to express the meaning and purpose of Christian worship";[63] and (2) "those components of culture that are able to re-express the Gospel . . . in an adequate manner should be studied."[64] And, if it is true that in the process of contextualization, "elements borrowed from local culture should always undergo critique and purification, which can be achieved through the use of biblical typology,"[65] does not the Virgin of Guadalupe, already consonant with an abundance of biblical typology, emerge as a preeminent example of what this process of contextualization is all about?

But, of course, Guadalupanismo is not a world religion. It is, rather, a religious tradition and practice that has been shaped as a particular and popular expression of Christianity, an expression, it would seem, that is highly consonant with the gospel. In fact, has not much of the contextual work on the Virgin of Guadalupe already been done by the likes of Elizondo, Espín, Goizueta, and Jeannette Rodriguez? And if their conclusions are correct, then, indeed, this Guadalupan reexpression of "the Gospel . . . in an adequate manner should be studied" by Protestants. For the vocabulary that is Guadalupe does seem to bear some dynamic equivalence to much of Protestant vocabulary expressed within the grammar of justification.

In light of the above, I would like to suggest that a Protestant (ecumenical?) theological approach to the Virgin of Guadalupe might be most appropriate under the category of parable, that is, "the Virgin of Guadalupe as parable of justification," or t"he Virgin of Guadalupe as parable of the reign of God." While scholars of the *Nican Mopohua* continue to debate whether it is Nahuatl prose or poetry,[66] I would argue that in either case it functions parabolically and that the literary genre of parable is a most fitting way to interpret it. In using the word parable here, I certainly do not mean to imply any critical judgment about the authenticity or historicity of the Guadalupan events themselves or to reduce the narrative to a particular literary genre. Nor am I using the word parable either as a mere true-to-life *story* designed to teach a central point or as a simple allegory in which each character is but a symbol of something or someone else. In both cases once someone gets the point of the story, the parable itself is no longer important and can be dispensed with quickly in favor of its meaning. Instead, by the use of the word parable, I mean how the Guadalupan story actually *functions*. That is, as modern New Testament scholarship on the parables of Jesus has come to emphasize, parables function as "stories that defy religious conventions, overturn tradition, and subvert the hearer's expectations"[67] about how God is *supposed* to act in the world and, in so doing, make room for the inbreaking of God's reign. One of the best examples illustrating this function is the parable of the Good Samaritan (Luke 10:29–37). According to John Dominic Crossan, one of the leading pioneers in the contemporary study of the biblical parables, the point of the Good Samaritan parable is not how to be a "good neighbor" to others. Rather, the parable itself, by making a hated and socioreligious outcast Samaritan "good" and "neighbor," shatters and reverses the expectations of those who heard the story, expectations based on their own cultural-religious worldview and tradition. Had Jesus wanted simply to teach the importance of how to be a good neighbor—even to outcasts—he could have told a story about a Jew reaching out to a wounded Samaritan. But he doesn't. As Crossan writes:

> The hearer must not be able to shrug it off by saying: "No Samaritan would act that way!" He must feel instead: I have just seen the wine and the oil, the donkey, and the inn. I have just seen the two denarii exchange hands and I have just heard the Samaritan discuss the situation with the innkeeper.... But whether one's mind reacts properly or not, the Good Samaritan ("the good terrorist," today?) is an attack on the structure of expectation and not a story which inculcates assistance to those in need.[68]

Consequently, he continues:

> Parables give God room. The parables of Jesus are not historical allegories telling us how God acts with [hu]mankind; neither are they moral example-stories telling us how to act before God and towards one another. They are stories which shatter the deep structure of our accepted world and thereby render clear and evident to us the relativity of story itself. They remove our defenses and make us vulnerable to God. It is only in such experiences that God can touch us, and only in such moments does the Kingdom of God arrive. My own term for this relationship is transcendence.[69]

If contemporary biblical scholarship is correct, the parables of Jesus, as reversals that make room for the advent of the reign of God as surprising gift and invite the action of response to that reign, point unmistakably to Jesus as the Great Parable of God himself. Indeed, it is precisely the Crucified One who functions as the ultimate parable of divine reversal and salvation, especially as this is proclaimed by St. Paul in 1 Cor. 1:22–31 (NRSV):

> For Jews demand signs and Greeks desire wisdom, but we proclaim Christ crucified, a stumbling block to Jews and foolishness to Gentiles. But to those who are called, both Jews and Greeks, Christ the power of God and the wisdom of God. For God's foolishness is wiser than human wisdom, and God's weakness is stronger than human strength. Consider your own call, brothers and sisters, not many of you were wise by human standards, not many were powerful, not many were of noble birth. But God chose what is foolish in the world to shame the wise; God chose what is weak in the world to shame the strong; God chose what is low and despised in the world, things that are not, to reduce to nothing things that are, so that no one might boast in the presence of God. He is the source of your life in Christ Jesus, who became for us wisdom from God, and righteousness and sanctification and redemption, in order that, as it is written, "Let the one who boasts, boast in the Lord."

The narrative and the widespread presence of the image of the Virgin of Guadalupe can certainly be interpreted as functioning parabolically in the same sense as the biblical parables themselves. For the Guadalupan story is a parable of the great reversals of God, the subversion of both indigenous and Spanish cultural-religious worldviews and assumptions, standing them on their heads, to make room for something new. Juan Diego is none other than one of the "low and despised in the world," who, in this Guadalupan encounter, becomes the prophet or messenger of the reign of God even to the ecclesiastical authorities and, as an indigenous *layperson,* subverts even the heavily clerical leadership structure of Spanish colonial Catholicism. It is no wonder that, increasingly, Juan Diego is becoming today the model for the ministry of the laity, the concrete example of the priestly ministry of the baptized—the "priesthood of all believers" in traditional Protestant terminology—especially within Mexican and Mexican American contexts.[70] Nor is it any wonder that early ecclesiastical responses to Guadalupe would have been so strongly negative. Then, as now, Guadalupe challenges the wise, the powerful, the noble, and the strong to a new conversion (as exemplified in Bishop Juan Zumárraga's response) to the presence of the reign of God as located in the weak, the lowly, the despised, and the rejected. This too is nothing other than a *theologia crucis.* For, like the parables of Jesus, the Virgin of Guadalupe, as parable of the reign of God, is connected to the great biblical stories of reversal that point ultimately to the great reversal of the cross. Thus, the narrative and image of Guadalupe belong, most appropriately, in close association with images of the Crucified One himself. For it is only in light of the image of Christ crucified that the meaning of Guadalupe is best revealed and appropriated.

A Protestant Guadalupan Veneration and Devotion?

Lutheran theologian José David Rodriguez is certainly correct when he writes that "the true intent of the [Guadalupe] story is not to bring people to venerate an image of the Virgin [but] to challenge people then as well as today to join in an ancient biblical tradition" and that the "good news" of "the story of the Virgin of Guadalupe . . . is that we are invited to be a part of that wonderful and meaningful story."[71] But, of course, for the good news or true intent of the story to be heard and the invitation to be made in this way, one cannot really separate the message or the meaning of the message from the narrative itself any more than one can separate the point of one of Jesus' parables from the telling and retelling of the parable itself. If the Virgin of Guadalupe, then, is to function parabolically in contemporary Protestantism as good news, the Virgin of Guadalupe as parable of the reign of God needs to be proclaimed. And closely related to the narrative is the Guadalupan image itself as the ongoing and permanent visible expression or iconographic representation of that parable. If, therefore, the gospel *message* of the Guadalupan narrative might be acceptable to Protestants in some form, the question is whether the Guadalupan *image* might also be acceptable for inclusion within Protestant places of worship. And, if so, might there then also be room for some kind of Protestant Guadalupan veneration or devotion?

With regard to the image, the question of its suitability in Protestant places of worship is, in part, moot. Her image is present already in a variety of, at least, Lutheran and Episcopal congregations in the United States. And for those Protestant traditions that are not iconoclastic in their self-definition or style, certainly a Mexican image or icon is as appropriate for inclusion as are European, Scandinavian, or African ones. But if Protestant churches in the United States (especially Lutheran and Episcopal), *unlike* those of Europe, Scandinavia, and England, have tended not to include Marian images in general (though there are certainly exceptions),[72] the increasing Hispanic-Latino presence in American Protestantism may lead to a reconsideration of this. Indeed, the image of the Virgin of Guadalupe is an indigenous American icon. I am reminded here of a comment made several years ago by the late Lutheran theologian Arthur Carl Piepkorn, who, in fact, argued in favor of "the devotional value of good, unsentimental representations of [Mary] in the arts, especially after the earliest surviving models which always show her with the holy Child" as appropriate for Lutheran worship spaces.[73] While it cannot be known whether Piepkorn would have found the Guadalupan image an "unsentimental representation" of Mary, surely both the overall Christocentric focus of the image and its close biblical associations to the woman clothed with the sun in Rev. 12 might well suggest its appropriateness.

Even if some Protestants might balk at an image of the Virgin like the Guadalupan one having a permanent place in their worship spaces, it would seem that at least during the liturgical season of Advent such an image might, indeed, serve as an iconographic focus for both the incarnational and eschatological orientations of the season. It is in the Advent-Christmas season that almost all Protestant traditions exhibit the important role that certain forms of popular religion still play among them, expressed by means of Sunday school Nativity pageants and public displays of the crèche, or manger scene, thus including at least images of Mary and Joseph in their worship spaces. It is hard even for the most ardent of iconoclasts to remain so, it seems, during Advent and Christmas.

But if some would still object that the traditional Guadalupan image does not appear to be explicitly Christological in its representation, the recent iconographic adaptation of the Guadalupan image called "Roses in December" by Brother Claude Lane, O.S.B., of Mount Angel Abbey, St. Benedict, Oregon, might well begin to answer that objection (see figure 5.1).

According to the description of this icon provided by the Printery House at Conception Abbey, Conception, Missouri, where it is available for sale in several formats,

> Mary has the features and dress of Our Lady of Guadalupe in this icon. She stands over the Creator of the Universe, manifested as a tiny, helpless infant. She is the agent of His Incarnation into the midst of His Creation, symbolized by her cloak covered with stars enveloping her and the manger of straw. The background of the center scene is a deep, featureless blue, symbolic of the pre-creation void. The black girdle which Mary had about her waist in the Guadalupe image has been transferred to the Babe as part of His swaddling clothes. It is a symbol of her pregnancy, and now she has given birth to Christ and He will give birth to His Church. Mary's right hand is in the same position of prayer as the Guadalupe image, but her left has dropped toward Jesus, directing her (and our) prayer to Him.[74]

This particular icon, then, while certainly representing the Virgin of Guadalupe, is actually an icon of the Nativity of Christ with the Virgin of

Figure 5.1. Roses in December

Guadalupe decidedly oriented to Christ himself. It would be hard, I believe, for any Protestant to object seriously to this particular Guadalupan
image. For, indeed, it is nothing other than an iconographic representation
of the Christocentric orientation and goal of the Guadalupan narrative or
message itself. Other iconographic representations of the Virgin of
Guadalupe with the Holy Child are available that some Protestants might
find more acceptable for appropriation. An example is the Byzantine-style
iconic depiction from the Shrine of Our Lady of Guadalupe in Coachella,
California, shown in figure 5.2.[75]

This is clearly an example of what Piepkorn called an "unsentimental
representation of [Mary] . . . especially after the earliest surviving models
which always show her with the holy Child."

If, therefore, the message of Guadalupe and at least some artistic adaptation of the Guadalupan image itself may easily be acceptable for some

Figure 5.2. Nuestra Señora del Programa Misionero

Protestants, especially during the Advent and Christmas seasons, might a similar case also be made for some form of veneration or devotion? Certainly the December 12 feast could easily be adapted and integrated liturgically along the lines already suggested above by the ELCA liturgical resource *Sundays and Seasons.* The biblical readings associated with this feast in the current Roman Catholic lectionary in Mexico, namely, Gal. 4:4–7 and Luke 1:39–47, could also be employed, especially if the Gospel reading itself were expanded to include all of Mary's Magnificat (through Luke 1:56). Similarly, there is probably not a more appropriate Protestant prayer of the day for such a celebration than the one already appointed in the *Lutheran Book of Worship* for the May 31 Lesser Festival of the Visitation: "Almighty God, in choosing the virgin Mary to be the mother of your Son, you made known your gracious regard for the poor and the lowly and the despised. Grant us grace to receive your Word in humility, and so to be made one with your Son, Jesus Christ our Lord, who lives and reigns with you and the Holy Spirit, one God, now and forever."[76]

But even if such a December 12 Protestant liturgical commemoration of the Virgin of Guadalupe would still be objectionable to some, surely a December 9 commemoration of Juan Diego as being, at the very least, the symbolic embodiment of Christianity taking root in the Americas would be appropriate. But, of course, one cannot tell the story of Juan Diego without telling the story of the Virgin of Guadalupe.[77] Nevertheless, while Protestants might object dogmatically to the Roman Catholic Solemnity of the Immaculate Conception of Mary celebrated on December 8, certainly, in light of concerns raised in the previous chapter about the place of Marian feasts during Advent,[78] the absence of any official Protestant liturgical commemoration of Mary during the Advent season of pregnancy and preparation seems a rather glaring omission, which either a December 12 commemoration of the Virgin of Guadalupe or the reintegration of both the Annunciation and the Visitation into Advent might serve to address.[79]

Apart from a December 12 liturgical commemoration, however, the possibility of some form of extraliturgical veneration and devotion must also be considered, especially because, as we have seen, devotion to the Virgin of Guadalupe in Hispanic-Latino contexts goes far beyond the specific liturgical celebration of mid Advent. What forms of Guadalupan (or Marian) veneration and devotion, then, if any, might be theologically acceptable to Protestants?

Certain forms of Roman Catholic veneration and devotion, in which the direct invocation of Mary and other saints is a characteristic emphasis, have, of course, long been rejected by Protestants either as detracting from Christ the One Mediator or even as idolatrous worship.[80] In fact, it has only been in recent years that ecumenical dialogue between, at least, Roman Catholics and Lutherans has led to the ability of Lutherans to ask themselves whether "Lutheran churches could acknowledge that the Catholic teaching about the saints and Mary as set forth in the documents of Vatican II . . . does not promote idolatrous belief and is not opposed to the gospel."[81]

Given this kind of history, the place that some form of Marian veneration held in the earlier writings of some of the sixteenth-century Protestant Reformers may seem rather surprising. In his first reform of the Mass, for example, the Swiss Reformer Ulrich Zwingli retained the pre-Counter-Reformation form of the Hail Mary (concluding with the words "blessed is the fruit of your womb, Jesus"), together with the Our Father, as preparation for the liturgy. And in 1522 Zwingli actually preached a sermon on the Hail Mary, noting: "When we say, 'Blessed are you among women,' as I understand it, one does not doubt what the word, 'blessed,' means, that is, 'You are highly blessed above all women.'... The angel in this greeting said nothing more than God greets you, full of grace; the Lord is with you; you are blessed above all women."[82] According to Zwingli, "*Ave Maria* is pure greeting and praise. Its value is grounded in the angel's words, which are a 'proof of her virginal purity.' It is a mirror of Mary's own Magnificat: 'The Almighty has done great things for me.'"[83] Several traces of continued Marian devotion are also discernible in the early writings of Martin Luther. These include his 1519 *Sermon on Preparing to Die,* and, of course, his 1521 *Commentary on the Magnificat,* which he concludes by asking that a proper understanding of this hymn might be granted by Christ "through the intercession and for the sake of his dear Mother Mary."[84] But, perhaps most important, Luther not only kept throughout his life both a crucifix and an image of the Virgin and Child (still the two most characteristic Hispanic-Latino devotional images!) in his study but also retained the traditional Hail Mary in his 1522 *Betbuchlein* or *Personal Prayer Book.* This prayer book was published in various editions until 1545, that is, one year before his death, and is clearly indicative of some form of Marian devotion continuing within early Lutheranism. In retaining the Hail Mary, of course, Luther, like Zwingli, did not interpret it as a prayer *to* Mary or as an invocation *of* her but as a meditation on God's unmerited grace showered *upon* her.

> Let not our hearts cleave to her, but through her penetrate to Christ and to God himself. Thus what the Hail Mary says is that all glory should be given to God. . . . You see that these words are not concerned with prayer but purely with giving praise and honor. . . . Therefore we should make the Hail Mary neither a prayer nor an invocation because it is improper to interpret the words beyond what they mean in themselves and beyond the meaning given them by the Holy Spirit. . . . But there are two things we can do. First we can use the Hail Mary as a meditation in which we recite what grace God has given her. Second, we should add a wish that everyone may know and respect her [as one blessed by God].[85]

That Luther retained the Hail Mary in his *Betbuchlein* led Arthur Carl Piepkorn to assert that, together with Luther's own theology of Mary as *typus ecclesiae,* "the analogy between the Blessed Virgin and the Church . . . makes it possible for a Lutheran to use the Magnificat as the canticle at vespers, and to say the first, pre-Counterreformation part of the Ave Maria . . . as memorials of the Incarnation."[86] Similarly, the late Lutheran theologian Joseph Sittler, in a published sermon entitled "Ave Maria, Gratia Plena," once said:

[I]f . . . the figure of Mary articulates in her song and demonstrates in her quiet life powers and dimensions of the action of God and the response of [humans], both our thought and our worship are the poorer for the neglect of her. It is not strange, but right and proper, that her meaning should be declared and her praise be sung from a Protestant pulpit. If we can find it in our competence in this place to hail the witness to the faith of Augustine, of Luther, of Calvin, or Wesley, how grudging before the gifts of God never to utter an *Ave Maria*—Hail Mary![87]

To the above examples might be added some of the explicit references to Mary appearing within contemporary Protestant hymnody. The classic Anglican hymn "Ye Watchers and Ye Holy Ones," sung in other traditions as well, addresses its second verse directly *to* Mary, saying: "O higher than the cherubim, More glorious than the seraphim, Lead their praises; 'Alleluia!' Thou bearer of the eternal Word, most gracious, magnify the Lord."[88] As John Frederick Johnson notes of this verse: "After invoking seraphim, cherubim, archangels, and angelic choirs, it invokes Mary as higher than the cherubim and more glorious than the seraphim. As bearer of the eternal Word and the most gracious, she is petitioned to magnify the Lord (as she once did on earth)."[89] And, of course, anyone who has spent time with the Guadalupan narrative and image, with its associations with the Magnificat and with the Virgin herself represented as enthroned above the angel at her feet, cannot but begin to make some imaginative connections to this verse. Similarly, at least ELCA Lutherans include in their *Lutheran Book of Worship* a version of the traditional sequence for the September 15 Roman Catholic feast of the Virgin of Sorrows, the *Stabat Mater Dolorosa* ("At the Cross, Her Station Keeping"), a hymn frequently sung by Roman Catholics between the stations of the cross. There can be no question that this is a devotional hymn commemorating Mary herself as La Virgen de los Dolores or La Soledad, in which her faith and devotion serve to inspire the worshiper on to a greater faith and trust in Christ crucified:

Who, on Christ's dear mother gazing,
Pierced by anguish so amazing,
Born of woman, would not weep?
Who, on Christ's dear mother thinking,
Such a cup of sorrow drinking,
Would not share her sorrows deep?

Jesus, may her deep devotion
Stir in me the same emotion,
Source of love, redeemer true.
Let me thus, fresh ardor gaining

And a purer love attaining,
Consecrate my life to you.[90]

Even the intense Hispanic-Latino devotion to the Virgin of Sorrows, especially on Good Friday, has some resonance here. And, as a final example,
the 1995 ELCA liturgical resource *With One Voice* includes the popular
"Sing of Mary, Pure and Lowly" in its Advent section:

Sing of Mary, pure and lowly, virgin mother wise and mild.
Sing of God's own Son most holy, who became her little child.
Fairest child of fairest mother, God the Lord who came to earth.
Word made flesh, our very brother, takes our nature by his birth.

Sing of Jesus, son of Mary, in the home at Nazareth.
Toil and labor cannot weary love enduring unto death.
Constant was the love he gave her, though he went forth from her side,
forth to preach, and heal, and suffer, till on Calvary he died.

Glory be to God the Father; glory be to God the Son;
glory be to God the Spirit; glory to the Three in One.
From the heart of blessed Mary, from all saints the song ascends,
and the Church the strain re-echoes unto earth's remotest ends.[91]

As in verse 2 of "Ye Watchers and Ye Holy Ones," so in this hymn is Mary
herself identified as one closely united to, and leading the praises of, both
the heavenly and earthly chorus of the church around the throne of God.

In response to Luther's theology of Mary, including his interpretation of
the Hail Mary, George Tavard asks appropriately, "Is it not possible on the
basis of justification by faith and on the strength of Luther's example to
count as a permissible *adiaphoron* a contemplative attitude before the mother of Christ, made of gratitude, admiration, and love?"[92] And is it not precisely such a "contemplative attitude before the mother of Christ" that
characterizes not only Luther's interpretation of the Hail Mary as a meditation but also the comments of Piepkorn (the Hail Mary as a memorial of
the incarnation) and Sittler, as well as those references to Mary in Protestant hymnody? If meditation or contemplation before Mary is not Roman
Catholic invocation of Mary, it also more closely resembles a form of prayer
than the characteristic Protestant emphasis on Mary and the saints being
"kept in remembrance so that our faith may be strengthened when we see
what grace they received . . . how they were sustained by faith . . . [with the
result that] their good works are to be an example for us, each of us in his
own calling."[93]

Since the Virgin of Guadalupe is, of course, also an image or iconic representation, the suggestion of permitting a "contemplative attitude before the mother of Christ" for Protestants seems highly appropriate in this context. One of the many stories told by Jeannette Rodriguez, in fact, points to such a contemplative attitude as one characteristic of Guadalupan devotion. She writes:

> I was with a Spanish priest, and he was showing me around the basilica and there was this old man on the side. The priest said, "Hombre, what are you doing here?" And the old man said, "I want to pray to the Lady." The priest replied, "Well, I don't see you praying." And the old man admitted, "Oh Father, I don't know how to pray." So Father said, "OK, here's a prayer book." The old man said, "I don't know how to read," and then the priest starts yelling at him, "Well, what are you doing here?" And the old man said, "You know, it's just enough for me to look in her face."[94]

This is precisely the kind of contemplative attitude long associated with the veneration of icons in the Eastern Christian traditions. In the foreword to her delightful book on the icons associated with the great feasts of the liturgical year in the Byzantine churches, M. Helen Weier says:

> The profound beauty of an icon is gentle. It does not force its way; it does not intrude. It asks for patience with the uneasiness of early acquaintance. It asks for time spent before it in the stillness of gazing. More important, it asks the one praying to allow himself to be gazed upon by it. One must yield space within himself to the icon and its persistent beauty. An icon is prayer and contemplation transformed into art. When exquisite art combines with prayer to become a work of worship and wonder, the art has become sacramental. It manifests to us the God who breaks through all signs and symbols with truth.[95]

If Tavard is correct, however, in saying that such a "contemplative attitude before the mother of Christ made of gratitude, admiration, and love" may, indeed, be permissible for Protestant spirituality, and if, with Luther's own theological interpretation of the Hail Mary as a meditation, it becomes possible for some Protestants "to say the first, pre–Counterreformation part of the Ave Maria . . . as [a] memorial of the Incarnation," then what about other widely practiced popular forms of Marian devotion, like the Angelus or the rosary, in which the Hail Mary is a central and traditional component? Is it permissible or possible for some kind of Protestant adaptation of these practices as well, especially when dealing with people coming into Protestant Christian communities who are already formed, at least *culturally*, by Hispanic-Latino popular religion? Does one simply say, "Throw out your images, stop lighting candles, dismantle the *altarcitos* in your homes, stop wearing medals, and stop reciting rosaries and novenas because Protestants don't do those things"? If this approach undoubtedly has been a characteristic of Latin American Protestantism in general, and one still vehemently supported by several Hispanic-Latino Protestants themselves, another approach must surely be possible at least in some Protestant contexts.

I know of one Hispanic-Latino Lutheran pastor who suggests to his parishioners that they substitute the traditional Jesus Prayer of the Christian East ("Lord Jesus Christ, Son of God, have mercy on me, a sinner") for the repeated Hail Mary's of the rosary. But isn't the core of both the Angelus and the rosary already Christological or incarnational in orientation? Take the Angelus itself, popularly recited three times daily, at morning, noon, and evening:

> V. The Angel of the Lord declared unto Mary.
> R. And she conceived of the Holy Spirit. Hail Mary. . . .
>
> V. Behold the handmaid of the Lord.
> R. May it be done unto me according to your word. Hail Mary. . . .
>
> V. And the Word became flesh.
> R. And dwelt among us. Hail Mary. . . .
>
> Let us pray.
> Lord, fill our hearts with grace: once, through the message of an angel you revealed to us the incarnation of your Son; now, through his suffering and death lead us to the glory of his resurrection. We ask this through Christ our Lord. Amen.[96]

The Angelus is less a prayer *to* Mary than a daily meditation or commemoration of the Incarnation itself, a meditation formed explicitly by Scripture. The concluding prayer is the same as the liturgical prayer of the day for the March 25 feast of the Annunciation of Our Lord in the *Lutheran Book of Worship.* And, if the pre-Counter-Reformation part of the Ave Maria is used for this devotion—without the invocation "Holy Mary, Mother of God, pray for us sinners now and at the hour of our death"— surely there is little here to which a Protestant might object. Is not such a devotion, in fact, centered as it is on the Incarnation of *Christ,* precisely a way to "recite what grace God has given [Mary]" and to "add a wish that everyone may know and respect her [as one blessed by God]" (Luther)?

Can a similar point be made with regard to the rosary, the most readily identifiable Catholic Marian devotion? The most common form of the rosary, of course, is divided into five groups (or decades) of ten Hail Mary beads and one, often larger, Our Father bead in each group. These are joined together by a small string or chain of five beads (one Our Father, three Hail Mary's, and another Our Father bead for the beginning of the first decade) with a crucifix or cross (for reciting the Apostles' Creed) on the end. After each decade the Glory Be to the Father is recited. What must be realized, however, is that, although the rosary is itself frequently recited in public by groups or in homes by families, it is perhaps best understood and employed as a form of private meditation or contemplation on fifteen salvific "mysteries" of *Christ's* birth, life, death, resurrection, ascension, and Pentecost gift of the Holy Spirit. These mysteries, corresponding to the five groups of beads, are organized as follows: (1) the *Joyful Mysteries* of the Annunciation, the Visitation, the Birth of Jesus, the Presentation in the Temple, and the Finding in the Temple; (2) the *Sorrowful Mysteries* of the Agony in the Garden, the Scourging of Jesus, the Crowning with Thorns, the Carrying of the Cross, and the Crucifixion; and (3) the *Glorious Mysteries* of the Resurrection, the Ascension, the Descent of the Holy Spirit, the Assumption of Mary, and the Coronation of Mary. It is upon these mysteries, often aided today either by the reading of the appropriate biblical texts associated with each of them (a "Scriptural Rosary")[97] or by adding a related phrase to each of the Hail Mary's in a given decade,[98] that the one reciting the rosary is to meditate and reflect. While Protestants might find dogmatically questionable the last two of the Glorious Mysteries (the Assumption and Coronation of Mary) and wish to substitute other biblical events for them,[99] and while they might, in general, be more open to an adaptation where something like the Jesus Prayer is substituted for the Hail Mary's, the overall focus of the "Mysteries of the Rosary" is, like that of the Angelus, Christological. In other words, understood in this light, and especially if only the pre-Counter-Reformation part of the Hail Mary is used, the rosary is not so much prayer *to* or invocation *of* Mary as it is contemplative and meditative private prayer *with* Mary *to* Christ. In fact, in what is clearly the best contemporary Roman Catholic treatise on Marian devotion, the 1967 Apostolic Exhortation of Pope Paul VI, *Marialis cultus,* both the Angelus and the rosary are especially commended precisely because of their clear and explicit Christological and liturgical associations.[100] And, together with that, it is quite interesting to read the following explanation of the Hail Mary in a recent Roman Catholic catechetical book for children: "The Hail Mary is not a prayer *to* Mary. It is a prayer we say *with* Mary."[101] Further:

> When we pray the "Hail Mary" we are saying: Our Father in heaven, we join the angel in greeting Mary. She is the beginning of the good news that Jesus came to us. You chose her and loved her to show us how chosen and loved all of us are. How blessed is the mother who gave birth to that child, and

how blessed is the child she gave birth to, through whom we know exactly
what you are like. We hold her hand as we ask you to accept us, now, and at
the testing time of our death.[102]

And I would be remiss if I did not mention here that one of the modern
spiritual classics on the rosary, *Five for Sorrow, Ten for Joy,* was, in fact, written by a Methodist.[103]

If, then, the *message* of Guadalupe and at least some form of the *image* of
the Virgin of Guadalupe might well be acceptable within a Protestant theological framework, a case can surely be made in a modern ecumenical context for recovering or redeveloping an evangelical interpretation of the two
classic Western Christian Marian devotions as well. Interpreted as prayerful
mediations on Christ and our salvation, like the biblical form of the Hail
Mary itself, both the Angelus and the rosary may well be compatible with
justification by grace through faith. Consequently, there may yet be room
in Protestantism for some form of Marian veneration and devotion.[104]

Conclusion

There are several approaches to the Virgin of Guadalupe that Protestantism
might take. The first, of course, is an explicit rejection of any form of the
Guadalupan narrative, image, and devotion whatsoever as absolutely inim-
ical to Protestantism. This kind of rejection may take one of two extreme
forms. On the one hand, it may be expressed by the ardent anti-Catholicism often characteristic especially of Protestant fundamentalism, which, as
Justo González has noted, may acknowledge the credibility of the Guadalupan events themselves but interprets and proclaims those events as invented by the devil "for his own satanic purposes." It is no secret, of course, that
many of the smaller antique Central American and other santos (wooden
saints) carved by indigenous folk artists, formerly present in homes on
altarcitos and now sold today in shops for collectors throughout the United States and elsewhere, have been rescued from the literal fires of fundamentalist purges in their evangelistic endeavors to destroy the vestiges of
Catholic "superstition," "paganism," and "satanism" in their converts. On
the other hand, the rejection of Guadalupe may also take the form of an
intellectual elitism or snobbery that looks down on her and other similar
popular symbols and forms of religious expression as merely the intellectually curious expressions of an "unenlightened" faith with nothing to offer
modern Christianity. Both forms of this rejection, I would argue, while admittedly extremes on a spectrum, are ultimately destructive of culture.

A second possible Protestant approach to Guadalupe would be the exact opposite of the first. That is, the Virgin of Guadalupe might be employed either as a conversion tactic in the evangelism or the proselytizing of newly arrived Mexican and Central American immigrants to various Protestant traditions in the United States or, among those whose liturgical-sacramental traditions are very similar to those of Roman Catholicism, she might be used to give the impression that a particular Protestant congregation is actually a Roman Catholic one. If the first approach is destructive of culture, this second one, while certainly dishonest, also displays a serious misrepresentation of what it means to be a Protestant Christian. If a Hispanic-Latino member of a Protestant Christian denomination sees him- or herself as a Roman Catholic or views this Protestant congregation as a Roman Catholic one, something has been miscommunicated. And the use of the Virgin of Guadalupe as an evangelistic tool or gimmick in such contexts is little more than a condescending manipulation of a highly cherished and revered symbol.

To be fair, however, many within those Protestant traditions, like Lutheranism and Episcopalianism, with a strong and central catholic liturgical-sacramental tradition, tend not to view themselves as really Protestant in either their denominational affiliation or their theological outlook. Anglicanism, for example, has a long history of understanding its identity as representing a via media (middle way) between Protestantism and Catholicism, and Lutheranism itself is probably best understood as an evangelical catholicism. That is, Lutherans are "catholic" Christians committed to an ongoing reform of the church catholic or universal and of themselves on the basis of justification by grace through faith for the sake of Christ. Hence, if the presence of the image of the Virgin of Guadalupe or another popular saint in an Episcopal or Lutheran worship space gives the impression that this congregation is a "Catholic" congregation, that impression is not totally inaccurate. Being "Catholic" is not synonymous with being *Roman* Catholic, and this needs to be understood especially by those who would interpret the presence of Guadalupe in a Lutheran or Episcopal worship space as dishonest or as a misrepresentation of what the denominational affiliation of a that congregation "really" is.[105]

A third Protestant approach to Guadalupe may be one of temporary toleration. In such an approach, the Virgin of Guadalupe or other forms of popular religion are merely tolerated among Hispanic-Latinos until such time as a more complete formation through catechesis can take place. While I suspect that this is the approach taken by many Roman Catholics in the United States today as well, it can also be rather condescending or elitist in orientation. If catechesis and Christian formation, especially for those immigrants who are often poor and illiterate, is absolutely essential, mere temporary toleration of popular religious symbols and practices is not the same as a serious and creative engagement with the content of what those symbols and practices express already. For that matter, the continuing influx of Mexican, Central American, and other immigrants across the southern borders of the United States suggests that the question of Guadalupe and Hispanic-Latino popular religion will not be a temporary question at all. Further, one does not simply tolerate a culture different from the dominant one by means of condescending or patronizing gestures masquerading as hospitality and welcome.

I have attempted in this chapter to offer a fourth possible Protestant approach to the Virgin of Guadalupe, one that reflects what might be called a Protestant-Catholic *Mestizaje,* a synthesis of popular Guadalupanismo and Protestant theological convictions. I have argued that on several levels the Guadalupan message, the image, and, at least some forms of traditional "Catholic" Marian devotion and veneration are easily compatible with the traditional Protestant theologia crucis and its doctrinal affirmation of justification by grace alone through faith for the sake of Christ. As such, I believe it is quite possible and permissible for one to be simultaneously both an evangelical Christian centered in the gospel, as understood and proclaimed within Protestantism, and a Guadalupano/a, one for whom the Virgin of Guadalupe functions as a concrete manifestation or cultural incarnation of that gospel message itself. A true Christian multiculturalism or ecumenical catholicity should be possible. Similarly, together with other elements, one of the gifts of the Virgin of Guadalupe to Protestantism, emerging from the changing cultural context of the United States, may well be the invitation for Protestants to rediscover the place of Mary within the Christian economy and within Christian spirituality and devotion, less as a theological abstraction and more as the concrete embodiment of God's unmerited grace and as a typus ecclesiae well worthy of "a contemplative attitude . . . made of gratitude, admiration, and love." If my approach is less than what Roman Catholics might want to affirm, it is more than what Protestants have tended to affirm, both theologically and devotionally, at least since the first decades of the sixteenth century Protestant Reformation.

Near the conclusion of his essay "Mary: A Reformed Theological Perspective," Daniel Migliore asks the ecumenical question: :

> Why not let Mary be what the Bible describes her as being: a woman of humble yet courageous faith from whom we might learn to praise the sovereign grace of God, to cry out against injustice, . . . to receive our commis-

sion to ministry from Christ at the foot of his cross, and to hope and pray without ceasing for the coming of God's Word and Spirit to renew the church and empower it for service?[106]

With Migliore's suggestion I couldn't agree more. But, I would hasten to add, such a biblical understanding of Mary is precisely what the Virgin of Guadalupe embodies.

Notes

1. Dwight L. Pentecost, *Romanism in the Light of Scripture* (Chicago: Moody Press, 1962), 26–27.

2. Faces painted on suns and moons in Mexican art are common. These faces, however, are never intended to be symbolic of Christ. And, of course, in the image of the Virgin of Guadalupe there is no face whatsoever on the moon. It could be that the author has carelessly conflated several Mexican images of the Virgin Mary in his polemical description or has misinterpreted the angel at the Virgin's feet.

3. Justo L. González, "Reinventing Dogmatics: A Footnote from a Reinvented Protestant," in *From the Heart of the People,* ed. Orlando Espín and Miguel Díaz (New York: Orbis, 1999), 224.

4. Interestingly enough, figures like Martín de Porres and Rosa de Lima and devotional practices like the Via Crucis (stations of the cross) were included in an earlier proposed version of the Libro but for some unknown reason were excluded from the final edition. Ironically, both Martín de Porres and a version of the stations of the cross appear in the African American Lutheran liturgical resource, *This Far by Faith.*

5. Justo L. González, *Mañana: Christian Theology from a Hispanic Perspective* (Nashville: Abingdon, 1990), 61; emphasis added.

6. González, "Reinventing Dogmatics," 225. On the "Catholic" roots of Hispanic-Latino culture see also Roberto S. Goizueta, *Caminemos con Jesús: Toward a Hispanic/Latino Theology of Accompaniment* (Maryknoll, N.Y.: Orbis, 1995), 8 ff.

7. González, "Reinventing Dogmatics," 228.

8. Theodore Tappert, ed., *The Book of Concord* (Philadelphia: Fortress Press, 1959), 30.

9. *Joint Declaration on the Doctrine of Justification,* 3.18.

10. Virgil Elizondo and Friends, *A Retreat with Our Lady of Guadalupe and Juan Diego: Heeding the Call* (Cincinnati: St. Anthony Messenger Press, 1998), 81–82.

11. Virgil Elizondo, *Guadalupe: Mother of the New Creation* (Maryknoll, N.Y.: Orbis, 1997), 113–14; emphasis added.

12. Alberto Pereyra, "The Virgin of Guadalupe, History, Myth, and Spirituality,"

Currents in Theology and Mission 24, 4 (August 1997): 353–54.

13. See Jaroslav Pelikan, *Mary through the Centuries* (New Haven: Yale University Press, 1996), 78, 180–81. In addition to the Spanish Virgin of Guadalupe at Estremadura, other popular European Black Madonnas include Our Lady of Montserrat (Spain), Our Lady of Czestochowa (Poland), and Our Lady of Einsiedeln (Switzerland). Several Black Madonnas are also to be noted in Central and South America (e.g., in Cuba and Colombia) and there are several images of the Black Christ as well, especially in Mexico and Central America. The most popular of these is probably the Guatemalan Black Christ of Esquipulas, a large image of the crucified Christ. While it is sometimes claimed that many of these images were originally of a different color but were blackened over time by the smoke from innumerable vigil lights burning in front of them, the recent restoration of the image at Esquipulas reveals that the original color of the image was, indeed, black. Shrines to the Black Christ of Esquipulas exist in the United States at the Santuario de Chimayo in Chimayo, New Mexico, and at the back of the Cathedral of San Fernando, in San Antonio, Texas, where it was installed to assist in the cathedral's ministry to Guatemalan immigrants. In Guatemala the date of the feast for El Cristo Negro de Esquipulas has for centuries been January 15, the very date of the national holiday in honor of Martin Luther King Jr. in the United States. However, while the Virgin of Guadalupe (called La Morena and La Morenita) is often classified as a Black Madonna, the fact is, as Jacqueline Orsini notes in her recent book, that "to replicate the tones on her face, an artist would have to use pale shades of natural [Caucasian] flesh tones and light gray, not brown or black." See Jacqueline Orsini, *Mary: Images of the Holy Mother* (San Francisco: Chronicle Books, 2000), xiv–xv.

14. John Macquarrie, *Mary for All Christians* (Grand Rapids, Mich.: Eerdmans, 1990), 128.

15. Macquarrie, *Mary for All Christians,* 119; emphasis added.

16. Harvey Cox, *Religion in the Secular City: Toward a Postmodern Theology* (New York: Simon & Schuster, 1984), 256–57. I owe this reference to Father Anthony Ruff, OSB, of the School of Theology, St. John's University, Collegeville, Minn.

17. Cox, *Religion in the Secular City,* 259.

18. José David Rodríguez Jr. with Colleen R. Nelson, "The Virgin of Guadalupe," *Currents in Theology and Mission* 13, 6 (December 1986): 369; emphasis added.

19. Ivis LaRiviere-Mestre, "Field Work Manual for Seminarians and Pastors Who Want to Do Outreach with Latino/Hispanic/Mestizo Families" (October 2000), 11. This excellent pastoral-liturgical resource needs to be published so that it might enjoy wider dissemination and use within the ELCA and other Protestant communities.

20. LaRiviere-Mestre, "Field Work Manual," 12; emphasis added.

21. Raymond E. Brown, "Mary in the New Testament and in Catholic Life," *America,* May 15 1982, 378–79.

22. Virgil Elizondo, "Guadalupe: Mother and Patroness of all America," *Celebrate!* 39, 6 (2001): 21.

23. See Martin Luther, *The Magnificat: Luther's Commentary* (Minneapolis: Augsburg, 1967).

24. Eric Gritsch, "The Views of Luther and Lutheranism on the Veneration of Mary," in *The One Mediator, the Saints, and Mary: Lutherans and Catholics in Dialogue* 8, ed. Herbert G. Anderson, et al. (Minneapolis: Augsburg Fortress, 1992), 236–37; emphasis added.

25. Gritsch, "Views of Luther," 241. On Mary as the "feminine face" of the church, see Sven-Erik Brodd, "From an Example of Virtue to the Feminine Face of the Church: Shifts in Marian Perspectives in the Lutheran Tradition," in *Mary in Doctrine and Devotion: Papers of the Liverpool Congress, 1989, of the Ecumenical Society of the Blessed Virgin Mary,* ed. Alberic Stacpoole, OSB (Collegeville, Minn.: Liturgical Press, 1990), 127–40.

26. Elrich Leupold, ed., *Luther's Works,* vol. 53, *Liturgy and Hymns* (Philadelphia: Fortress, 1965), 293–94. Unfortunately, this English edition does not refer to Luther's dedication of this hymn to Mary.

27. For a helpful summary of the Mariological concerns of both Zwingli and Calvin, see George Tavard, *The Thousand Faces of the Virgin Mary* (Collegeville, Minn: Michael Glazier), 104–9, 117–26.

28. Daniel L. Migliore, "Mary: A Reformed Theological Perspective," *Theology Today* 56, 3 (October 1999): 346–58.

29. Migliore, "Mary," 357.

30. Migliore, "Mary," 357.

31. Migliore, "Mary," 354.

32. Migliore, "Mary," 358.

33. Migliore, "Mary," 358.

34. Pereyra, "Virgin of Guadalupe," 350–51.

35. González, *Mañana,* 148–49; emphasis added.

36. González, *Mañana,* 149.

37. Goizueta, *Caminemos con Jesús,* 68–69. See also Orlando O. Espín, *The Faith of the People: Theological Reflections on Popular Catholicism* (Maryknoll, N.Y.: Orbis, 1997), 49–50.

38. Espín, *Faith of the People,* 71.

39. Virgil Elizondo, "Living Faith: Resistance and Survival," in *Mestizo Worship: A Pastoral Approach to Liturgical Ministry,* by Virgil Elizondo and Timothy Matovina, (Collegeville, Minn.: Liturgical Press, 1998), 16–17.

40. See above, chap. 3, 85.

41. See above, chap. 3, 79–80.

42. Leonard Boff, *The Maternal Face of God: The Feminine and Its Religious Expressions* (San Francisco: Harper & Row, 1987), 93.

43. Paul Tillich, *A History of Christian Thought* (New York: Simon & Schuster, 1967), 78.

44. Paul Tillich, *Theology of Culture* (London: Oxford University Press, 1959), 66.

45. Elsie Gibson, "Mary and the Protestant Mind," *Revue for Religious* 24 (1965): 397, as quoted in Elizabeth A. Johnson, "Mary as Mediatrix," in *The One Mediator, the Saints, and Mary: Lutherans and Catholics in Dialogue 8,* ed. Herbert G. Anderson et al. (Minneapolis: Augsburg Fortress, 1992), 324.

46. Elizabeth A. Johnson, "Mary and the Female Face of God," *Theological Studies* 50, 3 (1989): 519. The study noted is Catholica-Arbeitskreis der VELKD, "Maria: Evangelische Fragen und Geschictspunkte. Eine Einladung zum Gespräch," *Una sancta* 37 (1982): 184–201.

47. Paul Tillich, *Systematic Theology* (Chicago: University of Chicago Press, 1963), 3: 294.

48. Espín, *Faith of the People,* 10.

49. Migliore, "Mary," 354.

50. Berard Marthaler, *The Creed: The Apostolic Faith in Contemporary Theology,* rev. ed. (Mystic, Conn.: Twenty-Third Publications, 1993), 134.

51. See Macquarrie, *Mary for All Christians,* 81–83.

52. Marthaler, *The Creed,* 135.

53. Maxwell E. Johnson, *Images of Baptism,* Forum Essays 6 (Chicago: Liturgy Training Publications, 2001), 129.

54. See Frank Senn, *Christian Worship and Its Cultural Setting* (Philadelphia: Fortress, 1983), 79–80.

55. See Gritsch, "Views of Luther," 241.

56. Gritsch, "Views of Luther," 128–29.

57. George A. Lindbeck, *The Nature of Doctrine: Religion and Theology in a Postliberal Age* (Philadelphia: Westminster, 1984.), 74.

58. Lindbeck, *Nature of Doctrine,* 84.

59. Clare Veronica Johnson, "Paradigms of Translation: Implications for Roman Catholic Liturgical Inculturation," forthcoming in *Worship* (2002). I owe the above insights to Lindbeck from Johnson's fine essay. Of course, any application of Johnson's insight to the Virgin of Guadalupe is my own.

60. Lutheran World Federation, *Nairobi Statement on Worship and Culture: Contemporary Challenges and Opportunities* (Geneva: Lutheran World Federation, 1996), para.1.3.

61. Lutheran World Federation, *Nairobi Statement,* para. 5.2.

62. Lutheran World Federation, *Nairobi Statement,* para. 3.2. The use of the category of dynamic equivalence with regard to the Virgin of Guadalupe was first

suggested to me by my former graduate student the Reverend Mark Strobel, an ELCA pastor in Fargo, North Dakota. While the suggestion is his, any use made of it here, of course, is my own responsibility.

63. Lutheran World Federation, *Nairobi Statement,* para. 3.1.

64. Lutheran World Federation, *Nairobi Statement,* para. 3.2.

65. Lutheran World Federation, *Nairobi Statement,* para. 3.6.

66. See Lisa Sousa, Stafford Poole, and James Lockhart, *The Story of Guadalupe: Luis Laso de la Vega's* Huei tlamahuiçoltica *of 1649* (Stanford, Calif.: Stanford University Press, 1998); Clodomiro L. Siller Acuña, *Para comprender el mensaje de María de Guadalupe* (Buenos Aires: Editorial Guadalupe, 1989); and Jose Luis G. Guerrero, *El* Nican Mopohua: *Un intento de exégesis,* Biblioteca Mexicana 6 and 7, 2 vols., (Cuautitlán: Universidad Pontifica de México, 1996, 1998).

67. Nathan Mitchell, *Real Presence: The Work of Eucharist* (Chicago: Liturgy Training Publications, 1998), 48.

68. John Dominic Crossan, *The Dark Interval: Towards a Theology of Story* (Niles, Ill.: Argus Communications, 1975), 108.

69. Crossan, *Dark Interval,* 122.

70. See Roberto Piña, "The Laity in the Hispanic Church," in *The New Catholic World* (New York: Paulist Press, 1980), 168–71.

71. José David Rodriguez and Colleen Nelson. "The Virgin of Guadalupe," *Currents in Theology and Mission* 13 (1986): 369, emphasis added.

72. The ELCA parish where I am a member, Gloria Dei Lutheran Church, South Bend, Ind., for example, has on the wall behind its freestanding altar a large Christus Rex (Christ the King) crucifix flanked by images of both the Virgin and the Beloved Disciple. And in a garden area near one of the church entrances there is a statue of St. Anthony of Padua with the Christ Child.

73. Arthur Carl Piepkorn, "Mary's Place within the People of God According to Non-Roman-Catholics," *Marian Studies* 18 (1967):81.

74. This description is provided at www.printeryhouse.org/mall/icons/mary/ica11.htm; accessed August 2001.

75. This photograph was taken by Daniel Groody, C.S.C., who graciously gave me permission to use it.

76. *Lutheran Book of Worship: Minister's Edition* (Minneapolis: Augsburg Fortress, 1978), 175–77. The prayer of the day for the Annunciation of our Lord (March 25), p. 174, or for Mary, Mother of our Lord (August 15), p. 178, might also be appropriate. But because it draws attention to God's "gracious regard for the poor and the lowly and the despised," the prayer for the Visitation seems the better choice.

77. One wonders which of the two, the Virgin of Guadalupe or Juan Diego, is the more glaring omission within recent Spanish-language Protestant liturgical resources.

78. See above, 114–17.

79. Since 1985 the (Lutheran) Church of Sweden has dedicated the fourth Sunday in Advent to "Mary, Mother of the Lord," in order to "strengthen the place of Mary in Church life" (Brodd, "Example of Virtue," 131).

80. For a summary of traditional Protestant views, see James F. White, "Forgetting and Remembering the Saints," in *Between Memory and Hope,* ed. Maxwell E. Johnson (Collegeville, Minn.: Liturgical Press, 2000), 401–14.

81. Anderson et al., *One Mediator,* 62.

82. Text as quoted in Tavard, *Thousand Faces,* 106.

83. Tavard, *Thousand Faces,* 107.

84. Luther, *Magnificat,* 45.

85. Leupold, *Luther's Works,* 34: 39–40.

86. Piepkorn, "Mary's Place," 80; emphasis added.

87. Joseph Sittler, "Ave Maria, Gratia Plena," in *The Care of the Earth and Other University Sermons* (Philadelphia: Fortress Press, 1964), 55–56, 63.

88. "Ye Watchers and Ye Holy Ones," hymn 175, v. 1, *Lutheran Book of Worship* (Minneapolis: Augsburg, 1978).

89. John F. Johnson, "Mary and the Saints in Contemporary Lutheran Worship," in *One Mediator,* ed. Anderson et al., 309; emphasis added.

90. "At the Cross Her Station Keeping," hymn 110, in *Lutheran Book of Worship.*

91. "Sing of Mary, Pure and Lowly," hymn 634, in *With One Voice* (Minneapolis: Augsburg Fortress, 1995); emphasis added. It is most interesting to note, however, that there is a more pronounced Marian theology and devotion within some of the contemporary liturgical books of the Church of Sweden. Sven-Erik Brodd, for example, writes: "The recently (1986) ratified Church of Sweden Hymnal contains new hymns about Mary. What actually is taught about Mary in the Hymnal is not always easy to grasp, but at least the Church of Sweden now for the first time has got a version of Salve Regina, giving praise to Mary (no. 480), as well as prayer to her, 'O Mary . . . teach me to love Him who has passed through death and grave to the Kingdom of light" (no. 481, v. 4)." Sven-Erik Brodd, "Example of Virtue," 131.

92. Tavard, *Thousand Faces,* 117.

93. Augsburg Confession, Article XXI, in Tappert, *Book of Concord,* 46.

94. Jeannette Rodriguez, "The Gift of Guadalupe," in *U.S. Catholic* 64, 12 (1999): 22.

95. M. Helen Weier, *Festal Icons of the Lord* (Collegeville, Minn.: Liturgical Press, 1977), vii. It is the Virgin of Guadalupe as an icon that shapes the theological approach of D. A. Brading, *Mexican Phoenix: Our Lady of Guadalupe—Image and Tradition across Five Centuries* (Cambridge: Cambridge University Press, 2001), 361–68.

96. The Angelus is quoted here from Jorge Perales, ed., *Oracional Bilingüe: A Prayer Book for Spanish-English Communities* (Collegeville, Minn.: Liturgical Press, 1994), 8.

97. See Perales, *Oracional Bilingüe,* 75–93.

98. The Hail Mary during the first Glorious Mystery (the Resurrection of Christ), for example, may be prayed as "Hail Mary. . . . blessed is the fruit of your womb, Jesus, who died for our sins and rose for our justification." For additional examples of this model of the rosary, see Thomas McNally and William G. Storey, eds., *Day by Day: The Notre Dame Prayerbook for Students* (Notre Dame: Ave Maria Press, 1975), 147–51. A version of a devotion being called the "Anglican Rosary" also exists wherein the following petition is attached to the pre–Counter-Reformation part of the Hail Mary: "Son of Mary, Son of the living God, have mercy upon us, now, and at the hour of our death. Amen." On this see the website for Grace Episcopal Church, Pittsburgh, Pa., at www.usaor.net/users/grace/rosary .htm, accessed July 2001. On the rediscovery of various forms and adaptations of the rosary within modern Anglicanism, see also Anthony Price, *Reconsidering the Rosary,* Grove Spirituality Series 36 (Cambridge, England: Grove Books, 1991); Lynn C. Baumann, *The Anglican Rosary* (Telephone, Texas: Praxis, n.d.); and *The Rosary for Episcopalians* (Berkeley, Calif.: Incarnation Priory, 1992).

99. See the ecumenical Crown of Jesus Rosary, where the phrase "We adore thee O Christ, and we praise Thee, for by Thy Holy Cross Thou hast redeemed the world" is substituted for the Hail Mary's and where the final two Glorious Mysteries are "The Triumph of the Church in the Saints" and "The Adoration of the Lamb." *The Crown of Jesus Rosary* (Orleans, Mass.: The Community of Jesus, 1989).

100. Paul VI, *For the Right Ordering and Development of Devotion to the Blessed Virgin Mary: Marialis Cultus* (Boston: St. Paul Books and Media, 1974), 37–45.

101. Hubert Richards, *Some Catholic Prayers* (Collegeville, Minn.: Liturgical Press, 1992), 15.

102. Richards, *Some Catholic Prayers,* 16.

103. J. Neville Ward, *Five for Sorrow, Ten for Joy: A Consideration of the Rosary* (Garden City, N.Y.: Doubleday, 1973).

104. See also "An Ecumenical Office of Mary the Mother of Jesus," produced by the Ecumenical Society of the Blessed Virgin Mary and included in Macquarrie, *Mary for All Christians,* 139–60.

105. I attended a daylong workshop on Hispanic ministry a few years ago where the focus turned to a discussion of the signs often placed on the front doors or in the windows of Roman Catholic Hispanic-Latino homes that say something like: "This home is Catholic. We do not accept propaganda from Protestants or other sects." One Lutheran pastor in attendance stood up and said, in effect, "As a Lutheran I have never taken these signs as referring to me, since I too am Catholic, and I have been welcomed into them as one to whom these signs don't apply." In response, the primarily Roman Catholic audience applauded.

106. Migliore, "Mary," 358.

Conclusion

D id the Blessed Virgin Mary actually appear to a Juan Diego on the hill of Tepeyac near Mexico City between December 9 and December 12 of 1531? No amount of historical investigation and analysis will ever be able to determine objectively whether she did or whether she did not. But does the answer to the question of historicity really matter in the long run? As we have seen repeatedly throughout this book, that question pales in importance to the question of the theological significance of the Virgin of Guadalupe. What I do know is this: What the Guadalupan narrative, image, and feast incarnate is the reality that throughout history countless people, sometimes in spite of, rather than thanks to, the church, have heard the gospel's call to discipleship, to human dignity, and to prophetic ministry on behalf of the poor and the powerless in service to the inbreaking of the reign of God. Occasionally "Juan Diegos" have been raised up by the gospel and have taken up the ministry of that gospel to be prophets even *to* the church itself and to remind its leaders what the task of evangelization, cat-echesis, and service to that reign of God is all about. The abiding image of the Virgin of Guadalupe on the tilma of Juan Diego, an image reproduced over and again in such a wide variety of media, is, at the very least, a par-ticular cultural incarnation or inculturation of this call of the gospel as it took root in the context of Mexican Christianity and as it continues to live and come to expression in the lives of countless followers.

In the final chapter of this study I have argued that this traditionally Mexican Roman Catholic narrative, image, devotion, and feast are theo-logically compatible with at least some forms of Protestantism, including the central "Protestant" doctrinal affirmation of justification by grace through faith on account of Christ. As such, I have concluded that being an evangelical Christian centered in the gospel of justification and being a Guadalupano/a are not mutually exclusive, for it is precisely that gospel that the Virgin of Guadalupe embodies. In saying this, however, I am not naïve enough to believe that the Virgin of Guadalupe will ever be widely embraced by contemporary Protestants, even by Hispanic-Latino Protestants. Nor do I think, for example, that the Commission for Multicultural Ministries of the ELCA or similar offices in other Protestant churches will ever adopt her image as their emblem. What Justo González writes is undoubtedly true: "The notion that Cuban Catholics and Protestants will come together around the image of Caridad, or Mexicans around Guadalupe, may be very beautiful, but is made less than credible by our own histories."[1] Indeed, it is precisely those histories of polemic and mistrust expressed in both anti-Catholicism and anti-Protestantism that help one understand why it is that even an *optional commemoration,* much less a "lesser festival," of the Virgin of Guadalupe would have been rejected by those involved with developing Spanish-language Protestant liturgical resources even today.

But while I will continue to lament the absence of even an optional commemoration of the Virgin of Guadalupe in the ELCA *Libro de Liturgia y Cántico,* my approach in this book has not been based on the naïve assumption that Mexican or Mexican American Catholics and Protestants will simply "come together . . . around Guadalupe." Nevertheless, as we have seen, the Virgin of Guadalupe is *already* present as both image and feast in some forms of Protestantism in the United States, especially within various Episcopalian and ELCA Lutheran congregations. I could be wrong here, but I do not expect to see this phenomenon decrease at all in the coming years, especially with the expressed commitments to multicultural approaches to evangelism and worship in the so-called mainline Protestant churches. In fact, as already appears to be the case, I suspect that it will be primarily within the Episcopal Church, U.S.A., that her image and feast will become even more common. And, because the Episcopal Church, U.S.A., and the ELCA entered into full communion with each other in January 2001, I suspect further, as Episcopalians and ELCA Lutherans now together increasingly engage in joint ministries among Hispanic-Latinos, that the Guadalupan image and feast will become even more common among Lutherans. But if so, then most certainly the *theological* question of her compatibility with classic Protestant theology will also become increasingly important. Therefore I have not argued or proposed that the Virgin of Guadalupe must or even should be integrated within contemporary Protestantism. I have only argued, I hope convincingly, that such an integration is theologically, liturgically, and, in some form, devotionally possible and permissible for at least those Protestant traditions, like Episcopalianism and Lutheranism, that already share a common liturgical-sacramental heritage with Roman Catholicism. In other words, the Virgin of Guadalupe *can* be integrated into a Protestant theological context. Whether she will be or not is another question altogether.

Finally, the interpretation of the image of the Virgin of Guadalupe as a typus ecclesiae, an image of the church itself, may be one of the most profound Guadalupan gifts that Mexican and Mexican American spirituality can make to the church catholic. For the church being called into existence more than ever before in the United States is one called to be clearly multicultural and mestizo in form, and such a church appears to be already present proleptically in the mestizo face of the Virgin of Guadalupe. To gaze contemplatively upon her image, then, is to gaze at the future church in the making and to gaze at what we hope, by God's grace and Spirit, the church of Jesus Christ, racially, culturally, and even ecumenically, will become. Both Protestants and Catholics may be able to ignore or even reject the Virgin of Guadalupe, but neither group can afford to ignore the message of what her image and gospel-like narrative proclaim and embody. And because of that, at least this Anglo-Lutheran liturgist would like to say with both gratitude and hope, "¡Viva la Virgen de Guadalupe, Madre de Dios!"

Note

1. Justo L. González, "Reinventing Dogmatics: A Footnote from a Reinvented Protestant," in *From the Heart of the People,* ed. Orlando Espín and Miguel Diaz (New York: Orbis, 1999), 224–25.

For Further Reading

Anderson, Herbert G., et al., eds. *The One Mediator, the Saints, and Mary: Lutherans and Catholics in Dialogue 8.* Minneapolis: Augsburg Fortress, 1992.

Brading, D. A. *Mexican Phoenix: Our Lady of Guadalupe: Image and Tradition across Five Centuries.* Cambridge: Cambridge University Press, 2001.

Brown, Raymond E. "Mary in the New Testament and in Catholic Life." *America,* May 15 1982, 374–79.

Castillo, Ana, ed. *Goddess of the Americas, La Diosa de las Americas.* New York: Riverhead Books, 1996.

Dunnington, Jacqueline Orsini. *Guadalupe: Our Lady of New Mexico.* Santa Fe: Museum of New Mexico Press, 1999.

Elizondo, Virgil. *La Morenita: Evangelizer of the Americas.* San Antonio: Mexican American Cultural Center, 1980.

———. *Guadalupe: Mother of the New Creation.* Maryknoll, N.Y.: Orbis, 1997.

Elizondo, Virgil, and Friends. *A Retreat with Our Lady of Guadalupe and Juan Diego: Heeding the Call.* Cincinnati: St. Anthony Messenger Press, 1998.

Elizondo, Virgil, and Timothy Matovina. *Mestizo Worship: A Pastoral Approach to Liturgical Ministry.* Collegeville, Minn.: Liturgical Press, 1998.

Espín, Orlando O. *The Faith of the People: Theological Reflections on Popular Catholicism.* Maryknoll, N.Y.: Orbis, 1997.

Goizueta, Roberto S. *Caminemos con Jesús: Toward a Hispanic/Latino Theology of Accompaniment.* Maryknoll, N.Y.: Orbis, 1995.

González, Justo L. *Mañana: Christian Theology from a Hispanic Perspective.* Nashville: Abingdon, 1990.

Hanut, Eryk. *The Road to Guadalupe: A Modern Pilgrimage to the Goddess of the Americas.* New York: Tarcher/Putnam, 2001.

Icaza, Rosa María. "Spirituality of the Mexican American People." *Worship* 63, 3 (1989): 232–46.

Johnson, Elizabeth. "The Marian Tradition and the Reality of Women." In *The Catholic Faith: A Reader,* edited by Lawrence Cunningham, 97–123. Mahwah, N.J.: Paulist Press, 1988.

————. "Mary and the Female Face of God." *Theological Studies* 50, 3 (1989): 500–526.

Macquarrie, John. *Mary for All Christians.* Grand Rapids, Mich.: Eerdmans, 1990.

Madigan, Shawn. "Do Marian Festivals Image 'That Which the Church Hopes To Be?'" *Worship* 65, 3 (1991): 194–207.

Mexican American Cultural Center. *Faith Expressions of Hispanics in the Southwest.* Rev. ed. San Antonio: Mexican American Cultural Center, 1990.

Nebel, Richard. *Santa María Tonantzin, Virgen de Guadalupe: Religiöse Kontinuität und Transformation in Mexiko.* Immensee: Neue Zeitschrift für Missionswissenschaft, 1992. Also published as *Santa María Tonantzin, Virgen de Guadalupe: Continuidad y transformación religiosa en México.* Mexico City: Fondo de Cultura Económica, 1995.

————. *Viva Guadalupe! The Virgin in New Mexican Popular Art.* Santa Fe: Museum of New Mexico Press, 1997.

Pereyra, Alberto. "The Virgin of Guadalupe, History, Myth, and Spirituality." *Currents in Theology and Mission* 24, 4 (August 1997): 348–54.

Poole, Stafford. *Our Lady of Guadalupe: The Origins and Sources of a Mexican National Symbol, 1531–1797.* Tucson: University of Arizona Press, 1997.

Rodriguez, Jeannette. *Our Lady of Guadalupe: Faith and Empowerment among Mexican-American Women.* Austin: University of Texas Press, 1994.

Rodriguez, José David, and Colleen Nelson. "The Virgin of Guadalupe." *Currents in Theology and Mission* 13 (1986): 368–69.

Salazar, J. J. "'¿No estoy yo aqui, que soy tu madre?' Investigación Teológica-Bíblica-Litúrgica acerca de La Nueva Liturgia de Nuestra Señora de Guadalupe." 3 vols. S.T.D. diss., Pontificio Istituto Liturgico, 1981.

Schulte, Francisco. "A Mexican Spirituality of Divine Election for a Mission: Its Sources in Published Guadalupan Sermons, 1661–1821." Ph.D. diss., Gregorian Pontifical University, 1994.

Sousa, Lisa, Stafford Poole, and James Lockhart. *The Story of Guadalupe: Luis Laso de la Vega's* Huei tlamahuiçoltica *of 1649.* Stanford, Calif.: Stanford University Press, 1998.

Zimdars-Swartz, Sandra L. *Encountering Mary: Visions of Mary from LaSalette to Medjugorje.* New York: Avon, 1991.

Index

About the Author

Maxwell E. Johnson, an ordained minister in the Evangelical Lutheran Church in America, is professor of liturgical studies at the University of Notre Dame. He is a frequent contributor to scholarly and professional journals and author and editor of several books. His recently published books include *Images of Baptism* (2000) and, with Paul Bradshaw and L. Edward Phillips, *The Apostolic Tradition: A Commentary, Hermeneia* (2002).